I Came Home, But It Wasn't Me

CW01573084

I Came Home, But It Wasn't Me

The memoirs of a Vietnam Combat Veteran as a Recon Scout "LRRP"

By

Bruce Wm. Taneski

Other Books by the Author

Creatures Born of War

A Novel About the World Wars

&

Creatures Born of War

The Conflicts; Korea and Vietnam

Copyright 2015 © All Rights Reserved by

The author and publisher

Bruce Wm. Taneski

ISBN-13:978-1543192100

ISBN-10:1543192106

Table of Contents

Book Two, 5th Infantry Division (Mech Vietnam)

A note from the Author

All fairy tales start with "Once upon a time," every war story I have ever heard starts with "This aint no shit." These stories are just stories. They are my perceived recollections of the events and places during my year when I served as a US Army Infantry Recon Scout or "LRRP" in Vietnam. Perception is the operative word. I'm sure that all of the men with whom I served will recall some of these incidents but their perception will most likely be similar to mine but could also be decidedly different. The passage of forty-five years will do that. I cannot recall all of the names or faces, although if I see photos I can sometimes put a name to a face, but may not recall the exact time or place.

I never talked with my family in detail about Vietnam, having never been there they could not relate, although my brother in law was a US Navy Corpsman. He was assigned to the 3rd Marine Division. He and I have talked but only in brief conversations that never went into a lot of detail. Like me, he has PTSD, but has never been diagnosed as of this writing. I see the signs in him all the time, but he is content to bury the war as many of us do. My PTSD was initially diagnosed in 1982. My PTSD therapist thinks it's a good idea to share my war experience, so that's why I wrote this story. It is dedicated to all of my brothers who served in Vietnam, may they find some peace, happiness and purpose to life.

It's important to me to recognize the soldiers of the 27th NVA and 33rd NVA Regiments, as well as the 274th VC regiment with whom I had most of my combat experience with. In these stories, I have made a conscious attempt never to use the words "dink", "slope," or "gook." Today they are not a part of my everyday vocabulary. These are terms that are not befitting an enemy whose bravery, dedication and sacrifice against insurmountable odds was demonstrated every day. We too are brothers.

In addition, although the units were accurate I have changed some of the names of those I served with so as not to embarrass or make accusations against anyone. This is after all my story. I also made every attempt to use the exact locations I was able to gather from after action reports, maps and letters I wrote home. I did take some literary license with some of this writing but I tried to keep it as historically accurate as I could.

Some of the incidents I wrote about may not be in perfect chronological order although every attempt was made to do so. Forty-five years has clouded some memories but the reports, maps, and letters gave me some renewed clarity. I was very young when I enlisted in the Army I had just turned eighteen in November forty-nine days later, I arrived in Vietnam.

Physically I left Vietnam, but it came home with me. It has always been there, and hopefully these stories will explain why.

PROLOGUE

As individual human beings and as a species we are in a constant state of evolution. Who we are is defined by who we were yesterday and what we will live through today and tomorrow. The young men who stepped off the boats and the planes as they arrived in places called Tan Son Nhut, Cam Ranh Bay and Da Nang would forever be changed as a part of them died when they arrived. Larger parts of who they were would die as their tour progressed. Each day they would lose another part of themselves. They would leave behind the spirit if you will of the person they would have become had they not arrived in Vietnam. The person they would become as a result of their arrival would be defined by the day-to-day experience of their tours. Some would have it relatively easy; these were the REMFS, living in comfortable barracks with house girls.

They had three hot meals, each day, clean clothes and a basically secure area that might on occasion receive incoming rocket or mortar fire. Others would serve in the remote areas of the country on fire support bases or in military installations around the major cities. These guys would see more action, but the real soldiers to see the full effects of the Nam would be the grunts. The men who humped the boonies living in the mountains, jungles and rice patties, dealing with the day to day monotony of the heat and humidity, the bugs and the snakes, interrupted by a few minutes of terror, followed by the horror created by that terror.

Anyone who tells you the Vietnam War ended on April 30th, 1975 is a liar. The war and the place we call the big green hurt lives on. It came back with all of us. Buried deep in our psyche it rears its ugly head constantly. It's like the evil energizer bunny; it just keeps going and going. It never goes away. It comes back in many different forms, but however, it returns it destroys everything in its path. It returns through us as anger, anxiety, aggressiveness, emotional distress, memory loss, hopelessness, isolation, sleep loss, and nightmares. It produces alcoholism, assault, crime, child abuse, divorce, drug abuse, rape, homicide, and suicide. It affects not only the men and women who served there, but also the friends and family members of the veterans who came home. We all live with it. It is the silent killer of the society we all grew up in. The sad truth being we cannot stop it.

Every veteran of Vietnam and every family of a Vietnam veteran will experience one or more of these symptoms during their lifetime. Anyone that tells you different is foolish, plain, and simple. We cannot as a society raise our children to be good people, with an education, religious training, and a moral compass to care for one another, and then inject them into the meat grinder of Vietnam and expect them to come home and be as they were as if they never left. To think otherwise is madness. The Vietnam War will end only when the last veteran or the last family member of a veteran dies. Even then it will still be there if only in books, movies, and historical references and displays in museums and library's.

The veterans of the Vietnam War are unique. Unlike their predecessors in WWII and Korea, they came home as individuals. Isolated from the men they served with and injected back into a society that expected them to return to a normal existence and to blend back into life in 'The World' as we called it.

In some cases, and all too often men were in combat on Monday, leave the field on Tuesday, process out, fly home on Wednesday, and arrive back in "the world" on Thursday or Friday. I arrived home just twenty days after my last combat experience, where I was wounded and one man was killed and another seriously wounded. Many were ridiculed, spat on, and called vicious names upon their return. People would say, "Take off that uniform and forget the war your home now, and don't talk about it." Mothers thrilled that they are home would look into the eyes of their sons, and wonder, "Who are you?" They knew, this is not my son. It looks like him, smells like him, sounds like him, but there is something terribly wrong. Looking into his eyes deep inside the new soul of their son reveals a beast, and despite every effort to keep it buried it sometimes comes out into the light.

The psychiatric professionals call it PTSD, Post Traumatic Distress Disorder. It's listed in the DSM-5 used by psychiatrists as an emotional disorder. It is not a psychiatric disorder or illness. I call it Permanent Traumatic Stress Disorder. They claim that with medication, individual, and group therapy it can be treated. In some circles of the VA, there are some who claim it can be cured.

The basic premise is if the veteran relives his traumatic memories over and over and over again, that eventually, he will become numb to the effects of those memories. They want us to become emotionally numb to the events that made us emotionally numb. This is the same theory if you will that children who are raised by a civil society in a loving home will not be affected by the traumas of war. It is not surprising that the some of the same people who promote this stupidity have never served in the military let alone combat.

According to statistics tabulated by the United States 50th Commemoration of the Vietnam War more than 2.7 million American's served in Vietnam. All of them were affected by their service. To one degree or another, they all have had some type of problems since their return.

The war in Vietnam has been with me every day of my life. Some days are better than others, but there is not a day goes by that, I don't think of, or that I am not reminded of the Nam. These are my stories. The old me fights a war every day to keep the beast inside me at bay, it is exhausting and because it is, the old me rarely comes out. My wife and my family knew me before I left. My children and grandchildren never knew me as I was, they never will. They know only the new me, so for them, this is why I am, who I am today.

I Came Home, But It Wasn't Me.

Story One 199th Light Infantry Brigade

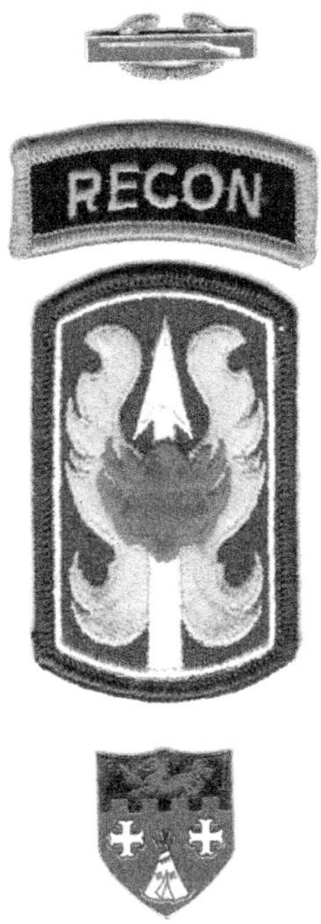

Chapter One, My Tour Begins;

The long twenty-four-hour flight on a chartered airliner from Fort Dix / McGuire AFB in NJ had two stops the first was Elmondorf AFB in Anchorage Alaska. This leg of the flight took just under eight hours. Here we all were dressed in jungle fatigues ready for the heat and humidity of tropical Vietnam, and allowed to run the 150 meters or so from the aircraft to the terminal in minus twenty degree Alaska. The fun is just beginning because we also had to get back on the plane. This was probably the only time anyone was in a hurry to get on a plane going to Vietnam.

From Alaska, we had one more stop after flying for another eight hours and landing at Yakota AFB in Japan. The base is located about twenty-eight miles northwest of Tokyo. The temperature there was a balmy ten or fifteen degrees. The aircraft pulled right up to the terminal so this was not as bad. Upon leaving Japan, we had a six-hour flight to Tan Son Nhut Air Base in Vietnam.

The pilot announced that we were preparing for final approach and flying over Vietnam and would land in about thirty minutes. Everyone was crowded around every window of the plane looking on down on the place where we would spend the next year of our lives. Assuming of course the worst did not occur.

We all made note of the vast jungle and open rice patty fields around the villages we saw below from 20,000 feet. We were also able to see dirt roads and black topped roads going from villages and towns.

As we got lower and slower we were able to see some of the Fire Support bases and airfields around the countryside, most of which were surrounded by large bomb and artillery craters. Large bunkers, observation towers, and seas of concertina wire surrounding their perimeters.

Upon final touch down, we zipped past hangers occupied by F-4 Phantom fighter jets C-130's and a variety of helicopters. We taxied over the tarmac and the aircraft came to a stop, it was mid-morning when the pilots announced over the paging system we were at our final destination, "Welcome to Vietnam and Good Luck. "

The Officers sat in the front of the aircraft followed by the Non-Commissioned Officers and finally in the back of the plane the enlisted cannon fodder.

The pilots shut the engines down as everyone was waiting for the mobile stairs to be put in position at the door at the front of the plane. The Vietnam sun was turned up full blast this afternoon with temperatures in the high nineties and humidity to match. It was getting pretty stuffy in the back of the plane and I thought I might actually pass out.

I finally made it to the door past the stewardesses who all wished us "Good Luck," and stepped out unto the mobile stairs. It was like walking out of pizza oven into a volcano, the blast of hot humid air hit me like truck and the first breath of air in Vietnam was not easy to suck in.

Then there was that strange smell in the air, everyone was making comments about, the Nam had its own distinctive aroma. Eventually we would get used to it, but would never forget it.

We boarded Air Force busses that would take us to 90th Replacement Company at Long Binh Army Post. The bus was not air conditioned but all the windows were open, covering the windows we saw steel wire mesh, the driver who was not armed told us the wire was there to stop mama san and papa san from throwing grenades into the bus.

We did see several native people wearing black pajamas and conical hats working in the ditches alongside the road and in the fields by the road. Many smiled and waved others called out in Vietnamese, which sounded like a very singsong language. One old man who looked like Ho Chi Minh himself smiled and waved, the young boy next to him laughed and drew his finger across his throat. Welcome to the Nam!

The barracks at 90th Replacement were like most of the barracks that you find in the so-called secure rear areas. They were one and two story units, with the walls about 6 feet high and on top about two feet of screening. They were really open-air buildings with sandbag walls around the base of the structure.

The roads around the camp were dirt but there were some blacktopped roads used as the main thorough fares throughout the base. Back in the barracks area, wood slate walkways were constructed and about every third barrack, there was a large bunker.

We were told to always know where the nearest bunker was at all times as these would be utilized during rocket or mortar attacks.

I was with Eric Delaney and Robert Ercalono both of whom had been with me from Basic, AIT, and Jump School.

After a brief orientation and chow, we made our way to the EM club for a few beers. The EM club had a live band, comprised of Filipino's that played all of the classic songs of the time", "Your Cheating Heart", "House of the Rising Sun", Good Lovin", "Paint it Black" "Let it Be" and of course "We Gotta Get Out of This Place." Quickly bored with this we left and went to the PX. We grabbed a six-pack and sat in an open field by the barracks as darkness closed in around us. We made quick note of the nearest bunker about seventy-five yards away and stared at the stars.

Light pollution in this part of the world was scarce and all of the lights on base were pointed down, so the stars were really prevalent. Off in the distance there was another light show, coming on the horizon there were flashes of light followed a few seconds later by the thump of outgoing artillery fire.

We were all quiet, not talking to one another each lost in our own thoughts. I remember looking and finding the North Star and looking eastward from that perspective knowing that was the direction of home. It was the one place I wanted to be right now but nothing was going to change where I was.

I felt so alone. I was with two other people who were good friends and I felt so small and so alone and isolated.

I have never felt like that ever again in my life. We left the field in silence returning to our barracks and tried to sleep.

The heat and humidity were still very oppressive making it hard to sleep and there was the constant drone of generators. The steady thump, thump, thump of artillery fire. I don't think any of us slept much that first night.

After chow the next morning, we were off to personnel to find out which units we would be assigned too. Robert and Eric were assigned to the 1st Air Cavalry Division, but were sent to different Companies.

I was sent to the 199th Light Infantry Brigade. I was familiar with the patch of the 1st Air Cav, the big yellow shield with the black horse head and bold stripe through it. A lot of our drill sergeants and other instructors wore this patch on their right shoulders. I had never heard of the 199th, nor did I have any idea what the patch looked like. The clerk whose desk I sat showed me the patch on a display of unit insignia's located on one of the walls.

We talked about the unit, he was assigning me too the 4th Battalion of the 12th Infantry Regiment located at FSB Nancy. He also let me know I would be sent that day to the BMB of the 199th.

The BMB I would later learn would actually be called Camp Frenzall-Jones, named for the 1st two-brigade hero's that were KIA's.

I met up with Robert and Eric back at our barracks and we collected our gear and said our respective good byes. We all promised to write each other. Shuttle buses would take us to our respective unit bases to begin our combat orientation training.

I arrived at Camp Frenzall-Jones the HQ of the 199th known also as BMB or Brigade Main Base, located on Long Binh Post.

The barrack area was pretty much the same set up; I noted the location of the bunkers and went to chow. After chow there was an orientation explaining that we would spend the next week getting familiar with the area of operations and tactics used by the 199th.

To my surprise, I bumped into Jack Meadon from Basic and AIT. There were only about a dozen of us that would go through the 199th's Jungle Combat Orientation or JCO. We later found out that Jack and I were the only troops assigned to the 4th of the 12th at FSB Nancy.

The combat orientation training was much different from Basic Combat and Advanced Combat Training Jack and I had been through. The instructors pretty much told us to forget some of the stuff we had already learned. The talked about the tactics used by the enemy, we also learned at that time, the Brigade dealt mostly with NVA units, and that the VC was not very active in our AO. This meant we would be fighting against North Vietnamese Regular Army Units and not farmer by day, guerilla fighter by night VC.

The NVA units we were told were well equipped, with AK47's, RPG's, mortars, and .51 Caliber machine guns, they were also well trained, motivated and were some truly bad ass soldiers.

The instructors taught us about the booby traps, bunker complexes used by the NVA, as well as their favorite of flanking units during firefights, and getting in close so our artillery and gun ship support was tough to deploy against them. Booby traps were something we all needed to pay attention too. Their presence was an indication we were approaching an enemy position.

In the hamlets and villages, the local dog population would alert everyone in the village that strangers were approaching by their never ending barking. Even today, barking dogs drive me out of my mind. In the boonies, a booby trap was just as effective, either by the sound of the explosion or the painful screaming of a wounded victim.

Some of the more common used in the 199th's AO were the Cartridge Trap, Whip Trap, Grenade Trap, and the infamous Punji Stake Trap.

The cartridge trap was simple in design. All firearm ammunition is fired when a firing pin hits a primer in the base of the cartridge. This trap would have a cartridge usually a .51 caliber round inserted into a piece of pipe with a wooden or metal plate at the bottom with a large nail sticking up about an eighth of an inch high. Buried in the ground an unsuspecting GI would step on the head or bullet of the cartridge and his weight would force the cartridge down unto the nail pushing it into the primer. The round would go off and cause terrible wounds in the foot and leg.

Because the round had no barrel to guide the path of the bullet, it just exploded upward, tumbling and shredding everything in its path as it went.

The Whip Trap was easy to make, just take a long low-lying branch of a tree or shrub attach some Punji Stakes to the end and bend it back away from the target area.

The trip wire if activated would release the branch and it would whip back to its original and natural position, the Punji Stakes impaling themselves into the legs of the victim.

The Grenade Trap was deployed with the same method but could be used above ground or under water. An old C-Ration can would be nailed to a tree or wedged between some roots under water. A trip wire would be attached to another tree or root and the other end attached to the grenade. A hand grenade activates and explodes when its 'spoon' is released from the firing mechanism. The grenade would have its pin pulled after inserting the grenade into the can, which acted like the human hand holding the spoon in place. Someone tripping the trap would pull the grenade out of the can allowing the 'spoon' to release and the grenade would explode.

The worst and most dangerous we learned was the Punji Stake Trap. Long spiked stakes were inserted into the ground and covered with leaves and small brush. The older traps that had the covers removed would be reclaimed by the jungle, which just over grew the trap. Walking through the jungle on old recovered trails was where these could be found. A newer version and more insidious was the use of a board three feet or longer in length. The stakes would be wedged into the board from the bottom and the board buried along with the stakes about twelve inches below ground.

The stakes would have notches carved into them about a half way down and pointed upward so that once the stake was impaled in the foot or leg it could not be removed because the notch would grab the flesh as anyone tried to remove the stake.

The entire trap had to be dug out by hand board and all so the wounded soldier could then be medevac'd. The NVA also loved to put these traps near spider holes or bunkers.

A clustered group of GI's assisting a trapped comrade was a prime target for automatic weapons fire.

We learned that bunkers were not just holes in the ground that may be covered with logs and dirt. Some of these bunkers were built like a 'Z' in the ground. Looking if you could at a 'Z' bunker from the side you would see a five-foot deep hole dug into the earth the back wall of sloping at an angle away from the entrance. At the top of the back wall a ledge would be dug out so that you could then enter the back end of the 'Z' and be in another five-foot hole. Sometimes these back holes would also contain an entrance to a tunnel that may or may not be connected to another bunker or a larger and deeper tunnel complex. You could never know until someone went in to find out, usually the designated 'Tunnel Rat'.

If a grenade were dropped or thrown into the bunkers main entrance the grenade would explode in the first hole and the occupant hiding would be safe from the deadly shrapnel, although stunned and deafened by the blast they could survive. Spider holes were just foxholes with some camouflage covering. They were used as fighting positions or hiding places from troops on the ground or helicopters above.

The 199th was very active in its operations and successful in routing out and engaging the enemy. Upon completion of the training, we were sent to HQ of the 4th of the 12th for our final unit assignment. I talked with the clerk; he explained I was going to Charlie Company.

He told me it was a good outfit, they basically were choppered into the boonies for two to three weeks at a time and then came back to FSB Nancy and pulled bunker duty on the berm for a few days before going back out.

They rotated with the other Companies, Alpha, Bravo, and Delta but not Echo Company. I asked why and he told me Echo Company was comprised of three units. A heavy weapon and mortar platoon, a Recon platoon and the Tiger Patrol. Now, the Rat Patrol used to be a TV show about gun jeeps operating in the deserts of Africa during WWII. The clerk told me this was the same concept and the Tiger Patrol set up night ambushes and did convoy escorts.

They were not in the jungle or boonies for weeks at a time and did not have to stand bunker duty on FSB Nancy. They had their own hooch's, where they slept as opposed to the line companies sleeping in the bunkers when on FSB Nancy.

This sounded like good duty, the jeeps were equipped with M60 & .50 caliber machine guns, and one jeep had a 105mm Recoilless rifle. This was some heavy-duty firepower and they also deployed with snipers from M Company 75th Rangers.

I asked if I could be assigned, the clerk called the Battalion S1. New meat was always needed so I was on my way. I told Jack about the assignment and he got the same posting, we would be serving in the same unit.

We got a jeep ride to Echo Co 4th of the 12th met up with the Company Clerk with our orders and was introduced to the 1st shirt.

The 1st shirt is the Company First Sergeant; commonly known as 'Top' he is the highest-ranking non-commissioned officer in the Company. These old guys basically run the Army.

I have seen 2nd Lieutenants and other officers shake in their boots around these guys, they were not to be played with. They have the power to bring down a world full of hurt on you if you get on their wrong side. They were the ultimate 'old boy network'. A few phone calls and you had orders to report to some hole in the wall at the end of the earth or your pay started going to a guy that really didn't exist. Top seemed nice enough but definitely gave you the impression he was not someone you could get close too or fool with.

We drew our gear, canteens a rucksack and a weapon an M16, frags, magazines and ammo. Top told us a jeep would take us both out to FSB Nancy the next day at zero nine hundred. We were to report back to company HQ by zero eight forty-five hrs. Beyond that, we were free to go to the EM Club or the PX if we wanted. After chow, we arranged our web gear and loaded the fifteen magazines with eighteen rounds each, and got some sleep, tomorrow would be a big day.

We were on time and so was the jeep that would take us out to Nancy. The driver worked out of Headquarters Company for the 4th Battalion, he was delivering mail and returning an NCO from R&R who was assigned to Bravo 4th of the 12th. I was hoping there was some mail for me in that bag. My mail was on hold until a permanent unit assignment.

The jeep had no canopy top and with the returning, NCO Jack and I had to sit in the cramped back seat with the 4 large mailbags on the floor where our feet normally would be. Wearing our gear and our flak jackets plus the addition of our rucksacks, we were sitting with our knees up around our ears.

Eventually, after leaving BMB and the Long Binh base area we made it to smoother blacktopped roads and we were able to sit on the rear wheel bumpers.

We did see a sign as we left the secure areas that we were leaving Long Binh Post, "Lock & Load". Jack and I sitting in the back seat in our brand new fatigues, boots, and gear stood out like two guys in tuxedos at a biker bar. Everyone knew who the FNG's were.

While we were watching the Vietnamese people we saw on the drive out with great intensity, and clutching our M16 rifles ready to defend ourselves at any moment, the driver and the NCO from Bravo were very relaxed. Just another day driving in the sun to them.

As we passed through some of the smaller hamlets and villages it struck me how primitive the local population was. It was as if I stepped into the pages of National Geographic. Little children were running around naked as jaybirds playing whatever games they knew. Older men wearing boonie hats, ball caps or conical hats worked in the fields. Women tended to the shacks they lived in with openings for a doorway and windows but nothing in them. They were just openings. The thatched roofs covered shacks built from old ammo crates or even tin signs advertising beer, soda, or cigarettes.

Some of the larger homes were constructed from plywood and corrugated metal. Almost everyone was barefoot or they wore flip-flops or a plastic kind of slip on sandal. Older kids were in the rice paddies sitting on or maneuvering large water buffalo's. Was this 1970 or 1470? Adding to the surrealism of it all Honda Motor bikes zipped up and down the streets.

Buses packed to the windows and overloaded on top with everything from luggage, boxes, and farm animals. Culture shock to say the least.

The driver had a side arm in a holster and pistol belt by the seat and the NCO had his M16 across his lap. They seemed to be out for a Sunday drive, while we were on high alert, having listened to our instructors about Vietnamese tossing grenades or shooting at unsuspecting GI's.

I had been in Vietnam for about ten days now and had no idea what day it was, but this was no Sunday drive for Jack and me. We were in a combat zone and the thought of being killed or wounded was definitely something we were both thinking about.

FSB Nancy sits on a hill above the village of Dinh Quan in Long Khanh Province. Dinh Quan village was nick named 'Rock City' because of the huge boulders in and around the village. Some of these boulders were as big as houses, and in some places were stacked on top of each other as if some giant stacked them there like toys to amuse himself.

We drove up the hill to the main gate at Nancy just past Charlie, 2nd Battalion 40th Artillery and were dropped off at the Battalion TOC building.

We were directed to the Echo Company area, which was located at the far end of the road we came in on last building on the right. We would know it by the 105 recoilless rifle mounted on a jeep. Sure enough, the jeep was there and the sign on the small building noted we had arrived at our destination.

We checked in with the clerk dropped our gear and went to chow. We learned that Recon was OPCON to the Brigade for Special Operations and the Tigers were on convoy escort. We had the area to ourselves and we set ourselves up in empty hooch.

A hooch on the fire base was constructed of old wooden ammo crates filled with dirt stacked about two to three feet high running parallel to each other and about five to six feet wide. The top of the hooch was half of a corrugated steel culvert which if both sides were together would form a six-foot wide pipe. All of this would be covered and stacked with sandbags.

The only place to escape the afternoon sun was in the hooch. As the heat and humidity climbed outside the sun beating down on the hooch made feel as if we were sitting in an oven. Even today living in the city during the hottest of summers I have never felt heat like that before, we drank plenty of water and took our salt tabs to stay hydrated.

The Tigers returned just before evening chow and we were introduced to our new platoon members. One of these guys Bob Murray was from Philly and had been transferred from the 82nd Airborne when that unit was returned to Ft. Bragg. He was getting pretty short and was expected to go home in early March.

I was assigned to his jeep and would take over operating the M60; I had an expert rating with the M60 in AIT.

Bob sat with Jack and me and showed us some of the things we would need. One of the most important was that every C-Ration meal came with a P-38. This was a very small but most effective can opener.

Not much bigger than your thumb the little tool was surprisingly efficient in opening the cans. He also showed us how to make a small stove out of a used and empty meat C-Rat can. We used this to cook our meals in the field by using heat tabs or if you really wanted something hot fast a small piece of C-4 plastic explosive.

Bob let us know to be sure to take the weekly and daily anti-malaria pills, and to always have salt tabs and halogen tabs on us at all times. We went over basic strategies for convoy escort and ambush duty. We were scheduled to go out on a night ambush patrol outside the firebase in two days. We fussed around with our gear, wrote letters home.

Now that we were permanently assigned, the mail finally caught up. I got a stack of letters from my girl, my brother, and his friend Mary who agreed to write to me. There was mail from Susie Todder my friend's sister and their Mother Peg, who was like a second Mother to all of us in the neighborhood. I read all the mail several times and answered a few letters.

There was a barbershop on the base staffed by local Vietnamese. So, I got a haircut.

We also learned that for a couple of bucks per month a "house girl" would do our laundry.

The house girl was really a middle-aged local woman from the village. We took advantage of both.

There was not much to do on the firebase except clean weapons, eat, and sleep. This part of the war could be very boring. There was a canteen on the base called the 'Ti Ti' club that opened up in the late afternoon, you get beer and soda, but beyond that, it was just sit and wait for the next assignment.

Recon was still out on their mission and would not be back for days, they would return to the base and go on one more mission before I was reassigned, but I had no idea that was coming. The day of the ambush, we had a briefing in the afternoon. We were told that we would be setting up off the main road highway QL 20 northeast of Nancy. Back in December, they set up an ambush northeast of FSB Nancy where the Tigers had ten to fifteen NVA take a break just in front of their position. Once they set off the claymores and opened up with the machine guns, it was over quickly. That mission saw seven NVA killed and weapons and equipment captured.

Battalion was hoping for the same result based on Intel about enemy re-supply activity around Hill 251. We would leave about 16:30 hrs. Then we would drive northeast on Highway QL 20 to Tra Lam Cay and wait for dusk. Once it was starting to get dark, we would drive back southwest and set up our ambush off the road on the south side of the road around Hill 251.

Most of the major roads have had the vegetation cleared by the engineers from the roadside about 100 to 200 meters back from the road. This made it hard for the NVA or VC to set ambush sites on convoys.

We left Nancy and started heading northeast. There were three men to a jeep and we drove off the base with all three jeeps.

Aside from our own M16 rifles we had two M79 grenade launchers, claymores, a mounted M60 machine gun, a mounted .50 caliber machine gun and the M40 105mm recoilless rifle. Riding along with us was a sniper from M Company 75th Rangers.

After leaving Tra Lam Cay as it was getting dark we drove back southwest to Hill 251 and set up on the south side of the road about 100 meters from the tree line at the base of Hill 251. The hill itself was shaped like an "L" with the longer side running parallel to the road, the shorter side pointed almost directly at the road running north and south. In this position, we had 100 meters of open ground to our west and south, and facing north and east, we had open fields of fire for 400 to 500 meters.

The backdrop of the jungle on the hill would make it difficult to see us from the road, and any one coming out of the tree line was exposed in open ground. One other toy we had with us was an AN/PVS-2 Starlight scope. This big bulky device looked like a big video camera. When you looked into the viewfinder, everything was tinted green. It worked by collecting any light source from stars the moon or even man made light and used it to illuminate whatever area you were looking at in the viewfinder. We would all use the device during our assigned watch period to check for anyone moving around our perimeter.

We set up our claymores facing towards the jungle and also had the M40 facing the same way. We set up our jeeps in a triangle formation but in such a way, as any of the three jeeps would be able to pull out and drive away from the NDP if needed. We would all be inside the perimeter and between the jeeps. We were all setup by nineteen thirty hours and were waiting for the 2000-hour curfew to take effect.

There was very little traffic on the road but some people were getting back to their villages late. Once twenty thirty hours came, they could be engaged if they posed any threat to us.

The first guard watch started at twenty hundred hours and lasted until zero five thirty the next morning. We pulled one and a half hour shifts with the second guard starting at twenty thirty hours. This staggered the watch period so we had two men on watch throughout the night. My watch started at zero one thirty hours, the new guys always drew the middle of the night. The best watch times were at the start of the shift and at the end, either way you were able to sleep without being interrupted. My watch also overlapped with Bob and the sniper from 75th Rangers.

The night went by without incident but I can tell you it was hard to going to sleep at first. I just laid there at my position and thought about where I was and how much longer I would have to be there. I was still awake when Bob came over to let me know my shift was starting. We talked in whispers so as not to alert anyone of our position and we could not smoke. There was no around us and the night was quiet except for the animal and bird noise from the jungle. It's amazing how much sound carries over an open field at night.

One of the things I learned using my own eyes or the scope was not to look directly at an object. When you did that, your mind played tricks on you and you begin to see things move or take on a new shape. The trick was to use your peripheral vision and look over or past something. We did see an antelope or deer about 300 yards to our east grazing in the open field.

When Bob's watch was over the sniper and I talked some. He had a modified M14 designated as an XM21. It fired special 'match grade' ammo that was supposed to be perfectly balanced.

He was getting short like Bob and would be going home in early March. After my watch, I was able to get back to sleep, exhaustion finally set in.

We were all up and moving just before dawn, and packing up our gear. We brought in the claymores and pulled out to the road and parked on the side of it. Bob called in our position and the fact we were ready to RTB when Battalion notified us they wanted two men to stay. They wanted them to stay behind take up a position on Hill 251 and stay there all morning as an OP. Bob noted he would stay and picked me as the second man. We took our M16 rifles, a PRC-25 radio, and an M79 grenade launcher.

The Tigers left for Nancy, and Bob and I climbed up the side of the hill. Once we made it to the top we saw a heavily used trail that ran from the base of the hill by the road all the way to the top and along the top running south and then east. We walked along the trail finding nothing of interest and came back to a point where we could see the trail and the road. We set up our position about ten meters off the trail on the east side.

We also had taken some extra water and C-rations so we had something to eat.

We had some C rations for breakfast and talked about the unit and its operations. I had a boatload of questions. Bob had been in the 82nd Airborne in a line company so this new duty with the Tigers was a blessing for him. Riding up and down the roads all day beat humping in the boonies every time. I felt I had gotten lucky with this assignment.

Around mid-morning, we saw a Vietnamese man coming toward us down the trail from the south. He was wearing a soft boonie type hat and black pajama shorts. He was bare foot and carrying a long two-man saw. He did not have a weapon and Bob signaled to me to be still and quiet. We were on the east side of the trail about five meters into the brush. I set my selector switch to full auto and waited as he approached. He passed by us without his knowing we were there, he continued down the trail and hill went out to the road and started walking in the direction of Dinh Quan. Needless to say, my heart was pounding but Bob explained he was probably just a logger coming back from working in the jungle. This was my first experience in the field where I just watched a Vietnamese walk past me, it would not be the last, but at the time, I did not know that.

The rest of the morning was uneventful and around noon, we had radio info that the Tigers were on their way to pick us up. They arrived about twenty minutes later and we went back to FSB Nancy. We spent the rest of the day hanging around taking care of our gear and just relaxing.

More mail came in and I had another stack, from my girl, 'Mom Peg', her daughter Susie, Mary, and my Mom all sent letters.

The next day we were assigned to do convoy escort duty on highway QL 20. We would go to a pre-determined location and meet up with the convoy and escort them to another pre-determined point. This basically went on all day and we got to spend some time in some of the local villages. The kids would be the first ones around us and were always begging for stuff.

They would say things like "You number one GI, you souvenir me," some of the older people especially the women would point at me and say "you babiesan." Remember I had just turned eighteen the past November and the fact I was only about 110 pounds did not help. In addition, my boots, fatigues, and gear were all brand spanking new so this FNG stood out from the rest of the guys. We also had the chance to sample some of the local foods. The villagers were very eager to sell us all kinds of stuff.

There was plenty of cold Coke to be found and they also had a local beer called 33 and Tiger brands. Both were pretty bad so I was told and there was no drinking on duty anyway. Mixing some of our C rations with some local rice with chicken or pork made for a decent lunch. Within the local villages, it was pretty safe, most of the enemy elements we dealt with were NVA, the VC kept a low profile at this stage of the war.

Outside the villages on the highway was where the danger was. The NVA would routinely ambush large convoys travelling on the highways with quick hit and run tactics.

The early morning hours were the worst. The NVA at night would bury or plant near the road explosive devices and would denote these when large two & a half ton trucks got close to the device. Then they would fire RPG rockets, B40 rockets and strafe the convoy with .51 caliber machine gun fire while dropping some mortar rounds on the road. By the time, we started return fire on the suspected enemy positions they would run back into the jungle and disappear.

These types of quick tactics caused a lot of damage and casualties and would not give us an opportunity to respond with any fire support like helicopter gunships or artillery.

We did not have any trouble during our convoy escorts so those days were spent driving back and forth and spending time in the villages. The people for the most part were friendly and caused us no problems.

We were not aware at the time that the Tiger patrol was going to be disbanded and that convoy escorts were going to be handled by the 152nd MP Platoon and track and armor units of D Troop 17th CAV in our area of operations. I also did not know that I would later return to this type of duty with the 17th CAV while still assigned to Recon when the Brigades operations started winding down for its return to the US later in the year. It's funny my experience with Bob watching the logger on the trail would become part of my duty with Recon and my convoy escort duty with the Tigers would become part of my duty again with the 17th CAV.

Jack and I hung out on the firebase cleaned or weapons and worked with our gear.

A few days later I woke up around zero eight hundred. Got my boots on, grabbed my boonie hat, and started walking to the mess hall for breakfast. The mess hall was off the main road coming up from the main gate on the right just beyond the battalion TOC. Across the road is where the 2nd Battalion 40th Artillery was located. Some guys were off loading 81mm mortar rounds from a 2 ½ ton truck right by that unit.

I was walking down the road about to light the first cigarette of the day when there was a large explosion. The shock wave startled and knocked me on my butt. I checked myself to see if I had any injuries and finding none ran down towards the 2 ½ ton truck about twenty-five meters away. The first thing I saw was a GI sitting against a sandbagged wall.

I could not tell if he was white or black but he was naked and his skin was charred with, spots of red were there were open wounds. Smoke was still coming off his hairless head and he had a dazed look on his face. Both legs were missing from the hip and part of his penis was gone. He was reaching out with his left hand as if trying to grab something.

A medic from the base aid station ran up and started treating him. There was not a lot of blood near him the burns from the blast must have cauterized the wounds.

I looked at the cab of the truck where the driver was still sitting behind the wheel. He was slumped over the wheel and had lost his left arm, a large pool of blood formed on the ground running down the side of the door less truck he was obviously dead.

There was a lot of confusion, screaming and the barking of orders from everyone at the scene.

To the left and in front of the truck was another body. This man had no arms and one of his legs was gone the other severed above the knee. He was also naked the blast tore him in half and his insides were hanging out a sprayed across the ground. I was stunned and in shock at the scene before me, it was horrible. There was a lot of shouting as Officer's and NCO's started barking orders.

The first man I saw was on his back now the medic had stopped working on him, he was dead. A Sergeant grabbed me and said, "Here help me with this," he had a large rubber package in his hand. Together we opened his package, it was a body bag. We laid it next to the man's body lying next to, the truck. We lifted the dead man's body into the bag and as we did, more of his internal organs came out of him spilling over the ground. The Sergeant told me "We have to put all of his body parts into the bag." We were not wearing any gloves we just scooped up the slippery body parts with our hands and place them in the bag with the rest of his body.

Another soldier came over and placed another body bag on the ground next to the truck. The three of us pulled the driver out of the cab of the truck and placed his body in the body bag. I was wearing a tee shirt and my fatigue pants and was stained with blood and guts literally. The first NCO placed his hand on my shoulder looked in my eyes and said, "You did fine son their families will be grateful." This was my duty that day. As traumatic as it was it was done out of a sense of duty and comradeship.

These men were now going to graves registration to be identified and prepared for their return to the families that would grieve for them. They were going home.

I was now numb, a jeep pulled up with a short flatbed trailer behind it and we placed the three body bags on the trailer. I only remember putting bodies of two men into the body bags. Where or who had filled the third body bag I was not sure of. We hopped unto the jeep and drove down to the firebase LZ to wait for the chopper. I tried to light a cigarette waiting for the bird and the Sergeant who I helped with the first body pulled out his lighter. He was an older man about forty or so and a Master Sergeant. After lighting my cigarette, he asked "Are these your first casualty's son?"
I replied "They were."
He said, "They will not be your last, what you did today was not pleasant, but it had to be done and you did your duty for these men."
The chopper arrived and we loaded the three body bags onto the deck, and watched it lift off the LZ. I looked at the door gunner as it lifted off; he was eating peaches from a C ration can.

The jeep left without me as I told the Master Sergeant I would walk back up to the base, he said, "That would be fine and wished me luck."

I walked back up to the company area and saw Jack coming out of the shower. He saw my blood stained clothes and asked if I was OK. I pulled my boots off and stepped into the shower clothes and all and let the water wash the dead off me.

Afterward Jack and I talked about what I had seen and done. I did not know those three men, I had no idea who they were or what their names were. Having done what, I did for two of those men, is something I knew had to be done and by doing it I felt a strange sense of kinship with them both.

Jack had heard the explosion and was ordered by the Company Commander and some of the others from Echo Company to stay away from the area. Apparently, the men from Charlie Company 4th of the 12th who were killed were off loading some cases of mortar rounds from a forward base.

Not much more than a week ago, I was told I was going to Charlie 4th of the 12th. I could very well have been one of those men. As the new man, I would have been assigned to every work detail. I wonder today if one of them died in my place.

I would later learn that the mortar rounds were left overnight on the base LZ that is outside the perimeter wire. An 81mm mortar round has three safety devices to prevent an accidental discharge. This means that the unattended mortar rounds had to have been booby trapped by NVA sappers. I never did learn their names or where they were from. It would be nine months later and I would re-live this horror with a man I did know, and another fort-four years before it came back to haunt me again but in a much deeper and disabling way.

My memory is of three men killed, when in actuality, it was thirteen men killed from Charlie Company 4th of the 12th and several more wounded. My perception and recollection of this incident was focused on the three men

I had to deal with. This was the worst accident in the Brigades history. Learning of the additional casualties and learning all of their names from the Brigades documented KIA list was shocking, but I still could not say which of the thirteen names listed on the wall in Washington DC on Panel 14W Rows 51 to 56 were the two I helped to return to their families. I was shocked at the damage done to the bodies of those young men. The reality of the war had really been driven home that day, I knew that it was possible I could be killed, but to be killed in such a way was disturbing.

These poor men had lost their lives not to enemy fire but because of an unfortunate decision to leave the mortar rounds unguarded and available to enemy sappers.

The Nam was a very dangerous place, I had been here just seventeen days and had to be here for eleven more months, and I had no idea how or where I was going to finish my tour. I never did get to breakfast and lunch was not on my mind. I spent the rest of the day thinking about my future and wondered if I had one.

For the next three days, the Battalion practically shut down its operations while it investigated the incident that had claimed the lives of so many young men needlessly. I was interviewed and several other men also were interviewed, including the Master Sergeant I worked with that day. There was also a memorial service held on the base. Seeing the thirteen boots with a helmet on top of an M16 all lined up is something my mind has blocked out. I know it happened but I don't remember it. It will most likely come to me in the night as I sleep, another suppressed memory woken by the beast within me coming out into the light.

The 'Tigers' spent the rest of the month escorting convoys. We were up and down QL 20 from Xa Gia Tan southeast of FSB Nancy to Madagui hamlet to the northeast. The NVA were laying low as if preparing for another TET offensive like they did in 1968. This year TET would fall on the 6th of February and would be the year of the dog. Hopefully the dog would sleep, not bark and would never bite. This is Vietnam however and the dog is not looking for a nap. You might here a growl now and then but eventually all dogs chained in the junk yard will bite.

This year would be no different. Before the Brigade would stand down and go home 112 more Redcatchers would be added to the total list of 757 killed in action. They would return to their homes in silence, their voices heard no more and a nation would forever ask why.

Chapter Two, Changes & Reality;

The new month would start out with some unexpected disappointments. Jack and I would learn that the battalion had decided to disband the Tiger Patrol. Once we got the official word, we had some apprehension because we had no idea what was going to become of us. Assignment to a line unit was not a good option; M Company Rangers was an option as well as Recon.

Recon was still out on one of their missions and had just left Nancy when the word came down. We would have to wait for them to return before we would know what was to become of us.

Even then there was no guarantee we would be assigned, it was really up to LT. Kamble and SFC Snead, and they handpicked their people. So it was hurry up and wait.

Just before TET on the 6th, Jack and I got the word that Recon was coming back to Nancy. It was getting to the time when we would know what our fate was going to be. The Company area was now filled with people, Recon had returned to their assigned hooch's and was getting busy with cleaning weapons, opening mail, getting showered and into clean uniforms.

Jack and I stayed by ourselves in our own hooch's to let these guys settle in. We had not met any of them before so to them we were just a couple of 'newfers' or FNG's. The next morning Lt Kamble and SFC Snead came to see Jack and me.

They asked us the basic questions, how did we get into the Army, how long had we been in country and whether we had any combat experience. Our answers were pretty much the same except Jack had been drafted and I had enlisted.

We talked about our work with the Tiger Patrol and we also discussed my involvement with the mortar explosion two weeks ago. They explained that Recons mission was to be deployed to areas where Battalion S2 had Intel about enemy activity. They were choppered into an area as a platoon and once they reached their destination point or NDP, they would then break off into six or seven man teams and run clover leaf patrols from that area.

The main function was to find and track the enemy, look for base camps, supply points and set up live and mechanical ambushes.

We had no idea what a mechanical ambush was and they explained basically they would take claymore mines and daisy chain two or three together and use a mouse trap, battery and a tripwire on a used trail.

The enemy would trip the wire causing the mouse trap to engage, two metal screws on the mouse trap would be wired to the + & - battery terminals so when the trap was sprung the lever would contact the two screws completing a circuit allowing current to flow to the blasting caps that touched off the claymores. Recon would be set up at its NDP 100 to 150 meters away. We let both know we were not interested in being assigned to a line company.

At that point, we learned we were now part of Echo Recon 4th of the 12th.

One of the guys 'Red 'Sanderson, was going back to a rear job at BMB; he was getting out of the field. He had a single, one-bedroom model hooch, right next to the berm on the northwest end of the base. He was in the process of moving out and I would be moving in when he was gone. 'Red' did not have much just his field gear an old portable radio his weapon and a case of beer. This would all be packed up in the jeep that was returning to BMB tomorrow after lunch. I got my gear what little there was packed up in anticipation of the move. Just after evening chow, we got word of a platoon meeting in a mortar pit just beyond 'Recons' area.

All of the members of 'Recon' were there and SFC Snead started the meeting. He let us know we were to go back out in about two days to the Xuan Loc area on a mission. Then he changed the topic, "It seems we have a thief among us," he said. "Someone has stolen a case of beer out of 'Reds' hooch, anyone have any ideas who could have done this?"

As he finished his sentence, he was looking right at me. I was stunned, I had no idea what he was talking about, but clearly, I was being accused of the theft. Everyone else was also looking at me and awaiting my response.

"If you're accusing me sergeant, you're wrong," I said. "I have no idea what happened to the case of beer." Why would I steal a case of beer and what in the world would I have done with it since lunchtime? I certainly didn't drink it; I'm as sober as a judge."

Snead said, "You, were with 'Red' when he packed, you knew he had the beer, you're the likely suspect."

I looked at 'Red' and said to him; "Look 'Red', I don't know what happened to your beer, why would I steal something having just been assigned to this platoon. It's not the best way to start out and if I did I would surely be out of 'Recon' and reassigned to a line company, which no one here wants to happen, to me, or to them."

'Red' responded with; "I believe you 'Ski', and I think it's obvious you haven't been drinking." Snead then said, "Well the beer is still gone and I guess we'll never know, so let's consider the matter closed."

"Not so fast sergeant, you just accused me of stealing in front of the entire unit the matter is not closed," I said. "I have no idea what happened to the case of beer, but I did not steal it, and for the record, the next time you accuse me of something, you read me my rights first, is that clear?"

Snead bristled I had just gotten into his face in front of everyone including the LT, who finally had something to say, "Ski I don't think you took the beer either. So let this be a lesson to everyone to secure your shit. "We have a mission in two days so everyone get ready and relax until we take off, meeting adjourned."

The LT left the pit followed by Snead and Woung. The rest of us were still standing around and I said again; "Red, I did not steal your beer." "I know" he said, "let's forget about it, I have one more night here so let's celebrate at the canteen." Ted Spancer chimed in, "I like the way you stood up to Snead, he was not happy."

"Yeah, you got in his face and put him in his place, sometimes he can be an asshole," said Tim Warden.

I joined the platoon that night for beers at the small bar on base. It seems everyone was supportive and there were no hard feelings, there would not be any problems with me and the guys. Snead however might be a different matter. In a few months, he would remember my challenge.

We would be at Nancy for two more days before we were assigned another mission, in the meantime Jack and I worked with the guys to get our gear in order for humping the boonies. One of the things we needed to do was to have the mama-san at the local village tailor shop add the 'Recon' tab above our 199th Brigade shoulder patch on our fatigue shirts. This was going to be easy enough because Recon members all wore 'Strikers' or cammo fatigues. We were issued two sets of new strikers.

What we both needed was an aluminum frame to hook our rucksacks too. This allowed us to carry the heavy packs more efficiently. The frame made the ruck sit higher and more squarely on the back and provided a strap across the small of the back. We were hoping to get the frames before we started the next mission but they did not arrive in time.

In addition to my web gear, I would carry a pair of two quart canteens of water as well as a five-quart bladder canteen. I also needed two ponchos and a liner two claymore mines, ten feet of detcord, a first aid kit, bayonet and 150 rounds of M60 ammo. In the ammo pouches of my web gear, I had ten M16 magazines with twenty rounds in each mag.

Add a helmet, boonie hat and enough C rations and LRRP rations for five days in the field. All of this including my 110 pounds would weigh in at about 220 pounds.

The pack and equipment weighed as much as I did. Humping this around the jungle in ninety degree temperatures plus the nearly 100% humidity was going to be tough work. If the enemy didn't kill me, the pack surely would. In a few weeks, however I would toss this pack around like a rag doll.

We were going to be inserted by helicopter into the Xuan Loc area. I was told there were rubber plantations in this area and it was known to be active with the 274th NVA regiment. On the day we left, it was hot as usual. I found I could barely lift my rucksack.

The rucksack had the two ponchos, two claymore mines, all of my food for five days and the five-quart bladder canteen tied to the outside. In addition, I had tied the detcord and a couple of smoke grenades to the sides of the rucksack.

First, I put on my web gear with the two, two-quart canteens ammo pouches, four fragmentation grenades and first aid kit.

Then the rucksack would have to be put on and I learned the only way to get my rucksack on was to sit on the ground put my arms into the straps, roll over onto my hands and knees I try to stand up. Once on my feet the M60 belt ammo was draped across each shoulder. Then it was the long walk to the base LZ to wait for the choppers. I walked like an old woman completely bent over from the weight of the pack and equipment.

By the time, we got to the LZ the pack straps were cutting into my shoulders and I was soaked in sweat.

SFC Snead gave me a brand new OD green towel to drape around my neck, I used this to wipe the sweat off my head constantly, and it was soaked in no time. The choppers finally arrived and the prop blast felt good. We needed three birds to get to our LZ in Xuan Loc.

I sat on the floor of the last chopper in the middle between the two doors. This Huey had the doors taken off so once we were airborne the air rushing in was a great relief. SFC Snead knelt down on one knee right in front of me. To my left was Ted Spancer the company net RTO.

Sitting on the floor to my left with their legs, hanging out the side was Sgt. Harry Soakley the "Hearts" team leader and Mark Malone the teams M60 gunner. Sitting the same way to my right was Lyle Laden the team's point man and Don Hardack.

The chopper ride was almost pleasant until the bird nosedived to tree top level and then continued to fly that way at high speed for a couple of miles. Looking out the doors it seemed as if the top of the trees would snag the bottom of the chopper and we would crash.

I later learned that this type of insert was used in sparse jungle and forest areas so the enemy could not determine where we would land. We finally broke into open ground and I could see explosions going off in the tree line we were headed for. Arty was prepping the LZ for us. We also had a 'Pink Team' escort us in. This is a three helicopter unit comprised of an OH-6 Loach with two AH-1 Cobra Gun Ships.

They were sometimes referred to as a 'Hunter Killer Team'. The guys who were sitting with their feet out the door were now all standing on the skids. The LZ itself was all thigh high grass as thick as a fairway on a golf course. The helicopter I learned would not set down onto the ground, the grass hid broken off tree stumps and the enemy would plant thick tree branches and metal spikes into the grassy area to spear landing helicopters. We had to jump out of the bird but it was only about three or four feet off the ground. The guys on the skids jumped off the bird almost at the same time, SFC Snead went out of the bird to my right.

Now here I am butt walking across the floor trying to get to the door opening to my right. The pilot is keeping the bird in a steady hover waiting for me to get my act together. I look over at the door gunner who is just grinning away, and enjoying the show I was putting on.

I finally get to the door opening and get my left foot onto the skid and just as I step off the pilot pulled ever so gently back on the stick. The Huey went straight up about three feet, I went head over heels, and flipped like a pancake into the LZ like a turtle on its back, I lost my helmet and weapon. I'm looking up at the door gunner who is now laughing his ass off. Welcome to the Nam newbie.

Snead grabs me by the collar hands me my weapon and helmet and shoves me in the direction of the tree line and yells "move." Once inside the tree line I am amazed at how hot and humid it is. You would think it would be cooler out of the sun, but was actually worse. The air here in the jungle was heavy with moisture and with no breeze, it just hung there as still as a statue.

We would find ourselves humping the rest of the morning before stopping. We went about a click or 1000 meters due south and away from LTL 25 the main road in the area.

We crossed the S Sau Creek and stopped for midday chow and set up a defensive position just south of the creek. I was soaked to the bone with my own sweat and crossing the creek actually felt good. I noted that I had scratches and small cuts on my arms because my sleeves were rolled up. Me and Snead were the only ones with our sleeves up, everyone else had the sleeves down. Now I knew why. Walking through the jungle with bare arms just asked for trouble. Once we stopped, I rolled the sleeves down. In addition, I learned to get rid of my under shorts and go 'commando' keeping them just caused a rash you wouldn't believe.

Now I also had some hitch hikers with me. I had leeches on my legs from crossing the creek. I pulled my pants legs up and used a lit cigarette to get rid of the blood suckers. Then I had to drop my pants to check other more sensitive areas. I had a lot of new little blood sucking friends.

Taking the rucksack off was quite a relief. There was no rest for the weary though, the Hearts team was being sent out on a clover leaf patrol. Basically, what we did is the seven-man team would walk about 300 meters to the south of our position then turn east for another 300 meters and then turn north for 300 meters so that when we turned back west we should come back to the original position.

Once we came back the Spades team would do the same although once they went 300 meters south they would then turn west instead of east.

Assuming of course that once we left our midday position we would be traveling south, we had already swept the area that we would be walking towards. The patrol itself was uneventful humping into the jungle without the rucksack was almost a blessing but the web gear and M60 ammo was still kicking my ass but we returned in about an hour.

It was now our turn to get some rest, water, and midday chow. We ate the C- rations first because they weigh the most.

Spades however had found an old NVA base camp with bunkers and hooch's. They left half their team at the base camp and the rest came back to our defensive position, then everyone packed up all the gear and met up with the rest of the Spades team at the base camp. Carrying the extra gear was definitely a pain but fortunately, we only had to go a short distance.

The base camp itself was small, only two hooch's but they were surrounded by six bunkers in the shape of a triangle. Three bunkers on each side of the triangle with corner bunkers capable of covering more than one direction of fire.

As we walked into the camp, I was amazed that I had come into the camp having totally missed seeing the bunkers and found myself standing in front of hooch.

The camouflage the enemy used was spot on. It was not like this in JCO at BMB, Snead pointed out the bunkers to me, and again I was amazed, I actually had to walk up to one before I could see it.

There was some equipment at the camp but it was obvious that no one had been there for some time. We found empty C-ration cans, canteens, ponchos, ammo crates, and web gear. All of it GI issue. We had a Vietnamese scout with us as a permanent assignment and his name was Woung. He was a former VC soldier who surrendered to the ARVN Army and went through the Chieu Hoi Program. My nickname was "SKI" and Woung had a hard time pronouncing it, so he called me "Soukie".

I learned later why Woung surrendered and changed sides and it was quite obvious he hated the communists. The VC came to his village one night and gave him a choice after already killing his sister. Join the VC and fight for them or his parents would suffer the same fate as his sister. Woung saved his parent's lives and fought with the VC but as soon as it was possible, he surrendered to the South Vietnamese Forces and became a Chieu Hoi Scout. Woung was very proficient in the jungle, new the enemy's tactics, how they moved, and the preferred terrain they liked to hide in. He was also dedicated and brave in any encounters we had with the enemy, everyone trusted Woung with their lives.

As we went through this base, camp Woung assured us that no one had been there in a while. We also found an overgrown trail just outside this base camp and the LT decided we would move away from the camp about 500 meters and setup our NDP or night defensive position.

Once we got to the NDP, we settled in and Sgt. Soakley showed me where to set my position and place the two claymores I carried. Soakley also explained the basics of our operations in the bush, he told me, "One of the most important things we do is to move like the enemy moves.

We never talk over a whisper we keep our gear tied tight to avoid any rattling or other causes of making noise. Clean up all of your trash don't leave anything out in the open bury or burn it. Learn to move through the jungle without disturbing it, step over things, go around things, and move through the jungle as gently as you can so you don't leave any signs of your presence.

Learn to look at the terrain around you take it all in anything that looks unnatural or out of place is a threat potential. If we run into an ambush Charlie will be so close, it won't be funny run at his position and try to get inside his perimeter or behind him. You're already in the kill zone when the firing starts going at the enemy's position takes away his advantage, any questions"? I had a bunch of questions but first I had to take in everything he just said it was a lot to process.

We set the claymores together, claymore mines have a back blast when detonated so they would have to be at least ten meters away and preferably, next to a large tree that would be between me and the mine. Both mines were linked together with the detcord so that when I set the primary off they both went at the same time.

I settled in by placing one of my ponchos on the ground, this would be my bed. The poncho liner served as a cover or blanket. I would use my ruck as a pillow. I had some more C-rations for dinner and waited for darkness.

Once I ate, I got word that Snead wanted to see me in the CP area that is located in the center of the NDP. I walked over to the CP and met up with Jack who Snead wanted also. Snead promptly sent us both back to our positions to retrieve our weapons.

Getting back to the CP he told us "When you are in the bush never go anywhere without your weapon," he also told us that we were to know the exact position of the man to our left and right at all times. If we had to go out forward of our position to relieve ourselves we took our weapon and let the man to our left and right know where we were going by holding up the toilet paper pack that was in every C ration box and LRRP ration pack.

In addition, he told us "The first magazine is to be loaded with all tracer rounds and should be fired on full auto whenever a fire fight starts, then you can use regular ammo on single fire." He continued, "Always aim your weapon about one to two feet off the ground unless you have a specific target, anyone we encounter out here in the bush is considered to be the enemy, men, women and even children any questions?"

We were too dumb founded to have any logical questions but he let us know to always check with the team sergeants when we were not sure what to do.

We would be pulling guard duty from our teams' RTO position and we were forbidden to sleep on watch. Situation reports or sit reps would be called in once every hour and when called all we had to do to respond was to key the mic twice or break squelch.

This indicated that everything was OK. No response or repeated keying of the mic indicated trouble.

I went back to my position and sat there thinking about the day's events. Now as a young kid, I had seen all the WWII John Wayne movies were the Marines would settle in for the night and listen to the Japs say things like

"Marine you die." As I'm sitting at my position, I can hear the rustling of leaves and bushes out in front of my position.

I look over to my left where the M60 gunner Mark Malone has his position. He's just sitting there as if nothing is wrong, off to my right Ted Spancer the RTO is setting up the PRC-25 radio for the coming night of guard watches. Am I the only one that hears this movement, just then it happens; "fuck……. Youuu."

I almost jump out of my skin, and then it happens again "fuck…… youuu." I look to my right Ted is settling in for the night.

Off to my left I see Mark looking at me. I point out to the front of me and it happens again; "fuck…..youuu." I'm wide eyed, shaking and pointing to my ear and to my front.

Mark gets up with his .45 pistol and comes over to me and says, "It's a lizard." "Fuck….. youuu." "A what? " I ask. "It's a lizard," Mark says. "In the central highlands there is also a Re Up bird." Re Up is GI slang for re-enlisting. Imagine hearing that conversation between two animals your first night in the bush. "Re Up"……..″fuck……youuu." It was going to be a long year.

The next few days were uneventful we humped to a location stopped at mid-day.

We ran cloverleaf operations from there. During this time, the LT wanted to evaluate my ability to walk point. Point men were important. They picked the path of movement for the entire unit and had to be aware of everything in front of them. I was a lousy point man.

Soakley worked with me giving me my azimuth directions and desperately tried to slow me down. I walked to fast, and struggled and fought with the jungle. There were these small vines, called 'come alongs', they somehow attached themselves to everything they came in contact with including me.

The red ants were also a problem. When they bite you, it hurts. I was walking along getting caught on vines and getting ants all over me.

On one of these, clover leafs while walking point I had just freed myself from some of these vines when I walked right up on a cobra. The snake made a hissing sound that sounded more like someone exhaling a deep breath through a tube. The snake was about three feet in front of me. It stood up and fanned out its hood its tongue flicking in and out and it was looking right at me. Its head was about three feet off the ground and slowly moving back and forth but it never took its eyes off me. I emptied the magazine of my M16 and blew its fanned head off.

Woung was with us and he ran up to see what was going on. Everyone else was lying prone waiting to see what was going on. Soakley was not happy he was on the radio explaining to the LT what happened. Woung on the other hand was very happy. "Good job Soukie, we have numba one dinner tonight." He had a knife out in seconds and was field dressing the snake that was about ten feet long, its headless body still slithering and coiling.

The LT was not happy, but hey what else could I do. My point walking days were over.

The pack was getting lighter but the heat and humidity were still kicking my butt. I was learning the disciplines of recon work, keeping your gear tied down tight, burying all of your trash and bowel movements, field stripping the cigarette butts down to the filters which were burned at midday or when we set up our NDP at the end of the day, but most of all learning to speak in whispered conversations and to use hand signals. My encounter with the cobra did not meet any of these standards.

As a small unit usually about twenty-nine men in total, we moved around quickly but quietly. The line units moving through the jungle ninety to 120 men made a lot of noise. One day we were told we would have friendly units operating close to our midday position to our west.

Due to the density of the jungle, we never saw them and they never saw us but we could hear them as they moved past us. After they moved on, we ran clover leafs again and my team crossed the line of march by the line company we heard earlier. We were about 600 meters west of our midday position and we could see the trail they left behind.

We found cigarette butts, empty c-ration cans, along with other types of trash, not to mention the path they used getting through the jungle was easy to spot. The NVA would have no trouble trailing this line unit and attacking its rear.

Sergeant Soakley worked with me when we moved in formation and ran clover leafs at walking drag. The drag man is the last man in the group. I had tried my hand at walking point but the LT said I moved too fast. A point man walking too fast is not going to last long.

Lyle Layden did most of the point work; he carried a 12 gauge Winchester Model 1912 pump action shotgun. The word was that Lyle could smell the NVA or native people in our area. He moved slightly ahead of the main group but always within sight of the NCO that walked behind him. The NCO was closely followed by a company net RTO. Lyle had the ability to see and hear things as he approached them. He was an excellent point man and the LT relied on his talents every time we moved.

Walking drag was a good spot for me because I had the problem of walking too fast. As the last man in the column, it was my job to hang back and be sure no one was following us. I had to keep and maintain sight of the man in front of me usually an NCO.

Some times that distance got to be as much as twenty or thirty yards depending on the density of the jungle. I also learned what every good point man needs to learn and that is what the terrain looks like after men have moved through it. Several times, I lost eye contact with the man in front of me but the new skills I was learning helped me to pick up his trail so I could rejoin the group. My ability to close up and get back within five yards of the man in front of me worked out well.

After we were out for four days, we got the word from the Battalion net RTO, Tim Warden we were going to be extracted out and going back to FSB Nancy.

We approached the LZ and worked our way around its perimeter to see if the NVA was there hoping to be able to ambush incoming choppers.

This is something they did often just setting up some fighting positions and holes waiting for the chance to open up on incoming birds. Seeing that the LZ was clear of enemy activity, we pulled back into the jungle about fifty meters or so to wait for the birds. The LT had arty prep the LZ just prior to the choppers arrival and once the arty stopped, we moved to the edge of the LZ. Communications were established with the choppers and we popped smoke and the pilots confirmed they had "mellow yellow" smoke.

The LZ was large running northwest to southeast 200 meters wide and a click long, it was more than enough for the three birds that landed almost at the same time we then ran to our assigned chopper hopped on and they lifted off.

This was another hair raising experience because in order for the birds to get off the ground the pilots tilted the nose of the Huey down so the rotor backwash pushed the chopper up into the air and helped it gain speed. It flew this way for several yards until it got up into the air and then we were well on our way back to Nancy.

Once back at Nancy it was time to relax and rest up. I was still struggling with my gear and I knew I had to come up with a better solution. Humping in the boonies with 100 lbs. of pack was bad enough but doing clover leafs still weighed down by equipment had to change. So from that vantage point I came up with a new strategy. I stripped my web gear down to the barest of essentials and then set it all up again trying to lighten the load.

On either side of the web belt buckle, I had first aid kit pouches then I kept the two ammo pouches one left and one right of the first aid kits. Each of these had five twenty round M16 magazines, and on either side of each, I carried four grenades two on each pouch. The pouches had a place to strap a M67 baseball type grenade to either side.

Then I replaced the two, two quart canteens with a pair of one quart canteens with a built in canteen cup and cover for both onto the web belt so that they road at my kidneys. In the small of the back, I had an open space for the ruck sack. Now when we ran cloverleaf operations I had two canteens, 200 rounds of M16 ammo, four grenades, and two first aid kits.

The suspender part of the web gear I taped my bayonet upside down on the left suspender. Now I was ready for clover leafs with a minimum load and all my weaponry. My helmet was comprised of four parts; the steel pot, a fiberglass liner that held the webbing that sat on my head, a camouflaged helmet cover, and a retaining band to keep the cover from sliding off.

Once the cover was placed on the helmet, there were four U shaped flaps that fit inside the helmet. Then you put the liner in the helmet slid the retaining band over the cover and you were done.

I kept my boonie hat in my pants cargo pocket and wore that on clover leafs instead of the helmet. The ruck sack was a different story. I emptied the entire pack and started over. The pack itself had a main compartment and three smaller external pockets. I left the external pockets empty to carry food. I found that most C-ration cans fit well in the external pockets if packed on their sides.

In the main compartment, I folded my second poncho, this was the one I would use as a tent cover if needed. Then I would pack all of the LRRP rations for that mission.

On top of those I packed the two M18 Claymore Mines, detcord, and the M57 detonating device or 'clacker'.

The pair of two quart canteens would go side by side on top of all that. Then I folded my ground poncho and liner. On top of that, I packed a one-pound block of C4 plastic explosive.

The last thing to go into the pack would be two belts of M60 ammo with about seventy rounds on each belt. I would wear these Poncho Via style when on clover leafs. On the outside, I tied a couple of smoke grenades. I thought that now I was ready to go.

When we stopped to do clover leafs I had all my combat gear two quarts of water and could open the main compartment of the ruck sack to get the M60 ammo. When we set up an NDP I unpacked the ground poncho and liner, the claymores my canteens and I had access to C-ration or LRRP rations. The LRRP rations were preferred over the C-rations because they were so light. These came in a pouch about the size of a book.

Inside were packets of coffee, cocoa, creamers, and sugar. In addition to the main meal like the C-rations, it had a small pack of toilet paper. The meal itself was freeze dried in a bag that you added hot water to. The varieties were spaghetti & meat balls, chicken & rice, chicken a-la-king, beef & noodles and beef stew.

The big fifteen ounce cans of C-rations had spaghetti & meatballs, beef stew and everyone's favorite, ham & eggs or as we called them 'pork & mothers'.

The turkey, chicken, & beefsteak cans were smaller about the size of a can of tuna fish, and C-rations came with small tins of peanut butter, cheeses, and jams with crackers. I was ready for my second mission but that would not come for another day or two.

Mail was delivered again and I had another stack of mail that caught up to me.

I heard from my girl, my Mom and got a letter from my Aunt Terry in Florida. I also got two additional letters from my brother's friend Mary.

I had never met her and the fact that she wanted to write and keep me up to speed about general things in Philly was appreciated. It was nice to have a pen pal and I always got mail from her. Susie Todder sent another letter and I even got a letter from 'Tackhead'. Her real name was Susan, but everyone in our crowd dubbed her with that nickname. She always had a crush on me and Elvis Presley's hit record "Falling in Love with You" was tagged as "Tackheads Theme". Her never ending love letters were getting old quick and I was writing home to try to get somebody to have her tone it down. Just the same, inbound mail is always welcome.

All through my Army training in basic, advanced infantry training and jump school, all of the Drill Sergeants and Instructors wore their CIB's or Combat Infantry Badge sewn on the left breast of the fatigue shirt.

It was impressed on me by the instructors that the CIB was the most coveted badge in the Army. I was told that no other combat decoration outside of the Medal of Honor or the Purple Heart was prized more and although anyone could be awarded either of these only an Infantrymen serving in combat could be awarded a CIB. The CIB was worn on the uniform over the top of all other decorations. The CIB was the one decoration were men had proven their commitment and bravery under fire to all others that they had marched into the hailstorm of combat giving the enemy as good as he gave and defended themselves, their comrades and the nation. It was the ultimate badge of honor.

I had yet to earn mine and I wondered if I would measure up to the men who had earned the badge before me with the same honor and distinction. I would no doubt earn the CIB before my tour in Vietnam was over the question was would I live to see it.

We would be going to the Tanh Linh area this time. Most of the guys told me that they liked this AO because the forest was easier to maneuver and see in and the jungle areas were not as thickly vegetated. This made humping a little easier. The new gear configuration worked better but I was still slipping into the pack while sitting on the ground and rolling over to my hands and knees before standing up. When we got on the birds I decided to not sit in the middle on the floor but would sit on the floor on the pilot's side in the doorway with my feet hanging out.

Sitting on the floor right behind the pilot I found I could hold on to the bulkhead framing that normally the door would latch to close with my left hand. This Huey like the rest had the doors and the seats removed.

I found out later that's why they are called 'Slicks', the floor of the Huey would be covered in blood making the metal surface slick. I was told by Sgt. Soakley that standing on the skid as the bird comes into the LZ and was about to land was better if the chopper was hit by enemy fire. If the chopper is hit say by an RPG then you would be pushed out of the helicopter by the blast. If you were not too high up when this happened, you had a better chance of survival.

Leaving the LZ at Nancy once again the pilots would lift off point the nose of the chopper towards the ground gain speed and altitude and then we were up and going. Cruising along at 120 mph and at an altitude of 5000 feet with your feet hanging out is quite an experience.

The 'Pink Team' was in formation behind us. It's actually a pleasant ride, the air is cooler the scenery is great but then the pilot nose dives to tree top level. Then he decides he is going to do some treetop high speed turns, one-minute I am looking up at the sky, and the next minute I am looking straight down at the top of the trees.

I could only hang on with my left hand and with the weight of the pack, I was amazed I did not fall out. Centrifugal force is what kept my butt on the floor but at the time I had no idea that was why I was not plastered in the tree tops. Finally, I could feel the bird start too slow and the nose started to rise a bit.

Arty was once again prepping the LZ and as we started to drop into the LZ, the door gunners opened up with their M60 machine guns strafing the tree line along the edge of the LZ.

I followed Sgt. Soakleys lead and stepped out unto the skid when we were about fifteen feet off the ground. He stepped off before the bird actually landed but I did not step off until we were about a foot off the ground.

I followed Soakley into the tree line and waited for the rest of the platoon to get caught up with us. The LT and SFC Snead got everyone moving and we were off on another mission. I was walking drag again with Soakley in front of me. The vegetation in this area was sparse and more open so we were all stretched out pretty good. We had two additional Kit Carson Scouts with us this time. They were up with the LT and SFC Snead; Woung was working with me and Sgt. Soakley walking drag.

We humped into the AO for about 400 meters east and setup a defensive position. Once we started up again we were going to continue east for another click.

Then we stopped at our NDP objective just south of the Suoi Ba Tay Creek. This was prime NVA base camp area so everyone was on high alert.

The 600-meter-high cliffs of the Nui Ong Mountain were to our northeast. Claymores were set up and watch schedules were set. The night passed without incident and we got an early start the next morning.

The plan was to walk due south for about a click set up a midday position and run clover leafs on the north side of Song Cac River. Now I was walking right flank with Woung further off to my right. Lyle was walking point at the head of our column off to my left. My job as a flanker was to be in a position to break up any ambush that the enemy might spring on us.

The plan was if an ambush was sprung from the west side of the column, Woung and I would be in a position to overrun the enemy's positions and break up the ambush.

The vegetation in this area was more like a forest than jungle. We had moved about 400 meters when I heard a loud, whoosh. I recognized the sound and the column of smoke going over Lyle's head as an RPG round. The rocket exploded in the trees towards the back of the rest of the platoon. The rocket had been fired head on into our column of march. I instinctively dove to the ground taking cover and then all hell broke loose.

Lyle was pumping rounds from his shotgun and the rest of the platoon was returning fire from their M16 and M60 machine guns. Green and red tracer rounds were flying back and forth through the air. The NVA were firing their AK47's and the LT was barking orders.

As for me, well I remember from science class in school that objects in motion tend to stay in motion. When I hit the dirt, I was trained to use the butt of my rifle to break the fall. I did this perfectly, I stopped, however my rucksack kept right on going, right over my head knocking my helmet off, and pulling the web belt and suspenders with it.

The web gear and the ruck sack were now sitting on my chest right under my chin and I was still in the straps of both so it was like wearing a straightjacket. The force of the ruck sack coming over my head also knocked my M16 from my hands. I was now desperately fighting to get the ruck sack and the web gear off me, and the entire time I'm doing this I'm on my knees with this fire fight raging and tracers flying all around me.

As I'm struggling to get this gear off me, I look to my right and see Woung leaning against a tree laughing at my dilemma. I was panicked; the gear had me wrapped up like package waiting to be shipped.

The fire fight continues and now I can hear our artillery rounds coming in over my head and exploding fifty to seventy-five meters in front of me. Finally, I get free of the gear and grab my helmet and put it on my head, except the steel pot and the liner had been separated and I now had a large steel bowl on my head with the cover flaps covering my face. I put the liner back into the helmet, put it on my head, and grabbed my weapon.

Woung is now in hysterics, if he laughs any harder, he'll need a medevac. I get into a prone position, click the safety of my weapon on full auto, and fire a burst into the tree line just a foot off the ground like I am supposed to. Now I have a pain in my ass not because I had been shot but because Snead is kicking me in the butt.

He is yelling "Cease fire goddammit get your gear and get over there with Lyle."
The fire fight had ended, not that I noticed. Woung walks past both of us wiping the tears from his face and trying to stifle his laughing. Snead just looks at him as if he has lost his mind.

When I get to Lyles position he tells me that he and the NVA almost had a head on collision. The RPG was fired less than ten feet from Lyle and fortunately, it went right over every one's head.

The adrenaline was now working overtime on me and my hands were shaking. I was trying to light a cigarette when Lyle took it and lit it for me.

He said; "Well Ski you just busted your cherry, and earned your CIB."
Woung came over to us still laughing patted me on the shoulder and said "You funny son of a bitch Soukie." So much for honor and distinction.

We packed up our gear and humped west for about 300 meters. Then we set up our midday defensive position. Spades ran an extended clover leaf with the LT the new Kit Carson's and Woung back towards the area where we made contact with the NVA. They did find a blood trail and the only other sign of the NVA was the spent shell casings at the scene of the fire fight. They followed the blood trail but lost it along the northern banks of the Song Cac River.

The LT was still calling in arty rounds around the area of contact and we were all on high alert. We had chow and waited for Spades to return. When they got back, they had the chance to get some chow and Hearts ran a clover leaf to the south of our position. Everyone was on edge including me but it was a relief that I was moving without the heavy ruck sack and I just had my web gear and weapon.

Clearly, the ongoing struggle with getting my gear straight needed to be addressed. The realization I could have been killed because of my gear malfunctioning was deeply disturbing. Once back at our position the LT had us move again to a location I later learned was in the center of all the incoming arty rounds fired that day.

These fire missions called 'Delta Tangos' were plotted and had their own designated code words. During the night if the enemy made an attempt to attack or even just to probe us the LT could call in artillery support using the designated code names and readjusting the incoming fire as needed.

We would spend the night surrounded by a ring of fire and hot steel. The night did go without incident and although our presence was now known to the enemy, we continued with our mission. Just before our midday stop for chow, we came across a dead NVA soldier. He had gunshot wounds and did not have any weapon or other equipment. He was most likely a casualty of the previous days' fire fight. We found another small and abandoned bunker site during the next couple of days. Sometimes if these bunker locations were used recently the LT would have arty fire two marker rounds at different locations. When each round went off, he would take an azimuth reading with his compass. Drawing a line on his map from the marker round locations back to an intersecting point would plot the location of the bunkers on his map.

This info was kept back at the fire control center and on occasion they would fire H & I or harassment and interdiction missions to these pre plotted locations. The purpose being that the enemy would never feel comfortable in his own areas or complexes. Another tactic used by the Brigade was to have aircraft mark these locations using small parachutes painted yellow and red. Hanging there in the upper canopy of the jungle, other aircraft on patrol or returning back to base could expend any unused ordinance on that location with the same result.

The enemy was laying low and we were running out of food and water so it was either re-supply or extraction. The LT and battalion command decided on the latter so we geared up for a RTB to Nancy.

We had arty prep the LZ to our north about a click away and the slicks held back until the last rounds were fired and we moved to the LZ and jumped on the birds. We left the LZ without incident and headed back to Nancy.

We got ourselves cleaned up worked with our gear and cleaned weapons. Mail was delivered and I had another stack from friends and family. I checked with the company clerk about getting a side arm but as a scout rifleman, it was not part of my TOE. Nonetheless I talked to Mark Malone one of M60 gunners who did have a .45 pistol.
"Mark, let me burrow your .45 I want to do some target practice."
"OK not a problem but you gotta clean it when you're done," he said.
"No sweat GI, thanks," I said. I went down to the area we used to zero and practice with our weapons and went through about fifty rounds. I was getting pretty good with the heavy M1911 and was confident I could use the weapon with proficiency. The next couple of days we just relaxed and took it easy.

A few days later, we got supplied for another mission to the Tanh Linh area. The NVA were getting active again and battalion wanted info on possible base camps and bunker complexes. We seemed to be getting into a routine of going out on four to six day missions and then coming back to Nancy for three or four days. We got ourselves together and headed for the LZ. The birds were on time and we were off the ground by zero nine hundred.

The insert was routine with the usual arty prep and cobra escorts. The Tanh Linh village is north of the Nui Da Ban Mountain and just west of the Nui Ong Mountains. The area we were headed for was flat with heavy jungle and light forest areas. There were some mountains between us and the village.

The LT had us moving southeast once on the ground and we travelled about a click before stopping for midday chow. We set up or defensive positions just north of the Suoi Phen creek. Spades and Hearts both ran clover leaf patrols along the northern end of the creek. We did find a trail that showed signs of recent use and set up a mechanical on this trail. The trail ran north to south and decided to use our midday camp as our NDP. The watch schedule was set up and we settled in for the night.

Another night passed without any problems other than the mosquitos and other jungle night crawling critters. We travelled about two clicks set up another midday position and ran clover leafs to our north and west. There were no other signs of enemy activity so we packed up and moved another two clicks and set up our NDP. We were getting closer to the N Lo O Mountains just west of Tanh Linh.

We continued to run our clover leaf patrols and found no more recent signs of enemy activity. We ended our mission at an old NVA base camp that the ARVN took over on top of a 200-meter hilltop that was part of the N Lo O Mountains. The position overlooked the airstrip at Tanh Linh that was just east of us. We had a commanding view of the valley below us to the north, west, and south. The eastern side of the hill was really a 200-meter-high cliff.

Not the best avenue of approach but we set up claymores all around us any way. We were resupplied and spent the next few days on the hill top.

On the second night there the NVA were feeling spunky and were probing the small air base in Tanh Linh. A C-130 'Spooky' gun ship was called in. This was quite a light show for us we could hear the big four prop aircraft but could not see it.

The mini-guns onboard when fired sent a solid line of red tracers into the jungle on the eastern side of the airstrip. It looked like someone took a paint brush and painted a red line from the sky to the ground. The muzzle flash would light up the big airplane and it looked like a shadow on the night sky. The sound of the mini-guns was surreal like a giant making a loud and long burping sound. We were on high alert that night but the NVA either did not know we were there or did not care.

The LT and Woung went back to Nancy the next day and got a briefing on a new mission in an area northeast of us in a valley between the Nui Long and Nui Bac Mountains. These mountains were steep and got as high as 700 meters with the lowest at 380 meters.

We were inserted without incident just northeast of RD 336 at the foot of the valley. We were to operate in the valley that covered about four square clicks and between two streams that flowed out of the mountains and feed the Suoi Lap Lai River. The point of the valley that began between the two mountains would be an ideal area for an NVA base camp.

It stuck out like a finger and the leading ridge line to the base of the mountains was 100 to 150 meters high and covered a full click. After the insert, we travelled due east for about a click to the river and then turned northeast and followed the river along its banks. This was all prime NVA base camp area with plenty of cover and an abundant supply of water and fresh fish. There was also plenty of other game to be found along the river banks.

We set up our first defensive midday position and ran clover leafs northeast along the river and also to our northwest. The Suoi Lap Lai River was fed from smaller streams that flowed off of Nui Bac Mountain. We were all on high alert but we saw no signs of the enemy.

The next few days were spent humping around the valley and running our clover leaf operations. We set up mechanical and active ambush sites without any contact. Whatever the people at Intel are drinking, we definitely want some.

There was no sign of the enemy anywhere. One of the assumptions was the NVA would use this area due to its natural food and water source potential. Once in the valley it was apparent the only way in or out was due west back to where we were inserted along the road. Steep cliffs that rose as high as 470 meters and no less than 300 meters were to the north east and south of the valley, it was a perfect horseshoe. During this mission, I had an opportunity to talk with Lyle about his point man skills. Not that I wanted to be a point man, I just wanted some insight of how it all worked.

Lyle took the time and explained that there was really nothing special. You just had to really look at the jungle and look for things that were out of place or different. One example he used was when approaching a tree line from an open field you see a wall of vegetation. If you look closely at that wall, you'll see 'doorways' that go into the tree line. These 'doorways' may just be game trails where animals enter the jungle from the field on a regular basis. Or they could be the spot where the enemy enters the jungle. Other telltale signs were an interruption of the plant life, as if something had pushed its way through. Branches that are broken off or bent forming its own little trail in a specific direction. I took it all in and found as I was walking drag I could see what Lyle was describing. The movement of the entire platoon as we humped through an area did leave its mark in the jungle. Some of the marks were permanent like a branch cut away with a machete; others were subtler like leaves pulled off branches that caught on our equipment as we all moved through the jungle.

We had finished a recon of the entire valley in four days and found nothing. We humped our way back to the western end and waited for the choppers to take us back to Nancy. The orders finally came from Battalion to RTB.

The big surprise for me and Jack was that when we got back to Nancy we found out that Recon was scheduled to go back to the Brigades BMB for stand-down. This meant we would leave Nancy the next day travel by truck in a convoy and go back to BMB for five days of cold beer, warm water showers, hot chow, clean clothes, a regular bunk, mail, the PX and did I mention cold beer.

We cleaned up our gear and weapons got showered changed into clean uniforms provided by the hooch girls and got some chow at the mess tent on base. The next day we left, for BMB around 10AM, joined up with a convoy headed west on QL 20 and we were on our way.

We arrived at the 4/12 battalion area of BMB just after lunch and got settled in. The supply clerk gave me and Jack an aluminum frame for our ruck sacks we had been waiting for. We put these with the rest of our gear and settled in for cold beer and steaks cooked on a grill courtesy of 'Top'.

We also had an opportunity to access our personal gear that was stored in the Company HQ building. This allowed us to get to any personal items we wanted to take back with us when we returned to Nancy. After some beer and steaks, we were off to the PX to buy all sorts of stuff we wanted, but did not have access to out at Nancy. Some of the guys bought Buck hunting knives or Seiko watches. I ordered a pair of stereo headphones. Shaving cream, soap, and spare socks were also high on the list. Cigarettes by the carton, new lighters, lighter fluid, sun glasses, candy, cookies and we also learned that each enlisted man was allowed one fifth of hard booze every two months. So along with our Seagram 7 we brought back cases of coke, 7 UP and stationary for writing home. Lyle also loaded up on Tabasco sauce that he put on just about everything he ate.

The EM club on BMB was called the Kangaroo Club. Its main feature was pitchers of cold beer and fresh hot pizza. The club also had live bands from the Philippines, Thailand, and Malaysia.

Along with the usual lead and rhythm guitars, the bands also had a bass guitarist, drummer and a lead singer usually a girl wearing very short skirts or shorts, with cleavage revealing tops. They played all of the classic rock songs of recent years but would always finish the night's final set with "We gotta get out of this place" a hit song originally done by Eric Burdon and the Animals. Once the club closed, everyone would stagger and sometimes crawl back to our barracks area and pass out on our bunks. The MP's always had a presence but was usually pretty restrained in their enforcements of drunk and disorderly.

In most cases even if the MP's took a GI back to the Provost Marshals Station the offending trooper would be allowed to sleep it off and return to his unit with a strongly expressed verbal warning.

None of our guys had this type of problem, and although we joined in on the nights' festivities with great enthusiasm we conducted ourselves in a matter that was nothing but complimentary to our unit. Ahem.

After the stand down was over we all boarded trucks that took us back to Nancy. Not everyone returned with us. Some of the guys were "short" and had secured jobs in the rear with the gear, in preparation for that coveted "DEROS" date. None of the Tiger Patrol members except me and Jack were returning to Nancy. Mike Gobelli, Gene Conley, & Mike Batista from Recon would all stay behind and return to 'The World'.

Chapter Three, General's, & FNG's;

I had the pleasure and honor to meet Brigadier General William R. Bond at FSB Nancy in Long Khanh Province. I was sitting outside my hooch arranging my ruck sack to the new aluminum frame I had just received while on stand down. The Echo company area was pretty deserted since all of the Tigers and four Recon guys stayed at BMB. I had moved into Red Sanderson's old hooch; this was a one-bedroom model so I had it all to myself.

Focused on the task at hand I never noticed the General, Battalion Commander and a bunch of other officers walking up the road from the TOC. I saw Lt. Colonel Black first but then noticed the star on Bonds collar. I jumped up and saluted but the General told me to be at ease after returning my salute. He actually sat down on an ammo crate outside my hooch and spent about fifteen minutes talking with me. He asked where I was from and how I came into the Army. He was pleased to hear I was Regular Army and had enlisted. I told him my story about my recruiting sergeant and how I was interested in becoming a 421A armament specialist. As an infantry rifleman, he noted I was going to be an expert with all sort of weapons US and NVA.

He laughed when I told him the recruiting sergeant's name was Kilroy. He claimed he knew about him from his WWII service, turns out the guy was everywhere, and let everyone know that "Kilroy was here."

He inquired what I wanted to do with myself when my tour was over. I told the General I wanted to be near home at Ft. Dix NJ. He had his aide take my name and service number and said he would see what he could do.

He was also interested to know if I had everything I needed, how much time I had been in country. He never gave an Army gong ho speech but let me know in no uncertain terms that he was concerned for my wellbeing and was proud of me and my unit. He wanted to know how I came to be assigned to Recon, and I let him know I had volunteered, after the Tiger Patrol was de-activated.

He probably knew at the time the Brigade would be returning to the US later that year but he never let on. My impression was he was a no nonsense sort of guy yet at the same time was very congenial. He was familiar with my home town of Philadelphia and said he had been to the city many times. We continued to talk about Philly landmarks and he told me he was from a small town in Maryland. He shook my hand and wished me luck and let me know he was always available to help the troops in any way he could.

I have to believe that my encounter that day with the General was why I was posted and assigned with the prestigious unit the 1st Battalion 3rd Infantry Regiment the "Old Guard" at Ft. Meyer Va. The Brigade already had the 2nd Battalion 3rd Infantry regiment as one of its units.

A little over a month later, the General would be killed in ground combat. The news of this event shocked and saddened everyone in the Brigade. General Bond was a career soldier having entered the Army during WWII.

The Brigade would get its orders to return to CONUS in late June. I am sure that General Bond would have been proud to bring the Brigade Colors back home with all of his "Redcatchers".

While we were at Nancy following, the stand down we got new people assigned to the platoon. John Lawder, Theodore Keiller, George Wilton, and Pete Black would join our happy little group. John was from California had been drafted and was considered an old man. Married with kids he was twenty-eight years old. A papasan for sure. Teddy was a new Medic from somewhere in the mid-west and like me was just eighteen small in stature, another babysan. George I believe was from upstate NY and Pete was from Baltimore.

There were plenty of empty hooch's for the newbies to pick from and they all got settled in. The new aluminum frame worked out well, everything else I kept the same, but I did practice a bit with the quick release tabs that would drop the entire pack and frame off when I pulled them. Soakley saw what I was up too, called over the new guys who all by the way were issued frames with their new gear. He demonstrated that when the crap hit the fan to just pull the right shoulder release with your left hand and then drop the pack off your left shoulder. This kept your right hand on your weapon, so we all practiced a bit with the technique with no loads in the pack. Soakley was pleased with our progress and told all of us this would dampen Woung's sense of humor during fire fights.

He looked at me and winked with a Cheshire cat kind of grin and left us to ourselves after that. Apparently, I was still the butt of private jokes in the platoon from my first combat experience.

The next day Sgt. Patchart showed up with a jeep piled high with ammo and food. We would be going out on another operation.

We were headed back to the center of Binh Tuy Province in the Tanh Linh district. This area was very active with the 33rd NVA regiment.

The 33rd was one of the first enemy Infantry Regiments to be deployed in September 1965 from North Vietnam into South Vietnam. Its first combat engagements against US Forces occurred that fall in Plei Me and the Ia Drang Valley against elements of the 1st Air Cavalry at LZ Albany and LZ X-Ray. In early November 1965, the regiment set up its headquarters on Hill 732 within the Chu Pong Massif. This regiment was tough as nails and combat proven and the area in which we were headed was very hot according to Lt. Kamble and SFC Snead. A few weeks later in this same district, Brigadier General Bond would be killed by a 33rd NVA Regiment sniper.

There was some apprehension about this mission we were headed back into a bad area. Supply had pulled extra ammo and LRRP rations for this mission, another indication this was not going to be a walk in the sun. After getting our gear packed up the LT let, us know that the slicks that would take us to the AO for this mission would not arrive until the next morning.

So we had one more night at Nancy. The next morning first thing as promised we were headed to the LZ to board our choppers. Once airborne the ride to the insert LZ was about twenty minutes. Tanh Linh is located about twenty-five miles south east of FSB Nancy in Dinh Quan.

Once again, we did the fast and low insert were the slicks fly at high speed at tree top level and then drop into the LZ just as the arty prep fire is stopping.

Once off the birds we took up our positions inside the tree line, the smoke and smell of cordite was still heavy in the air around us.

Noise discipline was stressed during our briefing and the LT got us moving fast to our north. Getting away from the LZ was important. Arty was also firing missions at other LZ sites in the area even though no one was landing in them. Our fast and low insert would be confusing to the enemy. He would of course hear the artillery rounds and the chopper blades but just what LZ was the question. After inserting us the slicks would do, some dummy landings in other arty prepped LZ's just too really throw the enemy off. A Recon platoon or smaller LRRP team's greatest advantage over the enemy is that the bad guys did not know you were there. We humped about 500 meters due south and then turned east for another 600 meters before stopping.

It was close to midday and the LT wanted to set up our clover leaf base of operations. We would be looking for signs of enemy base camps. These include sawed off tree stumps and branches. Trails and areas were the vegetation had been cleared. The enemy used the jungle and the surrounding terrain to hide and our job was to find him. Spades went out first to our north and found a trail with signs of a lot of traffic. All the brush alongside the trail was beaten back and the trail itself was hard packed with no recent plant life growing on it. Sgt. Tom Peady reported this would be a good ambush site.

The LT left our midday position and took Woung with him to meet up with Sgt. Peady at the trail site.

After looking over the site, the Spades RTO Dan White was told by the LT to call Ted Spancer the company net, RTO and have the rest of the platoon join up with him and Spades. So we packed up our gear plus all of Spades gear and met them at their position about 150 meters from where we were.

The trail itself ran almost due east and west with a small hill and ridge on its north side were the trail led east down along a dense tree line to its south into some heavy jungle. The platoon was set up on the south side of the trail in the tree line and SFC Snead was set up at the far eastern side where the trail went back into the jungle. Snead had M60 gunner Mark Malone, Tim Woodard and Spades RTO Dan White with him.

There was high grass on either side of the trail and the area between the north and south tree lines was a good fifty meters. From the hill on the north side to the end of the trail that went back into the jungle on the east side was a good 300 meters. Sgt. Soakley took M60 Gunner Mick O'Brian, Ted Spancer, Lyle Layden and me up on top of the hill on the northwest side the entire trail laid out in front of us right up to Snead's position. O'Brian's M60 had a clear line of fire from the base of the trail below us all the way up the northern side to Snead's position.

Malone's M60 had a clear line of fire on the entire trail plus the northern side right up to the base of our little hill position. Anyone coming down the trail from the west would be seen by the guys on the hill top position coming in from the open field below and would step into a cross fire from the M60 above and behind them and the M60 directly in front of them at ground level.

In addition, the entire south side of the trail was covered by claymores and M16 fire directed to the north side of the trail.

The LT had set up a perfect ambush with intersecting fields of fire. Even if an enemy platoon of twenty-five men walked unto that trail from either the east or west sides once they were in the kill zone they would be hit by claymore mines and small arms fire from the south and M60 & small arms fire from the east and west with the latter position elevated. The best laid plans however do not always work out. The NVA would show up, no shots would be fired and the only potential casualty was me.

After we got all this set up and we waited about an hour Tim Warden indicated his battery on his PRC-25 radio was failing. Soakley had a spare and was the closest to Warden's position. Soakley gave the battery to me and I was to go down the hill and walk east on the trail to Wardens position and deliver the battery. Then I would retrace my steps and climb back up the hill. Ted Spancer called Dan White on his radio to relay the plan. Once everyone was alerted to the plan of action I walked down the hill from the top to the bottom and started walking east on the trail looking for Warden.

The hill was only about 100 meters high but gave a commanding view of the entire area. Warden is now up from his position standing on the edge of the wood line looking for me. He can see me approaching but can only see the top of my head because of the height of the grass. As I draw closer he can now see me from the waist up, but I'm still thirty meters or so away from him but now he hears something to his right.

Warden sees two NVA scouts also standing on the edge of the wood line about fifteen meters to his right. One of those scouts is sighting his AK-47 directly at me.

Warden looks and sees his M16 just five feet away but in the direction of the two NVA scouts. He comes to realize if he breaks for his weapon, the NVA will then see him. Now he is frantically trying to get my attention. He cannot jump up and down or wave his arms his only chance was by sound. So now how to produce enough noise to get my attention and not alert the NVA to his position. So he starts to make "psst" noises. In the meantime, the NVA soldier is continuing to site down the barrel of his weapon leveled on my chest. "psst psst psst". I hear and see Warden off to my right, but so does the NVA.

Fortunately, they panic and start running east along the southern wood line right straight for Sgt. Snead and his position. Warden screams out "Snead there coming straight at you. "

At this point, everyone knows we've made contact because noise discipline has been breached. Knowing now something is wrong I cut into the grass to my right reach the wood line and trip right over Jack Meadon. No one on top of the hill can do anything, because to fire at the fleeing NVA they would have to fire into the platoons' positions on the south side of the trail. Not that it matters they don't see the NVA anyway. Snead can't have Malone fire his M60 because when all this is going down I'm still in the line of fire on the trail. Malone sees me bolt into the grass but has no sight of the enemy.

He can't fire into the wood line on the south side without firing on his own people. Because I'm in the kill zone on the trail the platoon can't set off the claymores.

The only one who knows anything for sure was Warden who is now screaming as loud as he can at Snead that "There coming right at you." By this time, Warden has retrieved his M16 but has lost site of the fleeing NVA. The two NVA scouts by this time must realize they walked right into an American position.

The NVA disappear into the jungle, Snead can hear them breaking through the jungle brush just to his left but can't see them. The LT is now out on the trail himself with Snead coming up from the east end. Once everything calms done, Warden tells everyone what happened.

Now keep in mind all of this took no more than a minute to happen, but it does go to show the skill and the training the guy's in this unit had. I'm sure in a line company the claymores would have been set off and the two machine gun crews would have fired on their own people. End result I'm dead with body parts all over the trail. Additional casualties would have occurred as well. This was the first time during my tour I came within a breath of being kllled. I would have this experience twice more before my tour was over.

Warden was really shook up over this but the end result was he saved my life. Beers were definitely on me! The LT had us take down the claymores and got us moving fast. The NVA scouts who wandered into our position now knew where we were located. The LT wanted to put as much ground between the ambush site and our NDP.

The LT pushed us hard and we set up our NDP almost a full click northeast of the ambush site and just south of Hill 222 on an another hill to the west of Tanh Linh. We set up a tight perimeter and made sure to stagger our claymores for the best effect.

We settled in for the night with strict noise and terrain discipline. There was to be no smoking and no cooking fires, everyone was forced to chow down on cold C-rations and no coffee. We also had a tighter perimeter than usual. Our position overlooked two intersecting trails about 200 meters to our east where we set up a mechanical.

Pre-planned delta tango arty missions were set in place around the NDP and given code names. The three missions were set up in a triangle formation around us and we could adjust fire wherever we needed it by giving the code name of the fire point and adding or subtracting meters from that point. We could also move incoming fire right or left as well. The three pre-plotted fire missions were designated "Moe, Larry, and Curly. "

The night passed without event and all of our sit reps were responded to. Battalion decided that since our presence was known to move us further south of the ambush site, we spent most of the next day humping two clicks south and another click east, and by the end of the day, we were spent. We set up our usual NDP on a center peak of a three peak hilltop with a saddle between each peak. The LT let us boil water for our LRRP rations and coffee.

The next day we moved west in the morning and then north in the afternoon, we ran cloverleaf's both mid-day and late afternoon with no enemy sightings or activities. We did find a trail that the maps showed that if you travelled north it would intersect with the trail we set the ambush on. The next day we moved back to the northwest that had us going back towards the ambush site.

We crossed the Suoi Tre Creek and came back to the platoon area and we set up for the ambush. I was going to pay later for my wet feet.

More clover leafs were run with no results although we did spot where the ambush trail intersected with another trail we saw running north and south. These were plotted for arty for their H&I mission. The LT decided to follow the trail northwest on the southern edge of the jungle which took us back to our insertion LZ and we were extracted out back to Nancy the next day.

Back at Nancy we cleaned, our weapons got caught up with our mail and just lounged around. There were letters from my girl, my Brother, Mary and some of the gang I hung out with at home. I also got an in-country letter from Eric Delaney. He was assigned to the 1st Air Cav.

I had a problem now with jungle rot on my feet. In the bush, we never take off our boots so you wear the same socks for all the days you are out. Even if you have spare socks, it cuts down the space to carry food or water so no one carried spares. Besides keeping, them clean would be impossible.

Soakley saw me standing in the chow line using the heel of my right foot to press down on the toes of my left foot because the itch is so intense. After chow, he took me to the aid station. After getting my boots off the medics saw that, my socks were stuck to my feet from the dried blood and puss. They cut the socks off as best they could then had to soak my feet in peroxide and cut away the remaining material before they started using tweezers and brushing my infected toes with soft bristle brushes to remove the remaining sock material, dead skin and scabs.

The entire time they did this, they rinsed my feet with water and peroxide continuously. Needless to say this was extremely painful and when finished I was not allowed to wear socks or my boots for a couple of days.

I had this condition for more than ten years after leaving Vietnam so whatever fungus I picked up stayed with me for years. I tried every type of athlete's foot medication on the market and nothing helped. Today it seems to have moved to my hands after years of lying dormant.

After my aid station ordeal, we hit the canteen for some brews, the beers were on me, and I could not thank Tim enough for saving my butt. That night I drank a lot of beer to help my aching feet and we were all getting pretty drunk. The LT and Snead had their sleeping quarters in the Echo Company CP shack. This is where the also did their drinking.

LT Kamble was a West Point grad and was Airborne Ranger qualified. Snead was a career soldier also Airborne Ranger qualified as well as a trained Pathfinder. When Snead was drinking some of the guys noted he was a nasty drunk, while Kamble was more playful. We were sitting around getting pretty loud when all of a sudden Kamble and Snead came running out of the CP. They both plowed into the group of us and the wrestling match was on. After a few minutes we all exhausted and laughing.

The only casualty was Patchart who had a little blood coming from his nose. We later found out it was Snead who got a little over excited during the match and had accidentally elbowed Patchart in the face.

The next day Woung came to see me and Jack. It was just before midday chow, "Soukie you and Jack come with me Dinh Quan for numba one lunch." We were both taken back a bit not sure, if we understood what Woung meant. Jack asked, "You want us to go into Dinh Quan with you for lunch?"

"Yes, you come now, bring M16 and ammo", Woung said, he was wearing his .45 on his hip and his Car15 was slung on his shoulder. We were skeptical not that we didn't trust Woung but we just didn't know how to take this. Jack and I took some extra magazines in our pockets and grabbed our 16's, I was wearing my new GI issue flip-flops, and we started to go off the base. We passed Soakley by the mess hall and told him where we were going and he said, "OK, no sweat."

With Soakleys blessing, we felt more comfortable and we walked off Nancy down the road into Dinh Quan. The village itself was on the main road of QL 20 running northeast from Bien Hoa up to Highway 333.

As I noted earlier the village was surrounded by boulders some as big as houses stacked on top of one another. Woung took us to a shack just off the main highway. It wasn't much of a house, just two rooms, one of which was a kitchen of sorts. There was a woman and a very old man and a young girl in the house. Woung had us sit at a small table and the woman proceeded to put out food.

There was some sort of soup, with meat, vegetables, and noodles. All the food was pretty good and Woung let us know that we could leave some money for the meal if we wanted.

"Woung how much should we leave?" I asked. "You can give $5 MPC, OK," he said. Jack and I both coughed up five bucks in MPC, which had more value than a five Piaster note. The woman thanked us all the way out the door; $10 in MPC was a lot of money for her and her family.

The old man and young girl did not eat with us but Woung let us know that the money we gave would last them a long time. "Who are they Woung, and why did you bring us here?" Jack wanted to know. Woung explained they were from another village that had been bombed by the US after the VC used it for supplies. They had come here to Dinh Quan and had nothing when they arrived. The woman took in laundry from the ARVN's and some of the GI's on Nancy to make ends meet. He had met them through an ARVN contact he knew. The woman was the young girl's mother and the old man was her father. She lost her husband when the VC came to their village. He sided with the village leaders to keep the VC out and he and the elders were all killed. Woung hated the communist's and now I think I knew why.

This sort of thing happened all over Vietnam this was just one sad case. So we also learned who was doing our laundry. Whenever we came back from a mission there was always clean uniforms for us, Woung loaded laundry bags with our dirty clothes into a jeep and brought them to this woman. She lost her husband, everything of value she had and her home and became a refugee and settled in Dinh Quan.

This was a typical story in Vietnam, the people who lived in the hamlets and villages around the country wanted only to tend their crops, provide for their families, and honor their ancestors.

They also wanted all the foreigners to leave so they could have their country to themselves. They were not concerned if the central government was capitalist or communist. They just wanted a united Vietnam. It was nice to know we were helping out someone who had it rough.

My feet still hurt but after seeing how these poor people lived and how they survived, I realized things could be much worse. I limped and Jack walked back to the base. Everyone was happy about my foot condition it bought us a few more days on Nancy.

The LT had everyone else checked their feet and there were a few more guys with the same problem but not as bad as mine. The medics gave us foot powder for our socks and boots but we ran out of that quickly. A lot of Recon guys were walking around in flip flops. I can only imagine what sort of parasite was in that creek we crossed.

Chapter Four, FSB DEN Attacked;

1 April, dawn we were still at Nancy I had just woke up, the morning sun brings the heat up fast. I was lying on my back in my hooch when I saw the curved tail with the stinger crossing my chest from right to left. Scorpion, a small one slowly moving across my chest out for its dawn stroll. I was under my poncho liner on my cot and when the little guy got to my left side, I threw the liner off me and bolted for the opening in my hooch. I dragged the liner off my cot and started to shake it out.

Never did find the little guy but a few months later he or one of his cousins would be back. I checked my hooch and my boots. Wherever the scorpion was he was long gone. I headed to the mess hall for breakfast. One of the mortar platoon sergeants was rotating home, so I moved into his hooch next to the Company HQ shack.

It was larger hooch and the departing sergeant left the hammock he used for sleeping. We were getting new guys so one of them took over my old hooch. Five new guys joined the platoon, Sgt. Andy Hooper, PFC Tom Kraus, Rich Howard, Bob Tipalty, and Ben Dayton. All of the PFC's added to Recon were just regular draftees except Dayton. He was an OCS washout from Ft Benning. He was a nice enough guy but everyone was curious about how he had washed out. He was not volunteering any info so everyone just let it go.

Sgt. Hooper was another story. He was from Mississippi and by his demeanor and that slow southern drawl he gave you the impression he was wearing the first and only pair of shoes in his life. We did not seem to like each other. In fact, our personalities would clash over the next few months.

We were told to pack up all of our gear, we were moving to a new fire base named, FSB Den. We would only be there on a temporary basis and then would chopper over to FSB Mace to run some operations in that area near the town of Ap Bao Chanh. We were also given the bad news that Brigadier General Bond had been shot and killed by a sniper near the village of Xo Xu south of Route 134. The 33rd NVA Regiment was stepping up its operations and the fact that they were able to kill a US Army General was unnerving. In addition, during this company-sized ambush by the NVA, we lost five men killed, eighteen wounded, and the loss of two M551 Sheridan Tanks and an M113 APC.

Once we arrived at Den, we were settling in and were informed that there would be a 'Mad Minute' the following night. During a 'Mad Minute' everyone lines up on the earth berm that surrounds the base and opens up with any weapons they have pointing to the surrounding area for a full minute. We were set up near an M42 'Duster'. This is a self-propelled armored vehicle used for anti-aircraft and had twin 40mm fully automatic cannons mounted on a turret.

Its primary use in Vietnam was convoy escort and perimeter defense. I wanted to see this thing do its business, it promised to be quite a show. The next day we cleaned our weapons worked on our gear and waited for the 'Mad Minute'. The LT. briefed us and let us know we could fire our weapons as much as we wanted.

We were also going to go on another mission after breakfast and that we had to reload our magazines and have our weapons cleaned and ready to go by eleven hundred. The signal to start the 'Mad Minute' would be a red starlight flare fired over the base. A green starlight flare would be fired over the base to end it. Kick off was scheduled for twenty-two hundred.

SFC Snead gave us a case of 5.56mm ammo for our M16's and a can of M60 ammo for each of the machine guns. He anticipated we would be firing off a lot of ammo. I decided to fire a magazine and then stop to watch the duster. Knowing that a 'Mad Minute' was on the schedule there was very little beer around. We had our evening chow and gathered around the berm waiting for the flare to be fired.

A few minutes past twenty-two hundred the red flare went up. All hell broke loose. The duster opened up on the wood line about 150 meters away. The 40mm tracer rounds could be seen leaving the guns and then impacting in the wood line. Each gun fired about eighty rounds each and the noise from the duster alone was deafening. I would not want to be an enemy soldier on the receiving end of this thing. Looking up and down the berm the rounds going into the wood line was frightening.

Any NVA or VC willing to hide in the wood line and then attack a fire support base day or night deserved every ounce of respect I could give.

I fired my one magazine just as the green flare went up and the officers and NCO's started to holler "cease fire."

Everyone was impressed and feeling invincible. No one could survive that kind of fire power. In a few weeks, we would learn that the enemy was not impressed. The next morning, I cleaned my weapon, reloaded my one magazine I had fired with all tracer rounds. I helped the new guys reload their magazines, they had gone hog wild the night before.

We got our chow and headed for the LZ to be inserted in to the LZ west of us that was about twenty-two clicks south at the mouth of the Suoi Yon River. The insert went without incident and the LT had us moving southeast of the LZ. We were following the wood line staying about fifty to seventy-five meters deep from the clearing to our west. The platoon had moved about three clicks that first afternoon and we set up our NDP. SFC Snead met with all of the new guys including Sgt. Hooper.

They were learning the all the basic operational methods we used as a unit. PFC. Kraus was assigned to the Spades team and was getting instructions on point walking from Sgt. Patchart. Sgt. Hooper was learning to maneuver and handle radio traffic while walking behind the point man. Hearts team was left to pull up the rear and I found myself pulling drag again.

The next morning, we were briefed that we would move another three clicks southeast following the wood line and would arrive at the village of Ap Bao Chanh.

This small village had a railroad line going right through the middle of the village. Lt. Kamble was to meet with some ARVN officers and another officer from 1st Field Force, along with the village chief.

The meeting was set for twelve noon so we had to cover the three clicks most rickie-tick, or pretty quick.
We took one fifteen-minute break and arrived in the village on the north side by eleven hundred. When we approached the village, the local dog population started raising a fuss. Dogs were the burglar alarms of every hamlet and village in Vietnam. The meeting was supposed to discuss the arrival of our battalion in this area of operations.

The NVA and the VC had picked up their activity in the area of FSB Mace that sat on the eastern side of Signal Mountain. This was usually the home turf of 3rd Battalion 7th Infantry 'Cottonbalers'. SFC Snead had us set our gear down on the north side of the railroad and we were right in the middle of the village. We felt pretty secure here there was a group of 'White Mice' or South Vietnamese Police, but Snead told us to be sure to stay alert around our gear.

Our arrival created quite a stir among the locals. Lt. Kamble took a fresh blouse from his pack and changed into it for his meeting. Sgt. Soakley and Patchart were left in charge and the LT took SFC Snead, Hooper, and Little Doc Kelly to the meeting. Woung stayed with us. Some of the guys took Woung and wandered off to the west following the railroad. The rest of us stayed behind to guard the gear. After a few minutes, the men returned and reported that there was a restaurant in the village but they would not serve them because we did not have an officer with us. The prospect of fresh hot chow was too much to pass up.

I saw the blouse that Lt. Kamble left behind and quickly changed shirts. Sgt. Patchart chimed in, "This is a bad idea

Ski if you're caught you'll be in LBJ." "Bullshit," I said, "What are they going to do send me to the Nam?"

Sgt. Soakley said, "Not everyone can go, half of us have to stay behind and watch the gear, so you guys will have to bring some of the chow back with you." Soakley had everyone who was staying behind provide a canteen cup to take with us. Now bear in mind Lt. Kamble is 6 feet tall and weighed in at 200 lbs. I was 5'10" and was 110 pounds with bricks in my pockets, add the effect of I was a very young looking eighteen years old, I looked ridiculous in Kamble's shirt.

Woung took off his pistol belt and side arm and we used that to tuck in the excess shirt material hanging on me like a blanket. The only thing going for us was the 1st LT. bar and the crossed officer's infantry insignia on the collar. We also took the LT's bar off his helmet cover and put it on my boonie hat. It would not cover the FTA on top of the hat but what the hell, who was going to notice. We were off to the restaurant with hot chow on our minds.

Going with me were, Woung, Sgt. Soakley, Ted Spancer, Mick O'Brian, John Lawder, Lyle Layden, and Dan Kiebler. The eight of us followed the railroad tracks into the village with me and Woung leading the way. Then we saw the jeep with a driver a passenger and a gunner manning a mounted M60 heading our way from the west. As the jeep came up to us, it stopped and so did everyone's heart. Sitting in the passenger seat was a full bird Colonel from 1st Field Force. He was going to the meeting. I snapped off the most military salute of my life and said, "Good Morning Sir." The Colonel looked me up and down, and so did the driver a Sergeant First Class.

"Good Morning, Lieutenant, Kamble," as he read my name tag. He also took note of the Ranger tab, CIB and Jump Wings sewn on Kamble's shirt. "Kamble, you're a West Point man aren't you?" He asked.
"Yes Sir," I replied, "Class of 68." I was still in high school in 1968; Kamble was a 1968 graduate of the Point.
"Not wearing your class ring I see," the Colonel said. The SFC driving the jeep just looked away rolling his eyes.
"Eh, no sir don't want to risk losing it in the field."
"Where you off to Kamble?" Everyone else was still at rock straight attention.
"Well sir the men wanted lunch at the local restaurant but they could not get served unless they had an officer with them, so I decided to join them, so they could get some hot chow." This was the truth but the Sergeant manning the M60 just rolled his eyes as well. The Colonel never flinched he just stared right into me.
"Well that's commendable, Kamble, happy to see that your taking good care of your men, carry on." He brought his hand up to salute and I returned it with my best West Point attempt. "Thank you sir," I said.

The jeep pulled off and he was gone. The collective sigh of relief was probably heard in Saigon. "Holy shit, holy shit, Jesus H. Christ," Soakley said. "Oh man, you're in deep shit Ski, that bird is going to the meeting where he's going to meet the real Lt. Kamble," Lyle said. "Well, we can't change anything now so let's eat, Woung lead the way," I said. "You too funny Soukie," he said.

We got to the restaurant and the old woman running it was not convinced I was an officer but she served us any way. We had a great meal of chicken, fish with noodles and rice. We ordered more food for the other guys, paid our bill and went back to our position.

Sgt. Patchart was the first to meet us, "Please tell me that bird colonel did not see you guys," he said. Soakley replied, "O yeah, he saw us talked with Lt. Kamble here about West Point".

I was getting changed back into my own shirt. "You think that colonel was going to the meeting?" Patchart asked. Soakley replied, "Why else would he be here, we going to catch some shit over this."

The guys were telling me they were thankful for what I had done but that I was in big trouble. The LT was sure to have my ass. He returned with the rest of his group around fifteen hundred, "Saddle up," he said, we have to move about a click west before dark. My gear was on the far western edge along the tracks. I would be walking drag again so everyone had an opportunity to pass me as we moved out. Spades was on point again, followed by the CP team and then Hearts.

Sgt. Patchart just shook his head as he passed me, some of the other guys just made some faces going by. Then came, the LT, "How was lunch?" He asked. "Eh, OK LT, not bad," I replied.
Woung was next in line and just smiled, and shook his head with his big grin, as he went by me, then came, SFC Snead. He just glared daggers at me.

We moved about a click west following the railroad tracks out of the village and then cut northwest to an area that was just into the tree line and set up our NDP.

The next day we moved out going northwest and broke out of the tree line into some high grass and brushwood. We were just about to go back into the tree line when we were attacked by wasps. PFC Kraus in his newbie wisdom decided to whack a wasp's nest with his machete.

We ran like hell in all directions, noise discipline was out the window and we found ourselves scattered all over the place. I met up with Soakley about 150 meters from where Kraus hit the nest. This was to be the rendezvous point for everyone so we waited for the rest of the platoon to show up. We were by a large clearing and as it turned out we would need it, most of Spades team got stung badly, but the worst was Krause. The LT called for birds to come get us and we were on our way back to Nancy.

Once back at Nancy the old drill of cleaning weapons and gear as well as ourselves was underway. Mail was distributed; I had letters from just about everyone.

We had a small open air theater set up by the 87th Engineers on Nancy, so we caught some of the bands brought out to play for us. We also had visits from the Red Cross 'Donut Dollies'. These were real round eyed young girls from back in the world who came out to talk and give out stuff like short timer calendars, candy, and gum and to play a variety of different games. Debbie Peyton was one of the girls who came out and everyone was in love with Debbie. She had these big round eyes and an easy going manner about her. She was transferred to the 199th from the 1st Infantry Division when it rotated home.

Just like us, they had a tour of duty too complete. "Donut Dollies' were always a welcome sight.

A few days later, we were back out in the bush. This time we were inserted by Slicks into an area south of Xa Duy Can village and east of Bien Lac Lake.

We set up our first NDP and ran cloverleaf operations on the western slope of Nui Ca Tong Mountain. That night my position was facing north and during my turn at watch, I heard movement out to my front. At first, I wasn't sure if this was some type of animal or not but then, I decided this may be someone probing our position. I grabbed the handset on the radio to let the CP know what was going on.

"Clubs Clubs Clubs, this is Hearts, we have movement, acknowledge, over," I whispered into the handset.

SFC Snead was on watch monitoring the radios when he heard my call. It was about zero four hundred and Snead responded right away. "Hearts, standby I'll come to your position, which, is this, over." "It's Ski," I replied. SFC Snead knew where everyone's position was and a few seconds later, I heard him coming up from the CP position.

He dropped in beside me we were both lying in a prone position facing north. "What have you got?" he asked. I told him I was hearing movement from the front of me about twenty meters out. We stayed there just listening when the movement started up again. Snead asked, "Where are your claymores?" He asked. "Straight ahead of us," I replied. We listened for a few more minutes and the movement was still there now moving right to left on front of us. I asked Snead, "What do you think?"

He was quiet for a few seconds the sounds of the movement still out there when he replied, "Light em up."

I hit the claymore clacker three times and the back blast of the two mines washed over us. WABROOOM !

After the noise of the blast settled down, I heard Snead spitting. He must have inhaled some debris from the back blast. "Christ, those are close, just like their supposed to be," he said. We lay there quietly listening for any additional movement.

Everyone else was now wide awake and alert and being the well-disciplined and effective unit we were they too just lay there and listened. Snead and I knew what had happened but for everyone else I can only imagine what they were thinking. Awakened by the claymore blast and then having to just lie there not knowing what has happened has to be unnerving. Everyone knew what to do, just stay put be alert stay quiet and wait for first light.

The light of dawn came up and Snead and I along with Soakley who was on my left and Dayton the new guy on my right got up and went out to the front of my position. The claymores cleared all of the low lying brush in front of my position and Snead commented again that the positioning of the claymores was excellent.

We found no blood trails or other types of human debris. Snead said, "Well that's disturbing, there was definitely something or someone here, I heard the same as you did." There was also no fur indicating an animal. Soakley asked, "Is this the spot you heard the movement?" "Yes," I replied. "It sounded like it was right here in the middle of the claymores," Snead said. The LT came over with Woung and Snead briefed him on the events earlier.

The LT decided to pack up and move right away and we headed up the 500-meter-high Nui Ca Tong Mountain. It took most of the morning to get up top and the LT had us set up an NDP. Snead checked everyone's claymore placement and again made the comment they should be in close like I had done.

My pack was now two claymores lighter and some of the guys were kidding me that I had developed a brilliant way to lighten my load. Midday chow was prepared as we did not eat anything that morning.

We set up our NDP and ran clover leafs around the mountain going all the way around. The mission was to check the mountain for any signs of enemy activity as the NVA were getting very active in this area around FSB Den. We would spend the rest of the mission scouting the mountain with no contacts and no sign of the NVA.

Waking the next morning on the mountain was surprising. Our sweat soaked fatigues and the surrounding areas of our NDP were frost covered. We were cold, really cold. The 500-meter-high mountain top was just over 1600 feet high. The air on top of the mountain was dryer as well.

Before long, however the sun would warm us all up and running our clover leafs helped but it was still much cooler on the mountain. Intel thought this was the most logical NVA staging area. It lay just northwest of Tanh Linh and the lake was only three clicks away but also fed the Dar Lang and Suoi Ray creeks that ran east to the base of the mountain.

Intel got it wrong again and we later found out the NVA were using the 300-meter-high Nui Rjinh Mountain southwest of Xo Xu village for their staging area and it was just four clicks from FSB Den. A few days after leaving the mountain and returning to Nancy the NVA would defy the display of fire power demonstrated during the 'Mad

Minute" and attack the fire base with 2 company sized elements from the 33rd NVA Regiment and a sapper company.

We were all at Nancy when the attack on FSB Den started late on the 17th. Illumination flares were constantly being fired over our firebase and the entire line was on high alert. We could hear the artillery rounds and small arms fire coming from FSB Den twenty clicks to our east. The eastern night sky was also glowing from the illumination and explosions at Den. The LT and SFC Snead had us on the southeastern berm line in our company area. Mark Malone one of our M60 gunners was getting instructions from Snead, "Turn your gun over to Ski Mark and get an M16". Mark replied, "Why Sarge this is my gun". "I know, but Ski is rated expert on the M60 your rating is marksman, you can stand in as the A-Gunner and call out targets." I took over Marks gun, he was not happy but orders are orders.

Snead then told us to focus our attention on the piece of wood line that stuck out a little on the edge of the wood line 300 meters away. The LT was on the radio with the XO at battalion TOC and was relaying orders to Snead.

Snead then told everyone, "Listen up, everyone except the M60's hold your fire, on my command I want every M60 to fire five round bursts at the tree line, this is a recon by fire." The LT relayed the command to Snead who then gave the command to us, "Commence Firing."

The entire perimeter opened up with all of the M60 and M2 .50 caliber machine guns. Tracer rounds were racing into the tree line and the concertina wire around the base. After I fired about 100 rounds, the command of cease fire could be herd around the base. The illumination flares were still going up but other than that, all was quiet. The NVA was not interested in Nancy tonight they were focused on FSB Den. We manned the berm all night the attack on Den ended about zero four thirty hours on the 18th.

The next morning revealed twenty-three enemy dead and a variety of weapons captured along with two wounded POW's. One artillery man was KIA and we had thirty-five WIA. The NVA poured a lot of mortar and RPG fire into the base causing the most casualties.

While the NVA may not have been impressed with the fire power potential to defend the base, I'm sure the AC-119G gunships that were called in did. This twin propeller driven aircraft is armed with four MXU-470/a Mini gun modules capable of firing 35000 rounds of 7.62mm M60 ammo per minute.

When these guns fire it sounds like a loud long burp and the night sky gets painted with a wide red line from the aircraft to the ground. The muzzle flash is the only way to spot the aircraft at night that is why it is nick named 'Shadow'.

Tim was getting pretty short and would be getting a job back at BMB we also got the news that Lyle Layden and Don Hardack were promoted to Sergeant. They had arrived in country together and were approaching the two-digit midget mark.

The entire platoon took it easy the next couple of days. Supplies showed up and we began packing up our gear. I found that by now I was able to pick up the pack and swing it onto my back I guess I was getting stronger. Good food and clean living will do that, right?

Two days after the battle at FSB Den, we were headed back into the field on a sweeping recon mission fifteen clicks east of the base and three clicks west of the Nui Long Mountain. The insert was routine with no arty prep but we did have a 'Hunter Killer Team' escort.

We had Woung with us as usual but we also picked up a Kit Carson named Son Tran Binh. He was tall for a Vietnamese and there was some faint freckling in his face. One of his parents may have had some western lineage. I got the impression from Woung that this new scout was not very good, or as he put it "numba ten asshole." We set up our day time and NDP positions and ran our clover leafs. We found some trails and signs of enemy activity but after four days had made no contact.

On the last day the LT brought us right up to the edge of the forest area we were in at the LZ site at a large null about 130 meters high. We set up our defensive position on the edge of the LZ facing to our north.

The forest area around the LZ towards the north curved around northwest about 600 meters.

In front of us was another tree line about 200 meters to the north that opened up slightly on the northwestern side. Through that, 200-meter wide opening you could see the next tree line a good 500 meters north of us. The area was open with high grass and old termite mounds that the grass had reclaimed. We ran a clover leaf towards that open area with SFC Snead, Woung, Sgt. Hardack, me and Jack Meadon. Snead wanted to leave Hardack, Jack and I at a point where the northern curve of the brush line that lined up with the opposite tree line that our defensive position faced. We were in a triangle shaped position with Jack on the southern side, me on the northern side and Hardack back in the tree line to the west.

Before we set up, Snead told us to "Keep your eyes open and be alert, Ski you watch the open area back here to the north and west, Jack you watch the area between that tree line to the east and the platoons position." "Hardack, you'll be back up support for these guys if they need it and you will cover their rear." I asked Snead, "What do we do if someone comes by?" He replied, "If they have weapons and their not GI's shoot em."

Snead and Woung left us at our post and we were on our own, somewhat. I could not see Jacks position; he had set up in a cluster of trees off to my right. Hardack was behind me to my right back in the tree line, and could not see him either.

The morning sun was getting higher in the sky I had to shield my eyes with my hand because the area I was supposed to watch was facing into the sun.

I took off my helmet because of the heat. All I had with me was my weapon and web gear. I had plenty of ammo and water but I wished I had brought some food with me.

There was an old termite mound just off to my right in front of me. It had grass growing over it. It curved around to my left a bit and it blocked my view if I was facing north or east. The only way to see over it was to stand up. I had clear view of the entire area I was supposed to watch to the northwest. Sitting on my steel pot and squinting into the sun, I heard some faint voices. At first I thought it might be Hardacks radio, but then I remembered he didn't have one, in fact neither did Jack or me.

It occurred to me that we had no voice commo with the rest of the platoon except to shout across the 200 meter LZ. I remembered what Snead said back at Nancy before our first mission, "Fire the first mag on full auto, reload, and switch to single fire if you have targets." I was shielding my eyes from the sun I could see that there was not anyone out to the north or east. The voices were not as faint now and I could tell by the sing song kind of language they were definitely Vietnamese. I got off my steel pot and was in a kneeling position when I heard the voices on the other side of the termite mound.

I tried standing up slowly but the grass on top of the mound prevented me from seeing anything and I dare not standup and reveal my position. Whoever was out there was having a relaxed conversation. I remembered something else Snead said, "Be aware of what the enemy is wearing, are they in uniforms, are there insignia's on the uniforms, what type of weapons, and what their demeanor is?"

I turned slowly to my right crouching down below the top of the mound as if I was following the sound of the voices, I was now facing east, and then they were there right in front of me coming from behind the mound no more than 10 meters away walking due south.

They had on shirts and pants of different colors, not uniforms, the first one had no hat the other two did. They were just boonie type hats, and the other two had rifles slung over the shoulder. I let the first mag go full auto as I brought the M16 up in front of me. I saw all of the tracers go through the closely packed group of three.

"Who's shooting, what are you shooting at?" Called Hardack I dropped the first mag and reloaded the second I had in my left hand. I fired this mag over the mound on full auto sweeping from right to left.

"What are you shooting at?" Hardack called again.

"Hardack, get your ass out here," I said.

Then I remembered what they taught us in jungle school, "The NVA and VC like to flank our positions." I loaded a third mag and let it go sweeping from left to right, in the direction of the open area to my left and rear facing northwest. This is called grazing fire.

Jack yelled out, "Hardack there's a VC out here."

"Where, shoot him," Hardack could not see anything from his position and I could not see the VC either.

"Hardack, get your ass out here," I yelled again. "Hardack what do I do with this VC in front of me?" Jack yelled.

"Shoot him," he replied. "He doesn't have a gun," Jack said. "I don't care shoot him."

The next mag I fired I was standing up firing over the mound into the tree line 500 meters away to the north. This mag also had nineteen tracer rounds and the LT must have seen these, because a minute or two later there was arty fire coming from the west into the tree line to my north.

"Goddammit Hardack get out here now," I yelled again. Then I heard a single shot from Jacks position, "Got Him."

Now the LT, Snead, Woung along with the Hearts team were coming to our position. "Cease fire goddammit," I heard Snead yell. The arty was working its way further into the tree line. I saw Woung first coming from my right followed by Snead.

They were right in front of Jacks position. They walked over to me, and Woung was looking around where I first saw the three VC.

"They walked right in front of me Sarge, there were three of them," I said. Hardack came walking up behind me.

"Glad you could make it," I said mockingly. "Knock it off," barked Snead.

Then Jack appeared from his position. Woung was following a blood trail towards the far off tree line to the north. Sgt. Soakley informed us the dead VC was unarmed, but had some documents on him. The LT walked up and let us know we were going to do an on line assault of the tree line. The rest of the platoon formed up and we followed the arty fire into the tree line.

The arty destroyed any evidence of a blood trail but we went into the tree line a good 150 meters. We found nothing else. We policed up the area, left the dead VC propped up on an old termite mound and waited for the slicks to arrive to take us back to Nancy.

When the slicks arrived, we all jumped on board. The chopper crews must have been told that we had contact on this LZ they seemed to be on high alert. Dan Patchart alerted the door gunner on his chopper and pointed at the dead VC. The door gunner opened up on the dead VC, the M60 rounds tearing into his body. We left the LZ and this AO, but a few weeks later, we would return.

Once back at Nancy we cleaned weapons, got showers, got into clean uniforms, and got our mail. The rest of the mail was from the usual friends and family and I read them all and answered a few as I went through them a second time.

Tim Warden was short and getting a rear job, so I was told I would now be the Hearts RTO. Tim went over the code books and maps he had and reviewed with me the use of the radio. He told me new code books were issued monthly and that once I had the new book I should burn the old one.

Sgt. Hooper was also assigned as the assistant team leader for Hearts and he sat in on the training with Tim and me. It was getting obvious that Hooper and I had a problem. Let's just call it a clash of personalities and leave it at that. We were going to have to work together and it was clear he was being groomed to take over for Soakley once he got short enough to leave the field.

We also got a surprise, the LT made arrangements for us to attend a training session on some new equipment at C3 A Company HQ of the 5th Special Forces Group. (Green Berets) Their camp was located in Bien Hoa. We loaded up on a deuce and a half and joined a convoy going south into

Bien Hoa. Once at the Green Beret base we were treated to cold cokes and grilled steaks.

The training was on a new type of sensor device comprised of three small stakes that you pushed into the ground. Each stake then had wires that fed back to a small base unit. One wire would feed back to another unit that you plugged a headset into. Once deployed on a trail the stakes would be placed approximately twenty meters apart. Enemy soldiers who walked on the trail would trigger the sensors. The sensors were placed in line as numbers one, two, and three. If the enemy approached the number 1 sensor, it would send a beep signal to the headset.

The signal sent would correspond to the sensor number. Beep..............beep.........beep...beep..beep.

The closer to the sensor the enemy got the closer the beeps. One soldier passing through the one, two, and three sensor array would sound like this in the headset.

Beep..........beep.....beep...beep beep...beep.....beep..........beep, as he approached the number two beeper the sound changed like this; Beep..........beep.....beep...beep-beep...beep.....beep............beep, beep-beep.........beep.....beep-beep, beep..beep-beep.....beep-beep....beepbeep.beepbeep.

This allowed you to track the movement of the enemy as he progressed down the trail through the sensor array.

All of the equipment was painted OD green and the sensors were numbered on top. This would allow us to set up remote ambushes on trails and fire the claymores at the most opportune time. It would also cut down the possibility that an animal would trigger a mechanical ambush.

After our day with the Green Beanies, we went back to BMB then would return to Nancy the next day. Upon return to Nancy, I had to readjust my equipment to accommodate the addition of the PRC-25 radio to my pack. I would no longer be required to carry claymores, M60 ammo, or blocks of C4 explosives. You would think this would lighten my overall load but the radio and its battery weighed about twenty-three pounds. Two claymores and 200 rounds of M60 ammo only weighed it at twelve pounds. My pack got heavier. In addition, when we went out on clover leafs everyone else dropped their packs I had to keep mine on, to carry the radio. The only other bright spot after returning to Nancy I learned I was to be promoted to Specialist 4 and be awarded my first Army Commendation Medal.

We took it easy for a few days Tim continued to train me on the radio and reported to Snead and Soakley I was ready. Eventually I would move up to be battalion net RTO that had greater advantages.

The company supply jeep showed up with water, rations and ammo for the next mission just south of FSB Den and in the area of Nui Rjinh Mountain.

This peak was in the middle of dense jungle and was 300 meters high with its western slopes being the steepest. The insert was north of the mountain and the terrain was dense and covered with ridges and ravines.

The 'Pink Team' we inserted with covered our southern insertion point with live rocket and mini-gun fire. There was a trail that ran northeast and southwest right through the LZ.

We moved south towards the mountain and took it slow, enemy activity in the area was still pretty hot. We moved about a click and set up our NDP. We had located the trail on the way in and set up a mechanical ambush on it. Everyone was on high alert. The night passed without incident and after morning chow and pulling down the mechanical we headed south again going about another click. The mountain was now due south of us and about 100 meters away. We set up for our midday break and had just settled in when 'Little Doc Keiller spotted 3 NVA walking into our position. He grabbed George Wiltons M16 and opened up on them. I was digging in my pack for a C-rat can when the fire fight started. The LT came up on 'Little Doc's' position and yelled for a line to be formed to his right. Me, Ben Dayton and Mark Malone formed the line and we went prone in an old dried up stream bed and started putting out grazing fire towards the heavy wood line about fifty meters in front of us to the west. Ben was on the far right of me and Mark was putting burst out next to me from his M60. He heard the LT yell, "I need a weapon, someone bring me a weapon." I turned to my left the LT was kneeling in front of an NVA lying on his back in front of him. I rose up my M16 to shoot the NVA but the LT waived me off.

I ran the twenty meters to my left and dropped next to the LT. His weapon an M15 CAR had jammed on him. The NVA was quite dead. He cleared his weapon and then I heard Mark yell he needed ammo for the M60.

"I'll get it," I replied and stared for the platoon's main position. I called out, "Snead, I'm coming in for 60 ammo." "OK," was his reply.

I came into the position and John Lawder gave me 250 rounds from his gun. Snead asked. "What's the sit rep?"

I told him that the LT had one NVA killed and we were putting grazing fire into the wood line. I left with the ammo and fell in beside Mark. We loaded up the M60 again and Mark started firing bursts when the LT called for a cease fire.

The LT told us to stay put and that he would send some more people up, he went back to the platoon's position and started putting arty rounds into the area the NVA ran too. He also sent Snead, Woung, John Lawder, George Wilton, and Ted Spancer up to our line to reinforce us. The arty was coming in close and then started walking further out. Snead and Woung checked out the dead NVA who had an AK-47 and some documents on him. After the arty mission was done the LT had us saddle up and started moving south towards the mountain. We moved slow and were on high alert this was the direction the other two NVA had run when they got away from us.

We passed through the impact areas that the 155mm artillery gun rounds left and did not see any blood trails or other signs of the enemy.

We got within twenty meters of the mountain when the LT decided to stop and set up an NDP and a mechanical. We reported our contact and document findings to the battalion TOC and settled in for the night. The plan for the next day was to check out the mountain.

At dawn, we pulled in the claymores and the mechanical and started up the mountain. Nui Rjinh Mountain was only 300 meters high but it was a steep climb. The first 200 meters were the worst. The mountain going east to west and north to south was about 750 meters. If you travelled east from its far western spot, you would cover 700 meters. If you travelled south from its far western spot, you would cover about 800 meters. The peak was flatter and covered about 200 meters. We saw a lot of trails that had just been used going up top. It took all morning to reach the peak and we found bunkers and hooch's all around the apex of the mountain. The NVA was here recently and it was determined from our recon of the mountain and the documents we later turned in to Intel that the NVA used the mountain to store its supplies for the assault on FSB Den.

There was no sign of the two other NVA scouts we encountered the day before. The apex of the mountain was marked on all of the TOC maps for regular H & I and air assault missions. We set up our NDP and spent the night on top and set up another mechanical on the trail most likely to be used to get to the top of the mountain. We used C4 to blow some of the bunkers we found and started down the mountain the next day. Battalion was eager to get a look at the documents we had.

Going down the mountain was rough for about the first 100 meters, and then it got down right dinky dao. You took steps and held on to brush and branches and if you took a misstep you covered ten or fifteen meters quickly aided by gravity. Then there was the domino effect, if one of the guys lost his footing and started falling he usually bowled into the man below him causing him to start falling. The wildlife on the mountain were entertained by us going down the steepest part of the mountain and also got an education on American swearing. By the time, we reached the bottom we were exhausted, bruised, and bloody from banging into each other and plowing into tree trunks.

The worst casualties were our hands. Everyone had cuts and blisters from grabbing vines and branches to prevent or stop a fall. We licked or wounds had midday chow and were instructed to walk northwest for two clicks to Highway 334 in the village of XA Vo Dat where we would be picked up by elements of Delta 17th Cavalry and taken to FSB Den. We would spend the night at Den and return by choppers to Nancy the next day for resupply and mail.

We got back to Nancy still sore from our decent down the mountain. Showers, clean uniforms, and hot chow soon had us back too normal. Mail was waiting once again and I went through the stack of letters in my pile. I had about five letters this time and started reading them when the LT came to my hooch. "Thanks for responding like you did during the last contact." "No sweat," I replied.

"You need to remember that going forward, you're an RTO, never leave your radio behind, understand."

"OK LT I'll remember," I said. "We all need you and the radio more than anything else," he said. As fast as he appeared was as fast as he left. Kamble was a man of few words, but when he spoke, everyone listened.

Chapter Five, R&R and Souvenirs;

We got two new guys with experience from Delta Company. Hank Waller and Jack Savicci were assigned to Spades. Both had been in country for a few months. Hank and I quickly became friends. He introduced me to a guy in Delta that was getting ready to rotate back to the world; he had a Ruger .22 caliber handgun he wanted to sell. I had our company clerk confirm that ammo would not be a problem and he got a 100 round brick for the gun. I bought it for $10. I attached a standard .45 pistol holster to my ammo belt and cut the flap to fit the peacemaker style of the handgun. I had practiced with the .45 every chance I got when we were at Nancy.

I had tried unsuccessfully to get one assigned to me. It was not part of my TOE so getting the .45 was not going to happen. Technically, as an RTO, I could request the pistol but at that time, the brigade was preparing to rotate back to Ft. Benning so adding new equipment was rough. We did not know this yet the announcement would not come until next month. The only other guys in Recon who had a pistol were the M60 gunners and Woung.

We got word from a variety of news sources that National Guard troops in Ohio opened fire and killed 4 students and wounded nine more. This did not sit well with us. Everyone here was either regular army or drafted.

National Guard troops while satisfying their military obligation to Uncle Sam did not have to worry about being deployed to Vietnam.

Only one National Guard infantry unit was ever deployed as a combat unit and that was 'D' Company of the Indiana

151st Infantry assigned to II Field Force HQ. Our feeling was if you joined the NG to avoid going to Vietnam then don't stay home and kill people protesting the war you avoided serving in. We were very pissed off over this, but the war here never stops.

A new mission was assigned we were heading back to the Xuan Loc area again. The insertion was uneventful; the usual arty prep was deployed as well as the cobra escorts. We landed on a large LZ just south of the S. Sau creek. There was also a marked footpath that ran through the southern end of the LZ right where we were inserted. 'Charlie' Company 2nd of the 3rd had been attacked in this area by a company sized element in bunkers a week ago.

Bravo Company 2nd of the 3rd also had contact with the NVA in this same area. That's why we were there to find the NVA base camps in the AO.

The LT had us moving east just south of the footpath and the creek and we moved about a click and set up a defensive position at the base of a hill. The hill itself was not steep at the top it was only about seventy-five meters high but the climb to the top would be on a thirty-degree grade. We ran clover leafs around the base of the northern side of the hill and then in the afternoon we climbed the hill to setup an NDP on top. When we got up top, we discovered the NVA had the same idea we found about a dozen bunkers still under construction.

The NVA were not at home, so we deployed our claymores, set up a mechanical on the footpath that crossed the top of the hill on the northeast side.

The foot path ran northwest to southeast on the hill top. The mechanical was on the northern side of the hill and we also deployed our new sensor toys on the southeastern side of the footpath close to our NDP.

The night passed quietly and after destroying what progress the NVA had accomplished on their bunkers we were up and moving the next morning after pulling in the claymores and sensors. We followed the trail southeast and came up on an intersecting trail running south. We followed the southbound trail into a clearing about a click away from our NDP and once we got on the far southern side decided to stop and set up a defensive position and run some clover leafs from a ridge position that pointed north into the clearing.

We had just started to settle into our individual defensive positions when firing started up on the east side.

I had yet to remove my pack. Sgt. Hooper was to my left and George Wilton was to my right. I dropped into a prone position pulled the release straps on my ruck, rolled it off me and fired my first burst of fire on full auto about two feet off the ground. I reloaded another magazine and switched to single fire when the LT hollered for a cease fire.

Turns out PFC Dayton had an accidental discharge when he set his weapon down. Everyone was now wondering if his washout of OCS was somehow related.

A few minutes later Woung came to me and said, "Soukie, you go see LT, now." I walked into the center area of our position Sgt. Snead, the LT were sitting there with Sgt. Peady the Spades team leader.

Snead spoke first, "Take a knee," I took a knee, I had my weapon but had left the radio, I did not think this was what the LT spoke to me about but I was sure something was up.

Snead spoke again, "Sgt. Peady is here as a witness, you have the right to remain silent anything you say will be held against you, do you understand your rights?" I looked at all three men, they were dead serious, and Sgt. Hooper was pacing a few feet away.

I finally spoke, "Are you out of your mind, what the hell are you talking about?" Snead asked again, "Do you understand your rights?"

"Yes," I said, "I understand my rights; now tell me what the hell you're accusing me of." Snead answered immediately, "You tried to kill Sgt. Hooper."

I burst into laughter. Now they were all looking at each other and at me like I was nuts. "You guys are beaucoup dinky dao," I said.

Sgt. Peady then spoke, "This is serious Ski, and Sgt. Hooper says you tried to kill him during the shooting. His pack is all shot up." I composed myself. "So where was Sgt. Hooper when the shooting started," I asked.

At that point, Hooper comes over and yells, "I went out front to take a shit and then you tried to kill me."

Now the entire platoon was aware of the situation and was watching closely.

Some of the other sergeants were trying to get the men to man their positions but no one responded they were watching this with great interest.

Hooper is clearly upset; his eyes are bugging out of his head and he had spittle on his chin from yelling out his words. I was quiet for a few seconds staring at him and then the LT looked at me and asked, "Well what do you have to say?' "Who was on your left Hooper?" I asked.

He just stood there, he looked confused and he could not answer. Snead stood up and looked over the perimeter and called for Sgt. Patchart.

When Patchart got there, Snead asked him, "Was Hooper on your right when we set up?' "Yes Sergeant," he replied.

Then I asked Patchart if Hooper ever gave him any indication he was going out front of the perimeter to take a dump. Patchart replied that he had no sign from Hooper he was going anywhere. I looked at Hooper and said, "You never said anything to me either, you know the procedure, if you're going out front to relieve yourself you're supposed to alert the man to your left and right, you failed to alert either one of us." Hooper looked like he could cry he was looking around for support but no one came to his defense, everyone just stared at him. He knew he was the one who screwed up, and the fact he made an official and serious accusation against an enlisted man he wanted court martialed made matters even worse.

Because we had our little issues in the past and now that I had been accused of a serious crime in front of the entire platoon and I was pissed I let him have it. "You're a sergeant, you're supposed to lead by example, you're supposed to know and follow the rules, because you either don't know the rules or you have decided not to follow them you put everyone's life at risk, you're nothing but an asshole with stripes."

The LT had heard enough, "Saddle up were moving, Peady your team has the point I want to cover a click by dark, take an azimuth of two nine zero, northwest."

Now we were moving and Sgt. Peady set a quick pace even though the jungle in this AO was as dense as ever. I was lost in my own thoughts. This was a serious situation and I was not sure what was to become of it. We moved just over a click when the LT called a halt and we set up our NDP.

I saw Snead talking with Hooper who moved to the far end of the Hearts section of the perimeter as far from me as he could get. We set up our claymores and settled in for the night. I set my radio for the watch details and started heating up water for a LRRP ration. Today's little incident caused everyone to miss midday chow and we were all hungry.

Soakley came over and talked with me. "This little war you and Hooper have going is not good, something has got to change," he said. "Look Harry, I know we have issues but what he did today is some bad shit," I said. "I almost feel like I should bring charges up on him.' Soakley replied, "That's a bad idea, Hooper could lose his stripes and you both would be out of Recon," he replied.

"I'm getting short, I want to go to my job at BMB when my time comes, I don't want to be stuck here because Hooper's been pulled out of the unit."

I asked Soakley, "You don't still think the LT will want Hooper to be Team Leader for Hearts after today, and this is not the first time he has done something stupid."

"The LT is not happy, I'm sure he's pissed that's why he had us move out after it was clear Hooper screwed up and if this goes official it will be a mark on his career too, don't forget he's West Point, the Army is something he worked hard for, these type of things destroy careers," Soakley said. "So what do you think I should do?" I asked. "At this point play it cool, we will be out here a few more days and then we'll head back to Nancy," Soakley said. "Ok," I replied. "I'm also slotted for R&R this month, maybe that will cool things down, but I need to know that when I come back, I'll be coming back to Recon."

"Well you go on R&R, you owe it to yourself, maybe when you get back it will all be forgotten, take the first watch, Kraus will relieve you." Soakley went over to see Kraus and left me to my thoughts.

I was still angry, but I did not want to do anything that would hurt the LT or get me packed off to a line unit after R&R. I did not know it at the time, but now I think that Soakley was working with the LT and Snead to keep this thing buried. I had a lot to think on.

We did not set up any mechanicals and we never deployed our sensors the night before so pulling in the claymores used for our normal NDP went quickly. The monsoon season was getting started and it began to rain.

We humped another click in the rain from our NDP and wound up at a point due west of our first nights NDP. From here after setting up a defensive position, the LT decided to basically re start the mission. We had midday chow and ran some clover leafs to the southeast.

After doing the clover leafs, we packed up and humped another click or so and came to the original NDP from the first night.

We set up a mechanical and deployed the sensors at the intersection of the trails we found earlier and settled in for the night. The heavy rain at times played havoc with the sensors and we had false readings all night long. The mechanical was still in place the next morning; apparently, the enemy had enough sense to stay in out of the rain. We pulled in the sensors and the mechanical as well as defensive claymores and the LT had us humping again another click northeast of our NDP and we stopped at a point just south of the S. Sau River and north of a large clearing.

We ran clover leafs southeast of the river and just north of where the trails we had seen the night before intersected. We were getting to know this AO pretty well we were spending enough time here.

We stayed at this position for the night and Spades ran recon patrols further southeast along the river. Hearts ran their patrols around the western edge of the clearing. The clearing itself was large it ran 700 meters north to south and 500 meters across east to west. It would be a great extraction point but then the rain really kicked up. We had been out for four days now and all but moved in to this AO.

We were running low on food and water and the LT decided to move us another click and a half east to larger clearing on top of a 100-meter-high hilltop.

We set up on top and placed our NDP on the northern edge of the clearing on top of the hill. The rain was not letting up and we could not get the extraction birds we wanted. Getting here, we had to cross the S. Sau River that at its deepest point was three feet but the river was starting to swell up from all the rain. We were now on the northern side of its banks. We used the claymores from the mechanical to strengthen our NDP defensives there were no trails anywhere in the area.

We laid low the next day and sometime around fourteen hundred the rain let up and the sun started to poke in and out of the cloud cover. Battalion decided to extend the mission and got us a re-supply bird. We got water and LRRP rations to last us three more days and mail. As part of the mail delivery, I got a small package.

Recon was excited not just because of the mail with re-supply but my package was the anticipation of packaged food items from home. I took my bayonet and attacked the cardboard box.

It was about foot wide ten inches high and about eight inches deep. I never looked at the return address. Once the box was opened, I dug in and pulled out a pair of stereo headphones. I was confused. I had forgotten that I ordered these at the PX on our last stand down. Needless to say, everyone was disappointed but we all got a good laugh from the surprise. I humped those headphones for the rest of the mission and even brought them home.

Battalion wanted us to cover the northern side of the river and the southern side of the ridge lines we were sitting on top of.

The LT had us run extended clover leafs in these areas to our southeast. We ran these patrols after getting the re-supply and the next day but packed up our NDP at midday and moved another click southeast keeping the clearing to our south.

The clearing was 200 meters wide and ran northwest to southeast for three clicks. The new hill top we set up our NDP on had a commanding view of the entire clearing. The LT had us run our patrols all along the northern side of the clearing, because the clearing was so wide he did not want to have us out in the open. The rain had started up again and we were all soaked. Now we had a new problem because we were so wet we started to get rashes and our feet were wet. This was causing blisters, so we fortified our defensive perimeter and hunkered down. We stayed in our NDP for two more days and had run out of food.

Water was not a problem, just stick your canteen cup into the rain and in about a minute, you had ten ounces of fresh water. In this situation, we also used our second poncho. We just strung it up over our sleeping positions and tried to stay dry. Sleeping in a puddle is not going to produce a restful night's sleep. To this day I hate being out in the rain.

We stayed the additional three days and were in need of re-supply again but the rain was relentless and with cloud cover, so low we could not get extracted or re-supplied. We were stuck in this AO.

A few more days went by we moved around a little but the shortage of food was taking its toll. On one of the clover leafs Woung came back with some fresh game.

He already had it field stripped it and had it ready for cooking when he returned.

Everyone was upbeat over the prospect of fresh meat until we saw what was on the spit. He had killed a monkey and the cooking carcass looked like a small child. Hunger is a great source however and we all ate the stringy meat. It did not taste like chicken.

A day or two later the weather cleared a bit enough so that we could be re-supplied again. We had been extended an additional five days. We spent the five days setting up our mechanical and live ambush sites, running clover leafs and moving around this entire area. In all the time we spent on this mission, we covered about five square clicks of area. We were crossing our own paths of travel more than once. We saw no signs of the NVA and were happy to hear we would be going back to Nancy. Upon our return, we were exhausted and weather beaten. Everyone had foot problems and we were all filthy despite being wet most of the time.

We smelled so bad the rats left our hooch's when we returned. A shower, clean uniforms and hot chow restored our spirits and of course, there was mail and cold beer.

We spent the next few days resting cleaning and drying out or gear. The incident with Hooper seemed to have quieted down and no one was talking about it.

I decided to take Soakleys suggestion and play it cool although I was still upset over what had happened.

A few more days passed and then the word came down we were headed out on another operation.

New supplies came in and we were off to another AO northwest of FSB Nancy in the Bao Loc District of Lam Dong Province. This was a new AO for us and we had never been there previously.

The insert was routine but this time we were dropped into an old LZ designated as Romo in a CH-47 Chinook. The big bird needs more room than the standard slick and it was able to carry the entire platoon. The crew consisted of a Pilot, Co-pilot and crew chief that doubled as a door gunner. We had the usual insert support from Arty and the cobras. Once on the ground we all ran, out the back door and headed into the tree line.

We were north of the Da R Holl River and just east of QL 20 the road that if we were to take it going southwest would take us back to Nancy. We humped west around the base of the Ba Da R Ting Mountain for about a click and then climbed up to a 300-meter-high null on the south side of the mountain and set up a mid-day defensive perimeter. The LT decided he wanted to check out the eastern side of the village of Phu Lam that was located on QL 20.

We had been inserted two clicks east of the village so as not to alert the local population we were there. We ran some cloverleaf patrols to our south and found trails leading into the village.

We set up a live ambush with the Spades team on the trail that ran east to west south of the mountain.

Once night started coming on the Spades team converted their deployed claymores into a mechanical ambush and then returned to our position, which we then deployed as an NDP.

The night passed without any trouble and the LT wanted to move a click today up to the top of the mountain another 200 meters higher than where we were.

Spades was sent out to retrieve the mechanical and had contact with a VC scout while taking down the mechanical. He was on the trail coming out of the village heading west. Spades had just finished taking down the mechanical down when he was spotted by Pillitary the team opened up and killed him with M16 fire. They also retrieved an AK-47 rifle.

The VC had no other usable Intel so we left the body and stared to hump up the mountain once Spades came back to our position. The LT had us moving due north taking a gradual climb up to the crest and after humping about 600 meters had us turning northeast towards the crest of the mountain. We humped another click that brought us to the 500-meter summit. The ground here opened up to high grass and bamboo so we stayed on the southwestern side still inside the trees. The true summit of the mountain was 584 meters high and it was north east of us about a click away. We set up an NDP and settled in putting out all of our claymores and setting up delta tangos.

We stayed here for two days and ran clover leafs all over the top of the 500-meter summit that covered a full square click. The mountain showed no signs of enemy activity and we broke our NDP and stared heading due south following a draw back down into the valley below.

This took most of the day the terrain going down was steep and when we finally made it to the valley floor, we moved north and east around the base of the mountain.

Here we found the trail the VC was using where it took a turn from running northeast to southeast. The Lt decided to set up a mechanical and we moved just south of the trail and set up our NDP. We waited out the rest of the day and that night with nothing to show for our efforts. We broke out of our NDP took down our mechanical and humped due west which took us back to LZ Romo. We called battalion and gave them an update and they decided to have us RTB.

The choppers came later that afternoon and were back at Nancy for just three days before Battalion was sending us back out to the FSB Den AO.

I would stay behind to begin the process of taking my allotted R&R trip to Bangkok Thailand. I caught a chopper ride from Nancy to BMB. While at BMB I had to get into my personal gear stored at Company HQ.

I would need my civilian clothes and some toiletry items as well as a small travel bag that I got at the PX. I was packed and ready to go and the clerk gave me a ride over to Tan Son Nhut Air Base. We were all put on a chartered flight to Bangkok, given the rules of engagement, and told to be sure to follow all instructions given to us about our return.

We had no choice about returning no one had a passport or US currency and possession of either was against the rules.

I stayed at the Miami Hotel in downtown Bangkok. I buddied up with two other guys whose names I'll never remember and we went to the hotel bar after checking in. This is where we met Todd who offered his tour guide and taxi service to us for the week.

We paid him $25 each and he assured us he would be available twenty-four hours a day to take us anywhere we wanted to go. He wasn't kidding. We took some of his suggestions about sights to see things to do.

His car was a 1955 Pontiac Starchief. We had plenty of room in the four door sedan and the one odd thing about the car and the driving in Bangkok is that it was all done on the English side. Sitting in the front seat was an adventure and the road rules in Bangkok are almost non-existent. I not sure which was more life threatening, driving in Bangkok or humping in the Nam.

We all agreed that we wanted to go to the beach and Todd arranged for us to take a private tour bus to a beach location on the tip of the southeastern side of the Gulf of Thailand. The location was just perfect. We sat on white sand beaches in a small lagoon that was wrapped around us on the north and south sides covered in lush green vegetation. The water was warm and every shade of blue, green and turquoise you could imagine. Standing in the water up to my chest, I could see my feet and small colorful fish swimming around me. To this day, it is still the most beautiful beach I have ever seen.

We also hit all the night clubs, drank plenty of booze and ate everything in sight. Todd took us to see the world's largest gold Buddha. It is about three meters high and weighs in at five tons. It is housed in a temple in Bangkok.

The week went fast and we soon found ourselves back at the airbase in Thailand. The chartered jet left Thailand and had us back in the Nam in about an hour and a half. We said our goodbyes wished each other luck and boarded busses to take us back to our units.

One of the things that were stressed to us about our return was that we were to report back to our unit by a date and time specified on our travel orders. To be late was met with serious consequences, like court martial and jail time at LBJ. Once you reported back in then the games began.

I reported back in on time and the company clerk noted my arrival in the company log and the daily report. Now all I had to do was avoid 'Top'. Since I had legally reported back to my unit, it was now up to 'Top' to make arrangements for my return to FSB Nancy. If 'Top' didn't see me then he had no idea I needed transport to Nancy.

Everyone played this game so it was no big deal in fact I think 'Top' went along with it to give the men a few extra days at BMB. I packed up all my civvies and stored them in my duffel bag that was kept at company HQ in BMB. After changing into a clean uniform I found out the Recon had found a cache of weapons near FSB Den.

The clerk that told me this did not have any additional info except to say Recon was still out on an operation and had been out for two days.

My goal now was to avoid 'Top' for at least a week so that when I did return to Nancy Recon would be starting another mission that I would miss and have some additional days at the firebase by myself.

Best laid plans as they say, 'Top' found me sleeping in the barracks at zero five hundred just two days later. I was promptly hustled off of BMB and on a convoy headed back to Nancy.

Upon arrival at Nancy, I found that Recon was still out on their operation so I headed to the mess hall for lunch.

My 'Striker Camouflage Fatigues' and my 'Recon' tab over my 199th patch identified what unit I was with and some of the line company guys gathered around me for info about the cache Recon had found. I had no additional info but the rumor mill was running at full speed and they were telling me that Recon found a boat load of weapons and supplies. After lunch, I went back to the company CP and asked for a sit rep. The CQ told me Recon found two caches on the 23rd and 24th and that arrangements were being made to bring the stuff back to Nancy that afternoon.

I was told to be on the LZ at fourteen hundred to help load the stuff off the birds. I drove a ¼ ton truck down to the LZ and waited with an NCO from the mortar platoon. Right on time we saw two slicks coming into the LZ. Onboard each of the birds was Pete Black and Hank Waller.

They jumped off the choppers once they landed and greeted me. The choppers were loaded with a lot of weapons and we started moving them from the choppers to the truck. Then we drove them up to the base TOC and started spreading them out for the PIO guys to take pictures for the brigade newsletter.

Here is what Recon had found;

10, 82mm Mortar Rounds,

10, Mortar Sights,

6, Light 7.62mm Machine Guns,

2, .51 Caliber Machine Guns with 2 extra barrels,

22, AK-47 Assault Rifles,

87, SKS 7.62mmx39 Chinese Chicom Rifles

11, 82mm Mortar Tubes.

In addition, they found uniforms, web gear, ammo and rice that were all destroyed on site. All of the weapons were wrapped in heavy paper and coated with Cosmoline. We had quite a haul. The line company guys were jealous; the SKS Carbines were a prized souvenir and could be taken home. We had enough for everyone in Recon and the rest of the company.

Recon made their RTB the next morning and we were all tasked with getting the weapons unwrapped and cleaned for a display for Stars & Stripes who were sending out a photographer and reporter. After all the weapons were cleaned they were all laid out on display in front of the TOC and the Battalion Command Staff came out for the photo op.

We had our own people there as well from 40th PIO they produced the story in the June 17th issue of the Brigade Newsletter.

Everyone in Recon completed paperwork to ensure that each of our SKS Carbines would be going home with us. I still have mine today. After the dog and pony show was over the weapons were again loaded on a truck to be returned to BMB.

During the cleaning process, I was asking about the mission and the guys were asking about my R&R. We were all excited and the conversation and stories were going back and forth. Recon's moral was very high, but it would not last, a few days more and all the rumors about the Brigade rotating home would be put to rest.

The official word would come down on June 1st, the 'Redcatchers' were going home to Ft. Benning Ga.

You would think this news would make everyone happy but it did not. The Brigade was indeed going home in October but that did not mean everyone would go home with the Brigade. Guys like me who still had more than fifty days left in country on October 1st would be transferred to another unit. Troops in other units with fifty days or less would be transferred to the Brigade so that it would return with its full complement of troops. The Army plays politics too.

All of this would be coming out later however and Recon would find itself working out of the old ARVN hill top at Tanh Linh. Another day, another mission. We were headed back to the boonies again and our old AO.

We got a new man for the platoon his name was PFC Jerome Ball. He seemed like a nice guy I think he was from Detroit. When I talked with him, I found out, he was a big Motown fan. No surprise there he was black. I had no trouble with this I was also a big Motown fan and as far as I could tell, no other member of Recon cared that he was black. Ball also was a big Beatles fan as was I and we became fast friends.

Recon was now integrated we had our first black member. I later learned that in 1969, there were blacks in Recon and I'm sure that they were black members who served with distinction in 1968 and 1967. Like I said no one cared about the color of his skin, we all bleed red blood except a certain Mississippi sergeant thought differently.

Ball was assigned to Hearts, and there were other changes as well. Sgt. Soakley was short and due to go to BMB for a rear job, Sgt. Patchart was to take over Hearts.

Tony Collard was working with Lyle on point walking so he had been moved from Spades. Hooper was moved over to Spades as assistant to Sgt. Peady.

I was now the Battalion net RTO. Dan White was the company net RTO the CP was now comprised of the two of us as well as the LT, SFC Snead, 'Little Doc' Keiller, Woung and the new Kit Carson Binh. We learned that the LT would leave us after this mission we had no idea who the replacement would be just yet. Woung was also going to a new assignment training new Kit Carson scouts and this meant we were left with Binh who was useless as an ARVN.

As battalion RTO, I had all the insight of the mission and what we were to do and most importantly when we would RTB or are scheduled for re-supply. I missed walking drag and working with Soakley but this was a prime assignment.

There were going to be a lot of changes in the next few weeks but for us the only real concerns were the missions and where they would be.

The next mission we took a CH-47 to FSB Den and then were trucked southwest of Den to the village of Cau Gia Huynh on RT 333. We met up with a Captain from 5th Special Forces who was in charge of training the Regional Provincial Forces or as we called them 'Ruff Puffs'. The Captain assured us this was a crack team of troops headed by an ARVN Captain.

The unit was about the size of a platoon around twenty men plus the ARVN Captain and an NCO. The game plan was Intel had information elements of the local VC unit would be coming into the village that night and the 'Ruff Puffs' would ambush them.

Our job was to protect the southern flank of the ambush team and set up mechanical ambushes and a live ambush on the trails headed southeast out of the village.

We set up the mechanical on the most southern trail leading out of the village and the live ambush on the one other trail on the southeastern side out of the village. The VC unit was supposed to be coming into the village from its northeast side right down the road. The 'Ruff Puffs' would set up their ambush about three blocks into the village.

The CP group was back at the ARVN base with Spades and the Special Forces Captain and me and Savicci and Dayton was sent out with Soakleys team for extra fire power. Hearts set up on the live ambush north of the trail were the mechanical was. Soakley had me Savicci and Dayton on the southern side of Hearts Team to cover their rear. Everyone was set the 'Ruff Puffs' were going to kick some VC butt. Well that was the plan.

The VC had to have known something was not right. First, the local dog population in the village barked continuously since we arrived. They never shut up. The local people also were in hiding. There were no children outside playing, all the livestock had been penned up, and the village looked deserted. Still the VC arrived at the northeastern end of the road around twenty-one hundred. The ARVN position three blocks away is only 450 meters from the far end of the village and the ARVN Captain decided to spring his ambush when the VC had made it about a block into the village. He does this by running into the middle of the road shouts, "Cai chet cho tat ca VC" (death to all VC) then empty's the clip of his .45 at the startled VC.

Now hitting a target at fifty meters with a .45 is quite a feat, hitting a target at 300 meters is just impossible. The VC cut between houses and run northwest out of the village towards the Suoi Chet River.

To make matters worse the 'Ruff Puffs' are calling in mortar support fire that is landing in the farmed fields southeast of the village not far from the Hearts and our rear guard groups position.

Not only is the mortar fire on the wrong side of the village the adjusted mortar fire was being walked back towards the village and us.

The LT was able to get to the TOC at the ARVN base and had them check fire their mission. We were not going to get much sleep tonight we were on high alert all night and the damn dogs never did shut up.
The next morning although bleary eyed we met with the Special Forces Captain and his little band of merry men and let him know how screwed up they were.
The ARVN Captains explanation was he was eager to demonstrate his bravery in the face of the enemy to his men. I suppose the ARVN NCO who called in the mortar fire was eager to demonstrate his knowledge of compass points too.
I think we were scheduled to run some joint operations with this group but I think the LT put a stop to that plan. We waited until mid-morning and caught a ride with tracks from D Troop 17th Cav back to FSB Den.
We stayed at Den for a day and got a new assignment west of the Nui Long Mountain. We had been there before last month and battalion wanted a fresh recon of the area. The insert was by CH-47 again and the usual arty prep and Cobra escorts. I hated these big birds they were slow and a most inviting target and the worst part was you were cooped up inside with the only exit being the back door. We landed on our LZ just east of the Suoi Tra Cap River and made our way into a high grass and low shrub area and followed the river southwest for about 800 meters. Then we crossed a small creek off the river and came into a lightly forested area where we set up our mid-day defensive perimeter.

Hearts and Spades ran clover leafs to the south and southwest along the river bank. No signs of the enemy were reported by either team and after mid-day chow; we moved south following the clearing to our east.

We made it to the southwestern side of Hill 130 and set up our NDP. Claymores were deployed and the watch schedule was set.
Soakley showed me his map and noted our position, we would be moving around the southern side of Hill 130 in the morning and move north after getting around the LZ we used to be extracted when I sprang the ambush on the three NVA we saw last month.

The LT wanted to check out the area the two NVA escaped in. We had another quiet night and we packed up our gear and started the mornings march around the LZ and Hill 130. We moved about 700 meters and came into the area where Recon had set up their defensive position on the day of the ambush. Soakley pointed out we did a good job of covering ourselves there was no indication we had been there.

We kept moving following the edge of the clearing and had turned north. We humped for another 300 meters and then stopped and set up for mid-day chow. Hearts was the first team out to clover leaf and I went out with them. Soakley wanted me along because this was the area the two NVA had made their escape. We went a good 500 meters following the edge of the tree line around the large clearing. Then we turned north.

The impact areas of the artillery rounds that were fired that day had started to grow over all ready. We moved another 200 meters or so. There were no trails or other signs of the enemy until Lyle held up his fist and took a knee calling a stop to our movement. Everyone was on high alert and Lyle turned to Soakley and pointed to the area we were about to move through.

He tapped his nose indicating he smelled something. Now everyone is on edge Lyles nose was famous for finding trouble. He moved cautiously forward and found what his nose had discovered. He motioned the rest of us forward and Soakley wanted everyone alert and to set up a perimeter. Everyone passed what Lyle had found and then quickly circled up. It was the body of a dead NVA soldier. He was sitting against a tree the only thing he was wearing was his pants.

The body was badly decomposed and the jungle critters had gotten to him as well. Soakley came up to me and said, "Say hello to your buddy, looks like you got one." I looked down at the body and thought to myself, I knew I could not have missed anyone at that range. It was still a weird feeling knowing I had probably caused the site before me that smelled so badly.

We started moving again and we were heading southeast before turning south to come back to our mid-day position. Soakley briefed the LT and Snead and the LT decided at that point to send spades out to our east towards the mountain. Spades went out on their clover leaf and came up on Rd 336 that basically ran north to south east of the base of the mountain. Still no sign of any recent enemy activity so we moved to our south about 500 meters.

We were just shy of a huge clear area that ran open south for several clicks. We set up our NDP and deployed our claymores and set the watch schedule. I was drinking my coffee after eating a chicken and rice LRRP ration, thinking about the dead NVA.

There was no concrete evidence that I had killed this man but this was the area where that ambush happened. The likely hood that anyone else had operations in this area was slim at best. I was starting to accept the notion that this man was one of the three NVA I had fired at.

It was hard to tell from the bloated decomposed body just what caused the man's death but arty fire could be ruled out because his body was still in one piece. We were also a good 200 meters away from the arty rounds impact area. I started the long process of accepting the fact I had taken one human life and was the cause of another to die as well.

The night passed quietly and everyone was up and moving at dawn. The LT had us moving east towards the southern base of Nui Long Mountain.

We climbed the southern side of the mountain traveling northeast to a 300-meter plateau and set up a defensive position for mid-day chow Spades and Hearts both ran clover leaf patrols around our position. Both teams reported no enemy activity or even signs of anyone in the area. We broke our mid-day position and started heading down the mountain traveling southeast. We humped for about a click and came up to the banks of the Suoi Lap Lai River that flowed off the mountain.

We set up our NDP for the night and settled in. Soakley was anxious to get this mission over with he was going to his job at BMB soon to finish up his tour. He had been in country for ten months now and was getting the short timer jitters.

One longer quiet night went by and we were all up by dawn had our breakfast and coffee and packed up our gear. We started moving southwest towards the road and following the river on its northern side. We still had seen no signs of the enemy and this mission was staring to look like many of the mundane missions we went on. Most of these missions were just humping through the jungle fighting the red ants, leeches and mosquitos. By mid-day, we found a bridge on Rd 336 to cross the river.
Better to use the bridge wading through the water to cross the river meant leeches. We set up a defensive position just inside the tree line and had our noon chow.
After we had lunch, the LT had us spread out and walking down the road south towards Dia Diem Dinh Diem Khac Can Village.

This village had been destroyed and was marked as such on the map. The distance from our position to the village was about five miles. We covered this in a couple of hours the road was really just a wide dirt path that cut through open grassy areas and some terrain with small shrubs and palms.

We set up our NDP in the abandoned village and set up a mechanical on one of the old roads cutting through the main part of the village. The place was eerie. You almost had the feeling that the ghosts of all the people who once lived there were wandering around; it was a long creepy night. The next morning at dawn, I got a coded message from battalion that we were going to be extracted at noon. This was one of the advantages of being battalion RTO. I knew before anyone what was in store for us.
We stayed put all morning there was plenty of open space around us to serve as an LZ.

By mid-morning, we pulled in the mechanical and prepared for our extraction. We packed up our gear moved west out of the village about 300 meters and waited for the birds.

The cobras came on station first followed by a CH-47. Once the big shit hook as they were called touched down, we ran to the open back door and were on our way back to FSB Den. We spent the rest of the day at FSB Den and were told we would be choppered back to FSB Nancy to clean out our stuff Nancy was going to be turned over to the ARVN as part of the process to send the Brigade Home. We were losing our hooch's.

Once back at Nancy we packed up anything we had that we could not carry so it could be sent back to BMB.

Needless to say, we were feeling a little low. We also had no idea where we were going to be when not out on operations.

1st LT. Albert Kamble was leaving Recon. Actually, he was taking over as Company Commander. His replacement was 1st LT John Coral. He came from one of the other line companies in the battalion and was an experienced platoon leader. He was also down to earth and everyone liked him. Sgt. Soakley was promoted to Staff Sergeant E-6 and would soon leave Recon as well. Lyle Layden and Don Hardack were promoted to sergeant.

The new mission came in a day later we would hop on a CH-47 to an LZ northwest of FSB Nancy. This would be the last time we would be at our old firebase.

It was a shame as we lifted off the LZ we could not see the base. Nancy would just have to live in our memories.

Chapter Six, Transition;

The CH-47 took us to an LZ about nine clicks northwest of Nancy. This was an area we had not worked in and the terrain was heavy jungle and a 200-meter-high mountain and a second 100-meter-high mountain to the south of the LZ. We were also north of the Song Dong Nai River. The insert was once again escorted by Cobras and the usual arty prep fire. The new LT had us moving southwest towards the highest mountain. We approached from the northern side where the climb up was more gradual. We reached the 200-meter summit just after thirteen hundred. We set up our defensive position and the way the LT had us deploy, it looked like we would NDP here. Another 200-meter peak was south of us about a click away and there was a saddle between the two peaks that reached up about 100 meters. Hearts ran a clover leaf down into the saddle found a trail and set up a mechanical. When they returned to us, we settled in for evening chow and set up the watch list for the night. SFC Snead and Staff Sgt. Soakley were briefing the new LT about the methods of our operations and the LT approved. The night passed without any trouble and we packed up to start our day.

We moved south into the saddle and Hearts took the point. Once we got to the trail, Heart dismantled the mechanical and then Spades took the point and began to climb the second peak. This was a steeper climb than the previous day and by mid-day, we were pretty spent.

We set up a perimeter and settled in for noon chow. PFC Ball was feeling the effects of his first real humping and the mountainous terrain added to his misery.

Ball was not a big guy he weighed more than me but only by twenty pounds or so. I felt bad for the guy. The LT sent spades out on a clover leaf to find out where the trail in the saddle went after it hit the valley below. They were gone all afternoon and we set up our perimeter for an NDP before they got back. Once they did return Sgt. Peady reported the trail went east and then turned south between the two peaks. The plan was to go down into the valley and set up a mechanical on the trail and then NDP on the other 100-meter peak. We had our evening chow and waited for dark. The watch schedules were set up and we passed the night without any problems.

The next day we moved down into the valley between the two peaks set up our mechanical and climbed the 100-meter peak east of the trail. It was only 100 meters but it was another steep climb. PFC Ball collapsed at the top he was fully spent. 'Little Doc' checked him out gave him some salt pills and water and reported he was OK. The Nam was kicking the new guys butt. We set up for another NDP and planned on spending the night. This peak was about 100 meters wide and 300 meters long so we had plenty of room to spread out. Despite everyone being tired, the LT had both teams' clover leaf the top. PFC Ball stayed back with the CP group just the same. There were no signs of enemy activity and the night passed without incident.

The next day we humped back down into the valley retrieved the mechanical and started moving east going around the south side of the mountain.

Once on the eastern side of the peak we cut due north heading back towards the LZ we came in on three clicks away.

We humped most of the day covering about a click and half through dense jungle and set up the NDP. There was no sign of the enemy and we settled in early for a long night.

After morning chow, we saddled up to move and I started to pick up my pack. Underneath the pack was a large black scorpion that was about six inches long. I used the butt of my M16 to kill it. In a few more months, I would meet his little cousin who would avenge the death of his family member. Everyone came over to check it out and we started to move out. We moved about a click and a half and settled in to another NDP. The new LT liked to cover a lot of ground and then call it a day.

Snead and Soakley reminded him our job was to move and clover leaf then move and clover leaf again. The LT was drifting back to his line company routine but he was getting the message. The long jungle humps were taking its toll on PFC Ball the poor guy was really beat. As battalion RTO, I was the first to get the coded message that we would be extracted from the insert LZ and taken to Tanh Linh the next afternoon. We did find another trail and set up our mechanical. The trail was about 100 meters north of us. We had our evening chow and set up our watch schedules. This was really more of the routine type of missions we were going on hump all day and set up an NDP for the night.

Eat your chow and fight off the insects, and the other creepy crawlers that called the jungle their home.

On these nights, we slept but were always half alert for any trouble.

I was on the western side of the NDP with Dan Kiebler next to me. About zero three hundred, the mechanical went off and now everyone was awake. The only thing to do now was stay alert and wait for dawn. As Dan and I, lay there waiting for first light we speculated whether it was the enemy who tripped the mechanical or an animal.

At first light the LT, Woung and the Hearts team moved out to check out the mechanical. I had the battalion radio so where the LT went I went. Once we got within about fifteen meters of the trail, we heard a burst of AK fire. Everybody hit the dirt and as I went down, I banged my knee on a rock. I was seeing stars from the pain but we started moving up on line towards the trail.

Woung found an NVA soldier lying on his back on the trail the AK-47 he carried was across his chest. His canteen was next to him. He had shot himself in the head.

He was quite dead. It became obvious to us that he was there all night by himself and he had suffered some nasty leg wounds from the claymore blast. His one ankle was barely still connected to his calf. He managed to tie a tourniquet to his leg to try and stop the bleeding. There was a lot of blood around his legs. He must have heard us coming and decided he was not going to be captured. We also found remnants of some of the documents he carried. He lay there all night tearing the papers into small pieces. I have to give the guy credit; alone and badly wounded he had enough dedication to try to treat his wounds so that he could destroy whatever Intel he was carrying.

Then knowing his fate, he decided to end his life on his own terms. We packed up our gear and left the NVA on the trail. To me it seemed like we should have done something with his body but no one seemed to care.

We had his AK-47 and his web gear with his ammo the only thing we left with him was his clothes. He did have a khaki colored uniform on. The LT informed battalion the NVA was most likely a courier. We were not able to determine what direction he had been travelling but the LT decided to start moving north towards the LZ.

We reached the LZ in the early afternoon and waited for the choppers. The 'Pink Team' showed up first followed by the chinook. Once the big bird was down we all ran to the open door and we were airborne a minute later. We would not be returning to Nancy instead we were on our way to Tanh Linh.

We ended our mission and were flown in to the airstrip at Tanh Linh. Now we had to hump a half a click to the old ARVN base camp we had stayed at before.

The old camp was on top of a 200-meter hilltop that was part of the N Lo O Mountains. The position overlooked the airstrip at Tanh Linh that was just east of us. We had a commanding view of the valley below us to the north, west and south. The eastern side of the hill was really a 200-meter-high cliff. Not the best avenue of approach but we set up claymores all around us any way. We were resupplied and spent the next few days on the hill top.

We heard that the 4th battalion 12th infantry moved its HQ to a new firebase called Eagle. We had no idea where this new base was but we were to find out in the next few days. Not having access to showers or clean uniforms was depressing. We were all a little ripe, but the re-supply had us stacked with plenty of C-Rations and LRRP rations. We also got mail, which was great, and because our location was so small, there were no details to worry about.

Then we had a surprise. We would pack up all our gear and be choppered back to Nancy one final time. It was great to be back at our old firebase it was like coming home but it would not last. The old girl looked deserted. One of the line companies was there to provide security but all the other units that were assigned had left. The base area that was taken up by 2nd Battalion 40th Artillery was deserted and the mess hall was empty.

Our task today was to pack up all of the Echo Company equipment and then we would be trucked to the new base FSB Eagle. Once everything was packed up we formed up into a convoy with the 152nd MP Group and headed northeast on QL 20 towards the new base. Eagle was located just off of QL 20 about ten miles away from Nancy between the villages of Trai Lam Cay and Xa Phuong Lam.

The new FSB was in its infant stages of construction. The engineers were already on site the berm had been completed but most of the bunkers were still under construction. It sat on a flat open area on the north side of QL 20. All of the vegetation had been cleared but there were still a few trees left on the base. We had to sleep out in the open on the ground but we did have access to showers. The old company area had already packed up clean uniforms for us so we were all fresh as spring daisies by evening chow. We did not have a mess hall yet but there was a field kitchen set up in a large tent so hot chow was available.

We still had a lot of LRRP and C-Rations left over from our little base at Tanh Linh so food was not an issue. The engineers were working into the night building bunkers and the next morning we were tasked with filling sand bags. It was hot in the open sun working to fill the sand bags but it was still better than humping the boonies.

The area outside the berm was open for 300 to 400 meters in any direction. The enemy would have to cover all that open ground in any attack and we had fire support on site from D troop 17th Cav as well as 2nd Battalion 40th Arty.

After a few days at Eagle, we were told of a new operation in the Tanh Linh AO. This would be Staff Sgt. Soakleys last mission he was going to be re-assigned to a rear job.

We got the usual arty prep and cobra support going into the LZ and the LT had us moving east towards the Nui Ca Tung Mountain a 500-meter-high mountain spread out over four clicks long and two clicks wide. The insert was two clicks to the west of the mountain through dense jungle. We covered about 700 meters and the LT stopped us for midday chow. We set up a defensive perimeter and Hearts went on a clover leaf to the east in the direction we were already heading.

The new LT caught on quick and Snead and Soakley were happy. Hearts went about 300 meters east then cut south and came back to the position from the southeast.

Sgt. Patchart was the new Hearts team leader and Soakley was back at the CP group inside the perimeter. Spades then went out going south and then cutting west before moving north and returning to us from the south.

We had noon chow and Patchart came to 'Little Doc' and asked him to check Ball. Everyone was hot and the humidity in the jungle was thick enough to cut with a knife but Ball seemed to be having issues again. His fatigues were soaked with his sweat and he was running a small temp. 'Little Doc' gave him salt pills and checked his water supply.

Hearts had found a trail on their clover leaf and the LT wanted to get on the eastern side of it before night fall. The hump was a good 300 meters again through thick jungle.

The trail ran north and south on the western side of the mountain and had an intersecting trail that ran southeast of the first trail. The LT's plan was to set up a mechanical on the two intersecting trails then set up an NDP north of the intersection and do a live ambush on the north south trail before dark. We packed up our gear and moved out.

Spades set up the mechanical and the CP group and Hearts set up the NDP. Once Spades came back, Hearts went out to set up a live ambush on the trail.

We had gotten to our objective by fourteen hundred that afternoon so Hearts would be out for about three hours before it started getting dark. We settled in for the night and set up our watch schedules. The tree line we were in was about 200 meters wide between the trail and a meadow to our east. We had plenty of concealment and the claymores were out and ready to go.

The night went by without any trouble and the LT decided to run some clover leafs to our north. Hearts went out and found the trail they had set their live ambush on had another intersecting trail going east. They followed this trail through the meadow and it looped around and came back to itself. There was also another intersecting trail going off to the north again. All of this area was covered with grass and small shrubs and a few trees. Once Hearts came back in the LT had spades retrieve the mechanical and then we were moving again.

We cut across country due east to the base of the mountain, we came out of dense jungle into a forested area and then into an open meadow with shrubs and high grass. We also started climbing up the foot of the mountain. The Hearts team set a fast pace to get back into the tree line. Once inside the tree line PFC Ball fell flat on his face.

'Little Doc' was called up and once we got his pack and some of his gear off we could tell he was having heat stroke. Snead told us, "Set up a perimeter and everyone drop off a canteen of water." We set up a hasty perimeter and 'Little Doc' went to work on Ball. He was semi-conscious and looked like he was in bad shape. 'Little Doc' opened up ball's shirt and pants and was pouring water over his head and torso. Snead was fanning him with a towel.

'Little Doc' said, "We have to get his core temperature down or he's going to be in deep shit." The LT and I were looking at the map and found we had a good LZ spot about 500 meters south of us. Everyone came over and dropped off a canteen when Soakley said, "Hooper bring over one of your two quart canteens." Hooper just sat there and said nothing. More guys brought their canteens over and Soakley was staring at Hooper.

Ball started to come around and Snead continued fanning him while 'Little Doc' gave him some salt pills and a little water to drink. "Don't guzzle the water just take a little you'll cramp up on me," 'Little Doc' said. Soakley walked over to Hooper and said something to him. We could not here what Soakley said or the reply given by Hooper. Based on the reaction of Soakley this was not a good exchange.

Soakley grabbed Hooper by the shirt and pushed him off the rucksack he was sitting on. Then he reached down and took a two-quart canteen off the ruck and brought it over to 'Little Doc'. Hooper got up and just glared at Soakley. The LT wanted an update from 'Little Doc' on PFC Ball's condition. "He needs to rest up and I need to get more fluid into him but slowly," 'Little Doc' said. "Roger that, OK, Sgt. Peady I want you to take your team due south of here and checkout this LZ," the LT said. He was holding out his map for Sgt. Peady. "Everyone else set up a defensive perimeter, let's move it," the LT said.

Spades left the position and Pete Black took over for Snead with the towel. Ball was awake and responding and it looked like he would be OK. The LT told me to prep a coded message to battalion that we were going to need a one-man extraction and why at the LZ we saw on the map. I broke out the code book and started to prepare the message.

I saw Snead walk over to Soakley and the LT soon followed. The three of them were in a hushed conversation and the LT was shaking his head. Snead was clearly pissed over whatever Soakley had told him.

I had the message prepared and let the LT know when he came back to me. "Ok," he said, "Little Doc, how's he doing?"

'Little Doc' told the LT, "He's going to be OK but I would not push him hard." The LT asked, "Can he walk a couple of hundred meters without equipment and some help?" "I can do it LT," Ball said. The LT looked at 'Little Doc' and he shrugged his shoulders and tilted his head to indicate 'Maybe'.

"White call Spades and tell them to call back when they get to the LZ," the LT ordered. Dan started calling Spades and we waited for them to come up on net. Spades got the message and responded they were approaching the LZ and would call back when they were there. PFC Ball was now sitting up but was still light headed. Spades called back and reported they had reached the LZ. Dan let the LT know and he relayed they were to check out the LZ for any signs of enemy activity. After about fifteen minutes' spades reported that, the LZ was clear with no sign of the enemy.

The LT took his map over to Dan and told him, "Have Spades set up a defensive posture along this line and wait for further orders." Dan called Spades and gave the orders to Peady.

"Ski call battalion send the coded message and ask them to send the bird for pick up at fifteen thirty hours," the LT told me. I recoded the message with the pickup time and sent it to battalion. The extraction was set up and we had 2 ½ hours to get Ball to the LZ. The distance was really about 600 meters but I kept that to myself.

We packed up Balls gear and passed it around so we could share the load. The only thing Ball was required to carry was his weapon. He seemed to be doing OK and Dan called spades to let them know we were on the way and we started at a slow pace.

We moved southwest on a downward slope through some light trees and kept an eye on Ball to make sure he was OK. 'Little Doc' was next to him as was Snead the entire way.

Once we had covered 300 meters, we stopped just to rest for ten minutes. Ball drank some more water and said he was OK.

We covered the last 300 meters and we hooked up with Spades in denser jungle on the edge of the LZ. It was fourteen fifteen and we had some time before the medivac would touch down.

The LT was taking no chances and had Spades run a clover leaf around the southwestern side of the LZ. Once they came back Hearts ran one going northeast around the LZ. It was now around thirteen fifteen and battalion called to alert us the medivac was enrooted with an ETA of ten minutes. Ball seemed to be OK but complained he was light headed and had a bad headache.

The medivac arrived on time and Ball was extracted without incident. The LT then had us move back to the position where Ball had collapsed to set up an NDP for the night.

LT Coral was an easy guy to get along with. He considered himself one of the men and from an operational standpoint, he asked everyone in the CP group their opinions. This was totally different from LT Kamble's approach but hey, everyone is different. Kamble was a quiet leader he spoke only when it was needed and expected his orders to be followed. Coral was more engaging gave his orders without hesitation but relied on the thoughts of his men as well.

The LT came over to Dan and me and asked our opinion as to who was the best replacement for Sgt. Soakley as platoon sergeant.
This seemed unusual to us but we both agreed Sgt. Patchart should be the new platoon sergeant. This also raised a question of when was SFC Snead leaving us. That answer came the next morning in a coded message from battalion. We needed to get to a clearing about one click south of us by mid-day. SFC Snead was to be extracted for RTB. This was most unusual; people were not pulled from the field to go on R&R or to go home. If the soldier scheduled for any event was within a few days of that event, they stayed behind and did not go out on the mission. The rumors were running around that on one of our last stand downs at BMB Snead had run into some troubles with the MP's. No one had any concrete evidence but if some type of official proceeding were pending Snead would only get a two or three-day notice. This all seemed to fit and feed the rumor fires but we never found out.

We packed up our gear pulled in the claymores and started moving southeast along the base of Nui Ca Tong Mountain to the designated pick up spot given us by battalion. We had to go about a click and the terrain was tough and steep along the base of the mountain. Battalion gave us a pick up point at the base of the mountain next to a lightly wooded area. Because of the rough terrain and the slow and deliberate pace set by the new point man Collard, we got to the pickup point just as the OH-6 Loach came on net.

The little bird hovered over the dense brush about six feet of the ground and Snead had to reach up and grab the skid to climb into the chopper. I watched Snead make it into the chopper and have to say I was impressed.
The man had to be forty years old and even with all his gear on he managed to climb into the chopper. "Rangers Lead the Way."

Now with Snead, gone Soakley was our platoon sergeant but this was to be his last mission. The LT had moving again to the southwest through the narrow patch of woods and high grass we were in. We moved and covered another click much quicker in this terrain and set up our mid-day defensive position alongside a small creek. We were on flatter ground and had good lines of sight around us. The LT called over Sgt. Patchart and Sgt. Layden and told them of the new assignments. Patchart would take over as platoon sergeant and Layden would be the new Hearts team leader. Soakley had no objections and he knew he was one step closer to going home. We ran some clover leafs from this position to our northwest and found the same trails we saw earlier.

After our mid-day break, we moved northwest and set up our NDP in the thicker wood line just north of the two intersecting trails we saw a few days ago. We set up another mechanical on the intersecting trails and set our watch schedules for the night.

Once we settled in I asked Soakley about his conversation with Hooper when Ball had collapsed.
"Let it go, Ski it doesn't matter now anyway," he said.
"The LT is aware of all the platoon politics and history from Kamble and Snead and has to make his own decisions," he added. Whatever was said in that conversation between Hooper and Soakley it seemed to me that something was about to happen as a result.
I had always taken Harry's advice before and I was not going to change now, I dropped the subject.

We had no luck with the mechanical and other than Ball's extraction and Snead's sudden departure, this was turning out to be another mundane mission. These was the way things usually went, hump all day in the heat and humidity and fight the losing battle with the local wildlife and insects. It was going to be interesting before it was over. Another night without any trouble so we pulled in the claymores packed up our gear took the mechanical down and started heading west back towards the LZ that got us started on this mission. This time though we came up to the LZ on its southern end. We had humped for about 500 meters and Collard found some bunkers. This was a small base camp with just three bunkers around it. There was no sign of any recent enemy activity but the LT wanted to check this camp out anyway. We found some sleeping positions in the base camp and what looked to be a tunnel entrance.

The LT said, "OK Ski, you got the pop gun and your small enough how about you climb in there and see what you can find". I was a little taken back but noted this was not an order it was more of a request. "Well OK LT, give me your flash light," I said.

The LT handed me his flash light and I dropped into the hole that was in the center of the camp.
I moved away from the hole entrance knowing I was highlighted in the day light and felt along the edges going deeper into the tunnel. It was about four feet high and three feet wide. Once I was about five feet into the tunnel, I cocked the pistol and turned on the flashlight. In front of me was what looked like the end of the tunnel but as I got closer, I saw it went in three different directions. I picked one and shined the flashlight down the shaft and saw nothing. I repeated this three times for each shaft with the same result. Now I had to pick a shaft so I took the one going to the right and followed it for about twenty meters and then saw day light. As I reached the end of the tunnel, I pooped up in one of the bunkers. Then I retraced my steps and headed back to the entrance I dropped into. I came out dirty and sweaty and informed the LT the hole led to a tunnel set up to access the three bunkers. "Alright, good job, Sgt. Soakley how much C4 do we have," the LT asked. "Should have close to 20 pounds between us sir," Soakley replied. "Great let's gather it up tie it all together and blow this tunnel," the LT said.

We pulled together the twenty-one-pound bricks of C4, took some of the wiring from our mechanical, and made a long line of wire. We did not have any tape but we all carried extra black nylon boot laces and used those to tie the bricks together. Then just to be sure, we wrapped the bundle with detcord from the mechanical.

Once the brick of C4 was prepared the LT asked me to go back into the tunnel and take the brick to where the three tunnels converged leading to the bunkers.

I went back into the tunnel and placed the brick in the center where the three tunnels were. Once I got out of the hole, the LT had everyone move away from the area and then used a claymore clacker to blow the C4. He called out, "Fire in the hole." Whoump!
The ground shook and smoke came out of the hole and the three bunkers.

In the center of the camp, the ground had collapsed into the tunnel and there was now large indented spaces were the C4 had been blown. The tunnels were destroyed and once in one of the bunkers you could no longer move to another one using the tunnel.

"Good job Ski besides being a half ass RTO you're also a half ass tunnel rat," the LT said. Everyone laughed and patted me on the back. I wasn't happy about the new duties I seemed to have been drafted for and I was filthy from being in the tunnel. Fortunately, we were going to be extracted the next day.

We set up our NDP at the base camp position and settled in for the night. After chow and over coffee with Soakley and the LT I asked, "LT suppose there was an NVA in that tunnel with an AK 47. An AK-47 against a nine shot single action revolver is hardly a fair fight." Then I added, "If I had been wounded how were you guys going to get me out?" Soakley laughed and said, "We just toss in some frags and have a memorial service." "Thanks pal," I replied, but the LT had thought about what I said and replied, "Ski, your right if anything happened to you we would be in deep shit trying to get you out. So from now on take Woung's .45," he said. They both laughed, but I was not going back into any holes any time soon.

The next morning, we got extracted back to FSB Eagle and would spend the next couple of nights in the bunkers around the berm. Showers, clean uniforms, hot chow and mail brighten up every soldier's day. We relaxed cleaned our weapons and just tried to take it easy.
Sgt. Hooper was heading for BMB for an R&R rotation. Harry Soakley was going back to BMB as well, he would be missed. He was a great sergeant; he did his job and made sure everyone knew what was going on.

Not known to us at the time is that Hooper would not return to Recon. Hooper would be reassigned upon return from R&R and we learned that Kamble our old LT was moving on as well. No explanation over Hooper's reassignment was ever given.

After a few days at Eagle, we got re-supplied with water and chow and we also found out we had a new addition assigned for this mission. A handler PFC Guntz from 49th Infantry Scout Dog Platoon and his canine 'Ranger' a 110 lbs. German Shepard would be going out with us. We would be headed for an area around FSB Libby further south down QL 20.

We were inserted by CH-47 again and this time we had no arty prep but we did have our cobra escorts. The dog was friendly enough around GI's but he did not like Binh our Kit Carson Scout. Just goes to show dogs are a great judge of character. The insert was west of Nui Dot Mountain and FSB Libby was just east of it on the other side of QL 20. Our assignment was too recon some intersecting trails in a lightly forested area around the Suoi Tia River that ran south from the Suoi Cha Rung River further north.

We moved about a click southwest of the LZ and set up a mid-day defensive position on a small hilltop in a lightly wooded area about 100 meters high. Hearts and Spades both ran clover leafs to our west and to the south.
The dog team went with Hearts on the western sweep and found two intersecting trails. Hearts set up a mechanical ambush on the intersecting trails and after mid-day chow, we moved 500 meters' northwest crossed the Suoi Co Creek to another 100-meter-high plateau in denser jungle and set up our NDP. More clover leafs were run to our north and west by both teams and the dog team went out with Spades this time. Binh stayed in the CP groups position the dog just did not like him and Guntz said he needed to eliminate the distraction.

Spades had gone out to our west and found another trail and the dog was actively sniffing around the trail. Guntz felt we had recent enemy movement on this trail.
We all settled in for the night the dog was deployed with Guntz on the western side of the NDP with Spades. The night passed without incident and Ranger came alert every time one of us moved to the radio position during the watch schedule.

At the crack of dawn, we were all up and had breakfast and coffee. After that, Hearts was sent out to retrieve the mechanical. Ranger sat up as they came back to our position and were still about a 100 meters out. The enhanced senses of the dog both smell and hearing was a great asset for us. We pulled in our claymores and left our NDP traveling west for about a click and came into a less dense forest area.

From here we turned north humped another click and crossed the wide but shallow Suoi Tia River. We set up our mid-day defensive perimeter and sent out our clover leafs to the west and north. The river was now to our east. Ranger went out with Hearts the idea being to get the dog used to the men on both teams. He basically stayed away from the CP group because of Binh but he was familiar with the rest of us. The clover leafs found another active trail to our west that intersected with another just to our north.

The LT indicated to us that he wanted to set up an NDP a few hundred meters north of us and to set up an overnight mechanical on the intersection. We broke or mid-day position and started humping north. We crossed a trail that ran east and west and continued north where we found another larger trail running north and south. We set up our NDP in an area that had the river now wider and deeper to our east and the north south trail to our west. The space between the two was about a 100 meters in thick jungle.

Hearts set up the mechanical on the east west trail just south of our NDP on the eastern side of where the two trails intersected. The terrain at the intersection was to open in a light forest area and the trip wire for the mechanical could not be concealed. You could see up to 125 meters from Hearts position. This also gave us the advantage of having the mechanical cover our southern flank. Claymores were set up all along the north of us and to our western flank. We had our eastern flank right up against the river.

We set up in a triangle shape with Hearts covering our south and western side, Spades covering our south and eastern side and the CP group at the far northern edge of our NDP. Both trails showed signs of heavy use and indications were that the east west trail had the most use. We settled in for the night and set the watch schedule. Everyone was on high alert except Ranger. He gave us no indication that there were any threats during the night. The LT sent Binh with Hearts on the south western part of the NDP. The dog spent the night with the CP group. Just before dawn, Ranger alerted. He stood up with his nose in the air and his ears up and pointed to our south. At first, we thought he was just getting Binhs scent but soon the hairs on his neck stood up and a low growl started. He was also nudging Guntz who indicated to us that something was up.

Then the call came over the net from Hearts RTO they were seeing movement to the south of their position and the intersection. SGT. Layden called into the CP, "Clubs, Clubs this is Hearts large NVA unit coming towards us from the south over." The LT was on the horn immediately, "Hearts this is Diamond how many over?" Lyle's response scared the crap out of all of us once we all heard.

"Diamond, this Hearts I see at least a platoon thirty men about 100 mikes away coming north."
"Hearts, hold your fire, do you copy, over?" The LT said. Lyle responded, "Copy hold fire."

The LT then called Spades, "Spades this is Diamond every one sit tight and hold your fire, acknowledge." Spades came on net and acknowledged the LT's orders.

We were in a wait and see situation, the enemy forces approaching our position was just as formidable as we were, but the advantage was ours because the NVA had no idea we were there. Lyle came back on net and the Spades RTO could also monitor his transmissions. "Diamonds, this is Hearts, enemy is moving north through the intersection, I can now see at least two platoons over." The LT turned to me pointed to a spot on the map and told me to get arty on the horn. I noted the position on the map where the river and the trail converged.

I gave the co-ordinates to the FDC and told them to stand by. This is just the type of fire mission red legs live for. "Musketeer 3, this is Eagle Warrior Four 3, standby fire mission large enemy force moving north at grid YT395300, over," I whispered into the battalion net radio handset. The response was immediate, "Copy Eagle Warrior Four 3, standing by with full battery over." I could just imagine every gun crew cocked and loaded waiting for the fire command.

Lyle came back on net, "Diamonds, this is Hearts NVA approaching our pos I count sixty and still coming, I say again six zero over." "Roger Hearts, stand down hold fire do you copy?" The LT said. Lyle came back right away, "Copy, hold fire."

We now had a large NVA force moving within 100 meters of us and travelling north. Our only advantage at this point was the enemy had no idea we were there and fire support. Behind the scenes at Battalion, they were monitoring our company net and hearing about the large enemy force they were salivating and preparing to feast on the unsuspecting NVA.

Unknown to us at the time battalion was already planning their air strike and arty fire missions. Battalions plan called for F-4 Phantoms to drop 500 lbs. bombs followed by a Hunter Killer Team at a point 300 meters to our north where the trail was between the river and a 100-meter ridge line.
The artillery barrages we had already plotted into the FDC would be used as a marker position for the Gun Target Line the Fox Fours would use.

Everyone in the meantime is holding their breath and laying low. The trail at far northern side of our NDP were the CP group was is less than twenty meters away. Even through the jungle on the trail, we could see the NVA soldiers.

I remembered what Snead had said months ago, "What are they wearing, what kind of weapons do they carry, and what their demeanor is." These NVA were well equipped. Uniformed in khaki wearing boonie hats or pith helmets, web gear with packs and all of them had AK-47 assault rifles, with some soldiers with RPG launchers.

"Diamonds, this is Hearts, end of enemy column approaching I counted ninety-two, I say again niner two, over," Lyle reported. This was a full company of NVA regulars. The LT made the right call even with our claymores and fire support we would have been in deep shit engaging such a large and well equipped enemy force.

It took the enemy column five minutes to fully get past our position and as the last enemy soldier passed the CP group, everyone was finally able to take a breath. "Hearts, and Spades this is Diamond hold your fire and position,"

the LT called on the company net. Then we got the call from Battalion letting us in on their plan. Three minutes after the last NVA passed the CP group 40th Artillery started firing at the grid co-ordinates I gave them. Those co-ordinates were just 300 meters to our north.
Then we heard the Fox Fours coming from the south of us. We were just 300 meters from the Gun Target Line. The roar of the low flying jets engines was deafening, but the explosions of the four 500 lbs. bombs dropped on the trail to our north was more impressive. The ground shook with each explosion and the bomb blast could be felt at our position. The canopy here was thick enough we could not see the jets or the dropping bombs, but the bomb blast knocked loose leaves in the trees off of their branches and it started raining leaves.

Once the Fox Fours were off station we could hear the Hunter Killer Team come on station. The low flying OH-6 Loach could be heard buzzing around the area where the bombs exploded but they were reporting on the battalion net they had no targets for the circling Cobras. The Hunter Killer team worked to the northeast of the bomb site and came up dry. The consensus was the NVA had broken west or southwest. Battalion wanted us moving to check it out. Hearts took down the mechanical and we pulled in our claymores. No breakfast or coffee today we were moving north to do a BDA on the trail and then try to find out where the NVA went.

Hearts had the point with Ranger and Guntz walking behind Collard who was on point. Lyle was behind the dog team. We went through where the arty had impacted and found no signs that the arty fire impacted the enemy column.

We moved up the next 200 meters to the bombing site slowly. Once we got within 100 meters, the LT had us go on line with Hearts on the west and Spades on the eastern side of the trail. The CP group brought up the drag.
The Fox Four jockeys dropped their bombs on both sides of the trail. There were four very large and distinct craters where the bombs fell and the trees and jungle floor around the impact area was covered in debris from the jungle. Amazingly, the trail itself was still there.
We checked all around the area and found no signs of any bodies, blood trails or the enemy. We returned to the area that the artillery had impacted because the LT saw a spot where we could cross the river when we passed through earlier. Once we crossed the chest high river we were on the western bank and moved north again.
Moving north and all of us back on line we found where the NVA had gone. They must have broken west when the arty rounds started impacting the trail.

We found multiple points along the river bank where troops had come out of the river and continued running through the jungle to our west. Battalion had the right idea they just had bad luck. The arty put the enemy in a controlled withdraw breaking through the jungle. We followed a few of places where we could see troops had broken down the vegetation and still found no other signs of the enemy. How far they ran and where they where was now a concern not only for us but battalion as well.

Some of the signs showed the enemy continued west until they came up on a lightly forested area. This is where we lost the enemy completely. We set up a defensive position on the edge of this forested area but stayed back ten meters or so in the denser jungle and notified Battalion.

They told us to stay put and we put out the extra claymores from the mechanical just in case.
Hearts and Spades ran short clover leafs to our east back towards the river to see if we missed anything or anyone, both came up empty.

Battalion notified us that two platoons from a line company would be inserted in an LZ two clicks to our west and another platoon would be inserted two and a half clicks to our southwest. They would be landing by late afternoon. The two platoons would move east towards us and the last platoon would move northeast towards our old NDP the next day.

The Battalion wanted to know where this NVA Company was bad. An entire company still moving at dawn must have been travelling all night. The NVA rarely moved in company sized elements during day light hours. We must be in an area where they planned to hole up. We were instructed to move back to the trails and follow them north to see where they led.

The LT had us moving south again to where we crossed the river and then back north again following the trails.
We stayed close to the river bank and continued north but then the river turned to the northwest and we were forced to follow the trail on its western side. We went a little over a click and found another trail intersecting with the one we followed. By this time, it was getting late and the LT had us set up our NDP. We set out all of the claymores and then posted our delta tangos with arty. There was to be no cooking tonight so we chowed down on cold LRRP's and C-Rats. The watch schedules were set with the first shift starting late. Everyone was on high alert.

It was a long night but it went by without any trouble. The LT was on the horn with Battalion in the morning and advised them of the river crossing point we used. The three platoons from the line company would converge there today and cross to our side of the river assuming they did not run into the NVA. Our job was to clover leaf around the intersection and follow the trails to see if they showed signs of recent use. Spades went out with the dog team first and found recent activity on the trail that went east and west. Ranger was sniffing at this trail and we believe the NVA must have run west after the arty impacted then turned north and picked up the trail again. The intersecting north south trail was the one we followed up.

This meant the NVA were probably picking up their original route that was headed in the direction of a saddle between a 145 meter and a 100-meter hilltop. This trail also crisscrossed the Suoi Cha Rung Creek that was fed off the taller hilltop. A perfect area for an NVA base camp. It took us most of the day to reach the saddle about a click and a half away.

The LT was now thinking the NVA had a day's travel in front of us and if we were following their line of march, they could be set up in a base camp waiting for us. He called arty and had them fire missions in front of us. Then we climbed the 145-meter-high peak to the north of the creek and trail and after arty plastered the top of the hill, we moved in and set up our NDP.

The three platoons from the line company had found our river crossing point and once on our side of the river set up their own NDP around the area where the trails intersected and north of where we saw the NVA. They were about two clicks away from us.

We were on high alert again, we had our claymores out we were on high ground and our delta tangos were set up. The LT would not allow any cooking again so it was another night of cold C-Rats and LRRP's.

To our east about a click was an open area and then a rubber plantation. QL 20 the road that would have taken us back towards Nancy was three clicks away. Battalion fired H&I missions all night to our east and the other peak to our south.

At zero three hundred, the line company NDP was probed by a large enemy force. The LT figured that the NVA suspected an American unit in the area spotted them called in the arty and air strike and with the line company making so much noise, the NVA assumed they were it. Our noise discipline had paid off. The NVA were not tracking us they were focused on the line company. The enemy broke off the contact just before dawn and the line company reported they were moving north after the contact.

Battalion had us stay put all morning while the line company pursued the NVA through a heavily wooded area. They had gone about a click and a half before they hit three different blood trails going north and northeast into the jungle. It seemed the NVA Company had split up its three platoons.

Battalion asked us to move south into the saddle and to check out the 100-meter-high ridge line to our south. We pulled in the claymores and started to move. We followed the ridge line from our NDP east and then turned southwest towards the ridge. We found a large enemy base camp that showed signs of recent use. There were about twenty bunkers and Ranger dug up some bloody bandages. While we stayed on the higher ridge, the NVA was still here in the area and moved during the night towards the line company.

All of this was reported back to Battalion. The line company was making contact throughout the day we could hear the AW fire off and on. The trail we followed led right through the center of the base camp. We plotted the co-ordinates of the base camp and followed the trail going east to the open area and plantations. We found more intersecting trails but no more signs of the enemy. It was getting late again and battalion decided to pull us out and we were RTB going to FSB Libby just three clicks away.

This mission was exactly what Recon was developed for. Find and track the enemy and let the line companies follow up and kill the bad guys. We never fired a shot but we observed and tracked the NVA movement and now the Battalion could deal with the issue. If we had fired on an enemy unit of that size equipped the way they were we would be looking at serious casualties on both sides. Instead of a pursuit operation, the Battalion would have been faced with a rescue operation. The discipline and professionalism of the platoon was outstanding. Additional line units were inserted north of our area and they made multiple contacts over the next few weeks killing several NVA and capturing weapons.

Whatever the enemy was planning was ruined by our finding them and the line units pursuing them.
The 33rd NVA Regiment was flexing its muscles again and was picking up its operations in our AO. We found one element and there would be more over the next few weeks.

Chapter Seven, New Leaders New Home;

Recon was basically homeless. The 4th Battalion 12th Infantry Regimental HQ was at FSB Eagle. It was moved from FSB Nancy when the new fire base was being built. Recon however would spend its days in the field and when not assigned to missions would be resting at FSB Mace, or spending time on our hill top position at Tanh Linh. We pulled bunker duty at Mace and if we were resting at Tanh Linh for all intended purposes, we were in the field. For now, we were spending a few days of rest at FSB Libby. Even though we were being bounced around when not in the field we had access to showers, clean uniforms and most importantly mail.

The Brigade was actively progressing its stand down operations in preparation for returning to Ft. Benning Ga. Operation Keystone Robin was moving along and before it was through entire units would be shuffled around.
While we were resting at Libby, we also had access to hot chow. The fire base was situated east of QL 20 and sat in the shadow of Nui Dot Mountain a 248-meter peak that stuck up out of the landscape like an over grown boil. We were lounging around and the subject of the mountain came up. Why was this fire base here? The mountain was the perfect location for the NVA to launch mortar attacks on the base. We all agreed that Charlie would need a tunnel and bunker complex to defend the position.
We wondered if our next mission was on that mountain. We stayed at Libby for two days the line company sent in to reinforce us on our last mission had been in constant

contact since we left. The NVA Company we encountered was still active and things were getting hot.

We were re-supplied and we were off again on a new mission further north Nui Dot Mountain would have to wait. QL 20 ran southwest from our old base FSB Nancy and crossed the 150-meter-wide Song La Nga River and then turned due west towards the Nui Tran Mountain. Once it hit the mountain, it turned south and then west again to get around the mountain. Then it continued southwest towards FSB Libby. Battalion reported in the briefing that the line company followed our north south trail the NVA used towards the Nui Tran. We were being sent in to check it out. The plan was to be tracked in by elements of the 11th ACR.

We would leave from FSB Libby travel north up QL 20 to RD 323 and go northwest into the tea plantation west of the hamlet of Ap Birh Hoa. A plantation service road intersected and went due north. We would dismount the M113 APC tracks when they turned around. The apex of Nui Tran was about a click away.

Once we hopped off the tracks we humped northeast up the ridge lines of the mountain and crossed the Suoi Bung Creek by mid-day. We found a heavily used trail and set up a defensive position. Hearts and Spades both ran clover leafs Hearts went north and Spades followed the trail southeast and found another intersecting trail.

We had our mid-day chow quickly and then the LT planned on moving northwest around the ridge lines of the mountain and then eventually turning east. We would set up a mechanical on the intersecting trails and then start the 225-meter climb to the top of Nui Tran.

We traveled northwest around the steep part of the mountain and then turned east to go over the top.
We reached the top by mid-afternoon and came into an enemy base camp. Collard from Hearts was on point followed by Sgt. Layden and his RTO. Collard stopped just as he came up on top and took a knee. This was a signal to Layden he saw something. He turned towards Layden pointed to his eye and then made a fist under his chin. "Enemy Bunker". Layden turned to his RTO and called Dan White to alert the CP group. Then he pointed to Wilton and pointed to his left and pointed at Kraus and pointed to his right. Each man in Hearts went left or right to come up on line with Layden. The CP group would bring up the rear as Spades was now coming past them to join Hearts.

Then there were bursts of AW fire coming from the top and green tracer rounds zipped over our heads.
The NVA on top had opened up with AK-47 fire but because of the steep incline, their rounds went over our heads. Hearts was already on line and opened up with return fire while charging the top of the hill to get behind or out flank the NVA. The top was occupied by three NVA and they bolted northeast off the hilltop. Hearts was in fast pursuit firing the entire time and the NVA could be heard crashing through the jungle as they went down the hill. Spades also took the top of the hill and found more bunkers and hooch's.
Hearts continued to fire down into the jungle on the northeastern side of the hill and the LT was on the horn with arty and started a fire mission at the bottom of Nui Tran. The LT called for a cease fire and we re-grouped to

check out the base camp. Hearts and Spades gave up a man each and they together with the CP group checked out the base camp.

Hearts and Spades set up perimeter defensive positions. Arty was told to stand down and we searched the camp. The camp was shaped like a "U" just like the top of the hill with the inside of the "U" facing southeast towards QL 20. There were twenty-five bunkers in total all with overhead reinforcement using logs and ten hooch's. Everything was freshly constructed. There were also thirty hammocks strung up in the camp.

Cooking fires were set up around the camp although none were in use now. This had to be where the NVA Company was headed when we saw them pass us on the trail.
No other supplies were found and due to it getting late, we had to NDP that night in the enemy's camp. Claymores were deployed and we were wishing we had the other five claymores from the mechanical. It was going to be a long night the NVA knew we were there and we had just broken into their house.

We settled in had our chow and set up our watch schedule. The LT decided to have two men on watch for each shift. The CP group would have to take two-hour shifts including the LT, Sgt. Patchart and Binh. We gave Binh the first shift no one trusted him to stay awake and he looked like he was about to blow his lunch.
The LT also set up delta tangos around and on the mountain just in case. The mechanical blew around twenty-three hundred hours. It was located at the base of the hill 500 meters south of us. We were not getting much sleep tonight. An hour after the mechanical blew we

heard movement at the base of the hill to our south. This was the area where the mechanical was. The LT called arty adjusted one of the delta tangos and set up a fire mission. Arty fired six rounds of HE at the base of the hill. We lay there hardly breathing staring into the blackness.

Around zero one hundred hours, we heard more noise to our north. It sounded like a large group was moving fast. The LT called arty again and they fired another six rounds of HE after adjusting another one of our delta tangos. We waited for dawn no one slept this night.

The next morning the LT called arty and readjusted his delta tango plots. Then he had arty fire some more HE rounds all around our position. The morning air was heavy with the smell of cordite and burnt vegetation. If the NVA were planning a dawn attack, the LT hoped to diminish the enemies resolve with the artillery. We were not attacked and the morning remained quiet. We had chow and coffee and the LT planned the day's events. Hearts would clover leaf going southeast and then around the inside of the "U" from one side to the other. Once they reached the other side of the "U" Spades would join them and act as backup as they went to check out the mechanical.

Collard set out on point and they took a very unhappy Binh with them. They were gone about thirty minutes when they called on the company net to report ten more bunkers in the center of the "U" below us.
All of the bunkers had just been constructed. They called again and reported they reached the other end of the "U". Spades then moved out to join up with Hearts. The CP group stayed behind. Hearts climbed down the steep embankment to where the mechanical was. They could

also see where the arty rounds impacted. They found several blood trails and pieces of bandages and it looked like the NVA escaped to the west.

Hearts then started coming back towards Spades position and found two caves that had been dug into the side of the ridges at the point of the "U". Layden reported these looked like some type of gun position. Spades was ordered back up top with us and Hearts was told to check out the inside of the "U" all the way around to the other side. They were about 100 meters lower than they had been when they first started out and reported finding three more of these caves in the center and two more at the other point of the "U".

The LT reported all of this information to battalion and we were ordered to move north to do a BDA of the arty rounds fired last night. After a quick mid-day meal, we got started and travelled due north down the steep side of the mountain. Once we hit bottom we travelled about 100 meters and found the impact points of the previous night's artillery mission. With nothing to report about the arty, we went another 150 meters and found a trail that had just been used and there were blood spots on the trail. It appeared the NVA were now moving east. We followed the trail along the southern side of it not wanting to us it. We moved the rest of the day breaking through the jungle alongside the trail and found ourselves looking across 150 meters of open ground to QL 20.
We had also seen another intersecting trail continuing east we followed the southern part of the trail. It was getting late and we needed to NDP so we crossed QL20 and climbed a 100-meter-high ridge line and set up our NDP there. The only other option was to move onto the "U"

shaped hill and sit in the middle giving the enemy the high ground in fortified positions. Besides everyone knew we were in the area anyway. Claymores were set up and the watch schedule set and we settled in for another long night after chow. Battalion notified us that they wanted us back on top of Nui Tran tomorrow so that we could secure the position for the 87th Engineers. They would be coming in to destroy the bunkers and those gun positions we found.

The line company that was brought in was still to our north and making sporadic contacts. They followed that north south trail until it cut east at RD 323 just north of the plantation. Their NDP was about a click and a half away and they would be moving east the next day while we reclaimed Nui Tran. The 11th ACR elements that dropped us off two days ago were also patrolling RD 323 and the plantation area west of the mountain.

The LT briefed all of us of battalions plan we had breakfast and coffee checked our gear and started moving out. We reached the base of the mountain by mid-morning and notified battalion we were on our way up.
We went up the softer southeastern side and reached the top by mid-day. We set our perimeter and let battalion know the site was secure.

The 87th Engineers trucked in from Libby and started their climb up to us. There were no problems and it looked like the NVA had left the area. Once the Engineers secured the hill top, we left to climb back down to QL 20. We hopped on a deuce and a half and we trucked back to FSB Libby.

Once back at Libby we waited for choppers to take us back to FSB Eagle.

Intel reported later the NVA were planning a large scale convoy attack on the east side of Nui Tran. There are several bends in QL 20 on the northeast and southeastern side of the mountain making it necessary for all vehicles to slow down to make the turns. Those dug out gun positions we found were most likely for .51 caliber machine guns that could cover the road from both tips of the "U" that faced the road. The NVA line company could ambush the convoy from the side of the road. Supported by the heavy machine guns and then retreat back to fortified positions on the mountain. We had found the NVA in the beginning stages of their plan and ruined their chances at a score on an American convoy.

Once back at Eagle we had showers, clean uniforms, hot chow and mail. We were assigned bunkers and we settled in for the night with some beer, soda and crackers and cheese tins from our C-rats. Smoking at night was a hazard enemy snipers would watch for. The glow of a cigarette as the smoker took his drag was an easy target so we learned to cup our cigarettes in our hands.

Bunker duty at night eliminated this problem so long as you stayed away from the open firing position. Boredom sets in quickly however and we decided to play a little game of Russian roulette with my Ruger .22 revolver.

It was a nine shot single action handgun and looked like a cowboy gun the old Peacemaker. How we played the game, we placed bets as to whether or not the player would lose by firing a live round into the ceiling. The top of the bunker was constructed with ¾" plywood that was then covered by 2x10 planks. Then the engineers covered the top with a tar type paper followed by three to four layers of sandbags. We figured there would be no way the .22 caliber round would make it through all that and we tested a spot to be sure. The beer of course helped with our logic and the game was on. I was in the bunker with Wilton, Kraus and Black. We also tested whether or not the shot could be heard outside the bunker. Kraus stepped outside as I fired the test round and then we inspected the spot on of the bunker and found out the round never made it through to the sandbags and the shot could not be heard over the drone of the generators nearby. We played the game for an about an hour and fired about three additional rounds. Once again, boredom set in and we finally went to sleep after deciding on a watch schedule.

The next day we checked our gear broke our weapons down for a good cleaning and just sat around to relax. We wrote letters home and walked around the base to kill time. We were not scheduled to go back out for another day or two and that was fine with us.

We had another night of bunker duty and we had strung hammocks in the bunker to sleep in. Then it rained.

The rounds we fired the night before during our little game may not have gone through the sand bags but they did make it through the plywood and the 2x10's.

That means they also pierced the tar paper. Our bunker leaks and rain water is coming inside.

The next day we had to pull up the sand bags and patch the three holes we found and then repack the sand bags.

It was a pain in the butt but it did help pass the time. We had a good laugh over the incident but we learned a lesson. Boredom, beer and firearms are a bad combination.

On our fourth day at Eagle, we got word we would be heading out on a new mission. We were headed to an area south of us and southeast of our old FSB Nancy. The insert was by CH-47 again in a marshy area about 150 across in either direction. The LZ was prepped by arty and we had the usual Cobra escorts who also decided to work over the LZ with rocket and mini-gun fire. With all the fire prep at the LZ and the big Chinook landing any enemy in the area knew we were in their back yard. Once on the ground and out of the big over grown noisy chopper we headed east 700 meters towards the Dar Tra creek. We set up our mid-day defensive position and prepared to send out our clover leafs.

Hearts went out first to the north alongside the creek and Spades went out after Hearts returned and went south. Hearts reported seeing sandal prints along the creek bed and that there were recent signs of cut branches and that one area seemed to be cleared of old dead branches and leaves. We were moving again after mid-day chow going north following the creek in a 300-meter-wide ravine. We humped about 600 meters and saw that the creek turned east and then north again into a tighter ravine about 100 meters wide. The LT decide to continue north to the top of the ridge line and we set up our NDP.

Once we had the claymores put out and the watch schedule set everyone settled in for the evening meal.

The LT was able to get us LRRP rations top last for five days and the lighter meals made the humping in the dense jungle easier. The LT called in the team leaders for Hearts and Spades and they discussed the plan for the next day.

Sgt. Patchart talked about continuing north but staying on top of the ridge line instead of following the stream in the ravine. The LT listened as the three Sgt.'s discussed the plan. Layden noted the ravine was a prime ambush location and Peady agreed. The LT liked what he heard and said, "I like your ideas men we'll clover leaf to our north and west in the morning and see if we can't pick a good ambush sight, in the meantime let's get some rest and brief your teams."

It was a quiet night and at dawn we had our breakfast and coffee and prepared to move out on our clover leafs. Spades moved about 500 meters and found a spot were the two opposing ravine came together to form a "U" shape and the creek cut right through it. There was a small pool of water at the base of the "U" and then the creek continued its movement downstream to the south. Sgt. Peady reported back to the CP and the LT changed our plans.

The LT then moved us about 100 meters west of Spades and we set up a defensive position. Spades stayed out and set up a live ambush on the western side of the creek. They had left their packs back with us so they did not have claymores. They just set up a line position along the top of the ridge. Sgt. Peady called the CP to advise the LT they were all set up so we all just sat and waited.

Tony Collard was set up on the far northern side of the ambush and the first to spot the two NVA coming south along the stream. They were each carrying four canteens. Both were armed with AK-47 rifles that were slung over their shoulders and web gear. Tony knew to wait until the two NVA got further into the Spades kill zone but the NVA were getting closer to his position.

They walked right up to him at a range of five meters the first NVA saw Tony. Before the enemy soldier could react Tony fired three rounds in rapid succession from his Winchester pump action 12-gauge shotgun. The first NVA fell backwards and the other took off. Tony fired three additional rounds at the fleeing NVA and had to reload. Then the first NVA got up and ran after his comrade. The other members of Spades opened up not knowing what was going on but they fired into their respective fields of fire until Peady ordered a cease fire. Tony had reloaded his gun and told Peady, "Sarge they walked right up on me there were two of them I got one for sure." They found blood where the first NVA had fallen and there were some canteens on the ground. These were two-quart plastic GI issue so Peady cut them all open with his bayonet the wounded NVA also left his AK-47 and Peady called the CP on the radio and briefed the LT.

The LT had us packed up and moving fast towards the northwest hoping to cut off the escaping NVA. Spades was ordered to swing around to the west and give us cover to our rear. We moved fast and got to the stream and found fresh boot tracks along the banks of the creek. We also found blood on the vegetation and the ground. Sgt. Patchart also found blood stained and torn web gear on the side of the creek.

Hearts was looking on the other side of the creek and reported back that there was no fresh activity. Convinced the NVA were heading north following the western side of the creek the LT called in arty. The fire mission came in danger close at first and then walked out further to the north. Once arty was done, the LT called Spades to have them return to us and we regrouped.

Hearts took the point and the LT had us moving north following the creek. The LT also pulled up Collard from Spades and had him walking right flank right on the creek bed and Meadon was out on the left of us. We moved up to where the arty rounds had impacted and followed the fire mission's impacts for another 150 meters and then they ended. Not seeing any signs, the arty had made any difference we continued another seventy-five meters and drew a burst of AW fire from our north. We all hit the ground but held back any return fire.

The LT brought Hearts up on line and started an online assault movement to our north. Hearts found the NVA lying on his back he had a bad belly wound and was dead. There was no sign of his friend other than a few spent shell casings but one other thing was on our minds. The two NVA had eight canteens between them and they were intent on filling those canteens. They wanted to use the spot where the creek formed into a pool and that meant there were other NVA in the area and quite possibly a base camp.

Knowing we were dealing with at least a squad sized element the LT had us moving again this time towards a small hill about 200 meters to our northwest. It was just passed mid-day when we found some spider holes and other signs of enemy activity.

Some of the normal debris found on the jungle floor was missing. Dead leaves small dead branches were cleaned out of some of the area behind the spider holes. The LT had us group up into a defensive posture and called for arty to come in and clear a path. The HE rounds came in real close and then the LT had arty walk the rounds out every twenty-five meters until they had fired into an area 200 meters in front of us. Once the fire mission was completed, we moved out again with Hearts on line followed by the CP group and Spades. We hit the top of the hill top and found the NVA base camp. We counted out eight covered and re-enforced bunkers as well as four-camouflaged lean too type hooch's. There were also two different fire locations and one was still hot.

The LT talked with Sgt. Patchart and they both agreed the NVA most likely left the area when the arty started coming in. We set up our defensive position in the enemy camp and also deployed our claymores. We were on high alert and the LT wanted to see if the NVA would be coming back. The LT gave instructions for each team to have mid-day chow one team at a time when one team finished the other would take over perimeter security and the other would eat.

We had enough C-4 to blow the bunkers and that was our plan. The LT also had Sgt. Patchart plot the exact location of the base camp for future H&I missions. The NVA never did return but the bigger question was where did they go? With our claymores deployed and the enemy bunkers still intact, we had set ourselves up in an excellent NDP. We were also on the crest of a small hill so we had the high ground advantage.

We did a though search to be sure there were no tunnels in the area the last thing we needed was for the NVA to come sneaking into the center of our NDP at night. The NVA did not bother us during the night or the next morning. After we pulled in the claymores, we burned the lean too hooch's and used eight blocks of C-4 to blow the bunkers. Then we moved out and headed northwest. We saw no more signs of enemy activity during day.

We set up a new NDP that same night on the southwestern side of the Dar Bou creek. Watch schedules were set and the claymores were destroyed. In addition, during our mid-day stop over the LT called in arty missions at the base camp just in case the NVA decided to access the damage we had done. The LT at this point had won the respect of all the men and NCO's and his style of command and asking everyone's input was looked on favorably. If we all had to hand pick a replacement for LT Kamble LT John Coral would have been it.

The next morning, we had our breakfast and coffee and the LT decided we were going to the top of another hill that was southwest of us. This hill connected with another to the northwest and was 200 meters high with open ground on top. We pulled in the claymores and Spades had the point.

The jungle was thick in this area and the humping went slowly. Collard was on point for Spades and by this time was showing he was developing into an excellent point man. Pete Black was working with Sgt. Layden on his point walking skills. We moved about 400 meters in the thick under brush and stopped for mid-day chow. We were all pretty spent. We set up our defensive perimeter and settled in for chow.

We had made it to the base of the hill and from what we saw on the map we were only another 300 meters away from reaching our objective. We broke up after a quick session for chow and made the climb up to the top of the hill in dense jungle by mid-afternoon. We set up our NDP and then started on running clover leafs to the west and northwest. Hearts went out first to the northwest and when they returned Spades went west.

Both teams came back with nothing to report. The NVA it would seem pulled off another disappearing act and vanished into thin air. We had no signs of them anywhere yet we knew there had to be at least a squad somewhere in the area. We all had our dinner and coffee and waited for darkness to set in and envelope us.

That night in the NDP, I talked with the LT and Sgt. Patchart about turning the radio over to someone else. The extra weight of the PRC-25 was kicking my butt. I was also looking to be in line as an assistant team leader that would give me a path to making sergeant. The LT and Patchart agreed it would be OK and they would move Dan White up to battalion RTO and find someone to take over either a team radio or the company net position.

I had now been in country almost eight months and with the Brigade getting ready to go home promotion slots would be hard coming.

Recon was down to twenty-five men including the LT and Binh. The prospect of dumping the radio made me feel better and even the thought of having to go out on clover leafs did not bother me much.

The next morning, we were up at dawn had breakfast and coffee and planned on moving northwest towards the 200-meter-high hill top that dominated the area. We moved into the saddle that was between where our NDP was and the hilltop and then started up the steep climb to the top of the hill. The saddle covered about 500 meters of dense jungle and by the time, we hit the top of the hill it was well past noon. Once on the top we stopped to catch our breath and the LT had us set up on line at the edge of the large open area. The clearing was about 300 meters at its widest point and a good 500 meters long. It would make a great LZ but first we had to be sure it was clear of any unwanted visitors.

We had a quick lunch break and then we started to patrol around the entire perimeter just to be sure, we were alone. The NVA so far had still evaded us and we were wondering where they were. By the time we had made it all the way around and having seen no signs of the NVA we set up a hasty NDP just before dark at a location that stuck out into the clearing to the southwest. We were tired, sweaty and dirty when we bedded down for the night. We were tired, sweaty and dirty when we bedded down for the night. We were also running out of rations.

We got word that battalion was pulling us out and that the extraction would be around lunch time. We left our claymores deployed the LT wanted to blow them just as the birds would be coming in. Just before noon, the Huey's came on net and we advised them we were going to blow claymores just prior to their touchdown. The Huey's were escorted by Huey type gunships and they joined in the fun.

The claymores all blew and the birds touched down and we ran to the waiting choppers, then the gunships fired rockets and fired mini-guns into the LZ as we lifted off. Any NVA in the area that had any plans of trying to shoot down a helicopter was discouraged from trying. We were RTB but we were headed to FSB Mace not Eagle.

Once back at Mace we had access to showers, clean uniforms, hot chow and mail. Then we were told we would be here at least for three to five days pulling bunker duty. We also figured out the radio set up. White would be the new battalion net RTO and Spancer would be moved to the CP group as company net RTO. Kraus would take over the radio for Hearts and Woodard would be Spades RTO. I was returning to Hearts as a rifleman. Both teams had two sergeants each. Layden and Hardack were with Hearts and Peady and Pillitary were with Spades.

I had become just one of the grunts again and Sgt. Layden let me know I would be walking drag again. The LT and Sgt. Patchart were pleased by their choices and I had to work with Kraus and White on getting Kraus up to speed. He was a quick study and we were all confident the new RTO set up would work out well.

I reconfigured my gear and sold my .22 revolver to a guy from D Troop 17th Cav for a case of beer. I had about 100 rounds of ammo left in the brick I had and let him have that with the gun. I got my gear reconfigured and was ready for the next mission.

The second night of bunker duty I was sitting on an ammo box on top of the bunker and around twenty-three hundred when we started getting incoming mortar rounds.

I had just started to doze off when the first round hit inside the base. Kraus was down inside the bunker. The rest of the guys assigned to the bunker were off trying to get something for us to eat. When the round exploded, I was startled and fell off the bunker on the berm side. This is a drop of about ten feet. Startled but unhurt I ran inside the bunker and called into the base TOC using the field phone and reported, "Bunker number ten that's incoming fire." Three more rounds had already dropped into the base by then and when TOC answered my call their response was, "No shit Sherlock." Kraus just laughed and asked if I hit my head. Feeling a little embarrassed I had no response. The other two guys showed up with some C-Rat tins of crackers and cheese. It was Meadon and Black and Kraus was happy to report I had a full understanding of our tactical situation and they need not worry. He then explained that the first incoming round knocked me off the bunker. We had some more beer crackers and cheese and the enemy only fired four rounds as it was. We all laughed but everyone stayed inside the bunker the rest of the night.

We spent the day light hours cleaning weapons and fussing with our gear. We were always looking for ways to lighten the load we carried into the bush.

We missed having our own hooch's we were living the life of a line company. We had very little personal items and what we had we had to carry.

Sgt. Patchart was basically in charge and told us the LT had been called up to Battalion TOC at FSB Eagle for some type of meeting. Rumors were flying and the anticipation of some sort of big mission was talked about by everyone.

The mystery was solved, three days into our stay at FSB Mace when the LT returned with another officer. A meeting was scheduled for thirteen hundred after lunch and everyone was adding fuel to the rumor fires because of the officer the LT returned with. We knew nothing about him other than he was from a line company from 2nd Battalion 3rd Infantry whose home base was FSB Blackhorse.

We all ate noon chow and waited for the meeting to begin. The LT showed up with Sgt. Patchart and the mystery officer. "All right Recon settle down and listen up the LT has an announcement," Sgt. Patchart said. The LT started his briefing, "OK Recon good to see everybody I have some news I need to let you all in on, this is 1st Lieutenant Chuck Parker your new platoon leader."

You could have knocked everyone over with a feather. "I have been reassigned by Battalion to other duties and LT Parker has been handpicked by the Brigade Commander to be your new platoon leader.

He has months of experience with 2nd of the 3rd and has spent the last couple of months with Brigade S2". "Chuck you're getting a good platoon and I know they will do their best, they are officially yours."

Then the new LT addressed us, "Hi guys, I want you to know that LT Coral and Sgt. Patchart have told me all about you guys and I'm proud to be leading such a great platoon. You should all also know that Colonel Collins the new Brigade Commander is aware of your achievements and will be using us for a special operation in a few weeks. In the meantime, I will make an effort to talk with each of you and get to know you all."

"Any official orders will be coming from Sgt. Patchart and your team leaders, does anyone have any questions?" Only about a hundred questions to start. We had just got used to LT Coral and now we were assigned a new platoon leader out of the blue.

There was no warning or even any speculation that this was coming and later we found that it was a surprise to LT Coral as well. All of the changes came from Brigade HQ that added even more mystery. This was all very unusual but orders are orders. Sgt. Layden asked LT Coral, "LT did you do something wrong?" "No sergeant this was a surprise to me but my reassignment is a career step up," he replied.

Some other questions were asked about future missions and stand downs and LT Parker replied "Recons mission remains the same and stand down will occur sometime in September". I asked if we were getting any new replacements and LT Parkers answer raised an eye brow or two, "We will not be getting any new people and everyone here is going to be here until the Brigade stands down." That meant anyone getting short was not getting back to BMB unless you had R&R that, LT Parker assured us was still moving forward as planned.

I had already had my R&R but Rich Howard one of our M60 gunners was scheduled for Hong Kong next week. He was relieved to know he was still going.

The new LT kept his word over the next two days he came and spoke to each of us. I was not sure about this new leader there was something a little odd and I could not get my finger on it but he seemed to be confident, knowledgeable and likable.

When we sat down, he asked me, "I understand you like to carry a side arm, why did you sell your pistol?" "It was not a good caliber for shooting people it was basically a snake gun," I said. "Well I can't get you a .45 with the brigade closing base's and getting ready to deploy home new weapons requisitions are not being processed, but I do know a pilot getting ready to go home he has a .38 would you be interested?" "Sure but I don't have a lot of money on me," I replied.

He said, "No sweat I think he wants about $10 for the gun and holster." Then I said, "LT I am really not interested in crawling into any tunnels if that's what you're driving at." He replied, "No any tunnel crawling will go to Binh it's about time he earned his pay." That really surprised me the LT seemed to know all about each of us as the conversation continued. He had knowledge of all our little quirks and he even knew what happened with Sgt. Hooper but he did not elaborate.

Later that same day a Warrant Officer came to see me in his hand was a Colt .38 caliber handgun in a black leather holster with twenty-four rounds of ammo.

The CW3 wanted $10 and after inspecting the weapon, I turned over the money. He was off to the world in a week from now so I was glad I could help him out.

Another day passed and we got word that we were getting supplied for a mission. The supply draws seemed to be a little light. Each man was given a claymore, and four M33 grenades. The only food we were given was two LRRP rations. Then we found out we would go off the firebase in the outskirts of Xa Gia Ray to a cemetery to set up an ambush.

Rich Howard would stay behind and catch a ride to BMB for his R&R. That meant someone had to tote his gun and the LT knew I had an expert rating with the M60 so I was it. Great I had just gotten rid of the twenty-five lbs. radio and wound up with a twenty-three lbs. machine gun and another ten lbs. of ammo. I also had my new .38 so Howard held on to his .45 and took my M16 to go back to BMB. Getting used to carrying the big gun was going to be interesting.

The M60 had a forearm cover in front of the main receiver made of heavy rubber. Most M60 gunners took an OD green towel folded it up to make a cushion and tied it to this forearm cover using black boot laces. Howard had done this to his gun. The M60 was carried on either shoulder with one of the bipod legs locked in the down position or you just held on to the barrel with both bipod legs locked back. A 100 round bandolier bag and box clipped on to the left side of the gun. Extra ammo was carried by the gunner Poncho Villa style or by slinging a 200 round ammo can over one shoulder. I used the Mexican bandit method. The only benefit to the gun was you did not have to carry a claymore.

Sgt. Patchart and the LT showed up and everyone started looking at one another. The new LT did not carry an M16 or an M15 CAR. He was holding an old WWII vintage M1 carbine complete with the canvas ammo pouches attached to the stock. For a jungle weapon, the M1 is not a bad choice. It is shorter and lighter than the M16. It is standard with a twenty round magazine like the M16. The LT's rifle had a single thirty round banana magazine and he was carrying extra twenty round magazines. The M1 is a semi-automatic weapon firing one shot each time you pulled the trigger.

That with his standard side arm the Colt .45 the LT was well equipped for jungle combat. That being said his choice of weapon was interesting. All Recon members could swap magazines with each other if one or more men ran short of ammo. Once the LT expended his ammo, he was on his own. The M1 took a different .30 caliber round the M16's all used the same standard 5.56 mm round and magazine.

He was also dressed in 'Tiger Stripes' not strikers like we had. With his clothing and choice of weapon, he had inadvertently set himself apart from the rest of us. This was not a good start. Then we learned the M1 was actually the M2 version capable of full automatic fire. Great this meant he would use up his ammo even faster.

The mission we were told was a night ambush on a trail leading into the jungle from a cemetery at a church in the village. The church was located on RD 333 heading northwest out of the village just outside the base. We would march off the base just before dark and set up our ambush and either return to base or run some clover leafs in that area during the next day.

The church was about a click away but we would be using the road through the village and should be able to cover the click in about an hour. Another mistake everyone in the village would be watching us.

Some of the guys were giving Sgt. Patchart the look that said watch this guy. As it turns out while we were watching him, he was watching all of us. We headed off the base just before dark and made decent time to the church. We moved in behind the church and passed through the grave yard and got into the jungle.

We had light packs so the hump was not as strenuous as the usual first day out. We set up in the jungle on the northwestern side of the trail deployed our claymores and settled in for the night. We had chow before we left Mace so there was no cooking tonight.

The three machine guns in the platoon were split up with one at each end of the trail and the other in the middle of our setup. My gun was the one furthest away from the village.

The night passed without incident and the new LT was impressed by our noise discipline and claymore placement covering the trail and our ability to move around from one another's position without tripping over each other during the night.

The next morning, we pulled in the claymores and the LT moved us about 100 meters further back into the jungle away from the trail and we set up a day time defensive position. Then we had breakfast and coffee. The LT briefed Sgt. Patchart that we would be moving back to the trail.

Then would proceed away from the village on a patrol. Patchart was then required to brief Sgt. Layden and Sgt. Peady who both passed the info on to us. It would seem a chain of command was being established. Every platoon leader has their own style Parkers was just more regimented. LT Coral had a more relaxed method and invited input from the men after all his decisions had an effect on them.

We packed up our gear and Spades had the point with Collard leading us down the trail to the southeast.

The trail turned south intersected with another trail and after some radio traffic Peady was informed to continue on the new trail heading south. Walking trails in the open and in broad day light was against everything we had been trained to do. Recon was supposed to hide and blend into the terrain just like the enemy. This was more like a line company operation and when you have 100 men in a company it tough to hide anyway.

The new southern trail went through some small brush and high grass and we covered a click in just less than two hours and found yet another intersecting trail. This one ran east and west and we headed west back towards RD 333 and the village.

As we came closer to the southern outskirts of the village, we started encountering local civilian population. I started thinking about what SFC Snead said about any people you encounter were supposed to be engaged. We had travelled another click in the open terrain and we were getting pretty tired. The LT called for a halt and we set up a defensive perimeter out in the open. There was just nowhere to hide.

Some of the men were making comments about this new tactical approach and expressed them to Layden and Peady. They told us to keep it down and that they would talk with Patchart.

There was plenty of military traffic as well both US and ARVN. The passing GI's would wave and the ARVN just looked at us. Then two white mice in a jeep saw us and sat there a minute or two just looking at us wondering what we were up too. We called them white mice because they wore white shirts and grey pants.

They were the Canh Sat or National Police. They were held in disdain by GI's because they were so corrupt.

After chow and about an hour of sitting in the sun the LT had us moving again back to the base. We walked right up the road to the base and then went in and dropped our packs. Layden and Peady were getting a lot of pressure to talk with Patchart about the new LT and his tactics so they went off on their own after we were dismissed. They were gone about an hour and came back to our area that we were assigned but had nothing new to add. After evening chow, the LT got together with his NCO's and briefed them on a new operation that would occur the day after tomorrow.

Line companies from 3rd of the 7th normally ran security operations and patrols around Signal Mountain as a matter of routine. Recon would take over some of these patrols on a day to day basis. We would patrol the mountain with elements of the 'Cotton Balers' who knew where the trip flares and mechanicals were set up. These would be set up and taken down on a random basis to keep the enemy off guard. These patrols would be day long excursions and we would not be out overnight.

We spent the next two weeks running these day time patrols around Nui Chua Chan Mountain. The peak itself is 837 meters high and the base of the mountain covers twenty square clicks. We went on patrol every other day and we were usually accompanied by a platoon from one of the line companies from the 3rd of the 7th. The patrols themselves were sweeping random type movements just to keep the enemy sappers discouraged.

On top were the 313th Signal Company and the 356th Radio Research Detachment. Their job was to insure the brigade had open and clear communications with all of its field elements.

These patrols were more of the type we were used too other than we did not expect to find any base camps. Confidence with the new LT was beginning to come together but he was still not combat tested in our eyes.

Chapter Eight, Special Ops;

We were lounging around on one of our days off from patrolling Signal Mountain when Layden and Peady came by with paperwork. Everybody got a mimeographed page of Vietnamese and English phrases. We were told to make ourselves familiar with everything on the page but were not given any additional info. Peady told us, "We know as much as you do and that's it orders are orders so get busy." Now we had some entertainment. Imagine eighteen guys sitting around attempting to speak the various translations we had on the page.

We already had a pig latin approach to the Vietnamese language so adding more fuel to the fire had everyone laughing in no time. But we did learn quickly. There were twenty-four different translations on the page and we already knew some of them. Dung lai meant stop, den day meant come here, dung yen meant stand still and everyone's favorite and used constantly was xin loi or sorry. Now we were getting a list that had greeting type translations. Cam on ban meant thank you, xin chao, meant hello, an meant eat, thuc an meant food and nouc meant water. Everyone tried his hand at the new phrase and we even tried to sound Vietnamese and mimicked the sing song type of dialect they all used. Too bad, we didn't have any beer we would have had a blast.

Patchart came by the next day to inform us we were going out on an operation. Choppers would take us thirteen clicks south of FSB Mace and Signal Mountain. The mission was to make contact with a montagnard chief who lived in a village on Be Bac Mountain.

We had no idea what we were supposed to do once we made contact we were not in the loop. Choppers were scheduled for zero eight hundred so we started to get our gear together. Patchart also brought our supplies for the mission and we noted we had rations for three days.

We got up early the next morning had breakfast and prepared to go to the LZ for the choppers when the LT showed up. He had an ARVN Ranger with him. He was introduced to us as Lieutenant Le Tran Lam. He was with the 3rd Ranger Group out of Binh Hoa. The ARVN Rangers were not your typical ARVN soldier. These guys were well trained and hard core.

The LT began the briefing by telling us the Brigade was actively engaged in relocating montagnard villages out of enemy controlled areas. He told us that sixty montagnard of the Cham tribe had been relocated by elements of the 3rd of the 7th near Ham Tan village along the coast back in July. The Cham were located throughout our AO and we were to meet with the village chief so that arrangements could be made to relocate this tribe. Then he asked LT Lam to continue. He spoke perfect English and told us, "There were about twenty to thirty people in the village and women and children are part of the group. Be very careful about firing your weapons be sure that you are shooting at a VC or NVA soldier".

He went on to tell us that these people are very primitive but were hospitable towards strangers. They are very protective of their women.

He added, "The women will most likely hide away to their homes. The men will be friendly and welcoming to strangers and may offer gifts usually some type of fruit or another treat. Accept anything they offer graciously.

You are not to enter a home unless invited to do so by one of the men and under no circumstances are you to leer or make gestures or comments about any of the women. The Cham also like to haggle and trade and they are a very honest people they will not try to hustle you." Then LT Parker added, "Remember these people are not the enemy and they are not Vietnamese, so be on you best behavior. When we move off the LZ Spades will take the point with LT Lam, Hearts will be on drag, Ski keep your eyes open on our rear." Sgt. Patchart then chimed in, "OK Recon let's saddle up and move to the LZ." We needed four Huey's to lift us off the base so we headed south to the LZ. There was no arty prep and no Cobra escorts.

We came in to the LZ fast at tree top level from the east and the 4 choppers set down simultaneously. We jumped off the birds and headed west towards Be Bac Mountain. I was in the last chopper and by the time I reached the wood line the birds were gone. From the LZ to the foot of the mountain was about a click due west.

We humped about 500 meters when we crossed a small creek and continued on another 400 meters and set up a defensive mid-day position at the foot of the mountain. We settled in for mid-day chow. The LT did not want to run any clover leafs.

I was at the eastern most point of our position and was heating up water for coffee when I looked up and saw two Cham tribesmen standing not five feet away from me.

Both had big smiles on their faces and large crossbows in their hands. They were both bare foot and wore loose calf high pants with tunic type shirts. I never heard them and never noticed them until I looked up. One used the Vietnamese greeting of xin chao for 'hello'.

I stood up and the speaking tribesman extended his hand and repeated, "Xin chao." I took his hand and said, "Hello." The other one also extended his hand and repeated after me, "Hello."

None of us were whispering which was normal speech mode for us in the boonies so everyone heard us talking. LT Lam came over and started speaking a language none of us heard before. I learned later the Cham used a Malayo-Polynesian type of dialect that was very ancient. LT Lam was starting to impress me. Greetings and handshakes went all around and the two tribesmen joined us for lunch. They ate their own food but drank no water until they were done eating. They were to be our guides up the mountain. One would walk point with Collard to point out booby traps and the second would walk drag with me.

When lunch was finished, we started heading up the mountain with our two new friends. It was a gradual climb up to the 324-meter-high peak shaped like a horseshoe. We went right up the center of the mountain on a trail and several booby traps were pointed out along the way. The point guide would either point out the location of the trap or disarm the trap depending on which type it was. The punji stake traps were inert and only had to be pointed out to each man as they passed them. The point guide disabled all the whip traps and my companion drag guide re-enabled them as we passed.

Upon reaching the top of the hill, we passed through some heavy vegetation through a small low opening and we were in the village. By the time, I got into the village all of the women had fled into their homes. The men were all standing around smiling and greeting all of us.

Some of the children could not suppress their curiosity and would peak out the doorways of the hooch's they lived in that were built up on stilts. The LT had us set up a defensive perimeter around the village that was about fifty meters wide and seventy-five meters long. This stretched us pretty thin usually when we set up an NDP each man is five meters apart; in this position we were stretched to ten meters apart. The village also had chickens, small pigs and a few goats in pens. LT Parker and LT Lam met with the village chief a very old guy with a long bushy beard. He smiled a lot and gave both officers fruit and flowers. They sat down outside the honcho's hooch and LT Le acted as an interpreter.

We were left mainly to ourselves and Patchart made the rounds with Layden and Peady. No one was to deploy claymores until we were told so it was just sit back relax and remember the rules.

The kids were funny they would peak out the door and if we waved at them they would retreat back into the house or their mother would yell something and they would duck back in. I had Wilton on my right and Jack Meadon on my left. Patchart came back around to each of us to let us know the old guy says there are no VC or NVA in the area. Nonetheless, we were to stay alert. The prospect of this being the NDP without our usual ring of claymores was unsettling. Add the fact we were twice as far away from each other didn't help.

LT Lam came around with Patchart and LT Parker and told us to deploy the claymores. No one was to fire a claymore without orders from LT Parker. Sometimes one of the animals may get out of its pen and they did not want us firing a claymore and killing a valued animal.

The village chief was sending three of his best men out tonight to patrol around the mountain so his guests would be safe. Based on my experience with these guys I was sort of confident they could do the job. We had our chow and coffee and settled in for the night. It was not a restful night the inside of the perimeter is usually dead silent to us; tonight it was filled with noise. Between crying babies, laughing children, squawking chickens, snorting pigs and the baa of the goats we were nervous. Despite our heightened alert, the night passed without any trouble. The three tribesmen sent out last night to protect us came back at dawn and reported to the chief no enemy activity.

We were told to go ahead and prepare our breakfast and as we were doing so, the village came to life. First, the kids could no longer be contained and despite the corrections from their mothers, they wanted to see each of us up close. Funny thing is all of the kids are bare assed naked.

I was sitting down on the ground eating some crackers with grape jelly when one little girl about five years old approached me. Her mother was right behind her and was dressed in a sarong that did not cover her breasts.

She was young not older than me and not intimidated or embarrassed at all. The little girl was curious about my crackers so I made her one. She took a tentative bite and I have to say the smile she made was worth all the value of the cracker and more. She turned and gave it to her mother who also took a bite.

The little girl finished the rest of her cracker and sat down next to me. Under the watchful eye of her mother, the little girl was fascinated by the patches on my uniform blouse and all of my pockets.

LT Lam came over and spoke to the mother and he told me she liked the cracker. The mother then held out her hand and called her daughter who reluctantly got up to leave. Before she left, she put her face behind my ear and made a snorting sound, laughed and ran to her mom. Her mom laughed and bowed said something in her language and left. LT Lam said, "The little girl liked you and the noise she made is how the Cham show affection, you did well soldier."

Jack Meadon saw the whole thing from his position and when LT Lam left, he started making snorting noises and kissing sounds and laughed his ass off. I was going to be the butt of jokes for the next couple of days. We sat back and got into a relaxed mode. The women in the village went about their chores and the children ran around playing their games. The village itself was clean. The jungle floor was devoid of any vegetation and the ground was packed hard and smooth. The huts were all built up on stilts because of the snakes and other jungle critters. The canopy here was very thick a Loach hovering right above us would not be able to see a thing.

The shape of the roofs was funny almost like a Popes Mitre, but we were told they were very waterproof. Some of the men left the village to check the traps they set to capture game.

Later about mid-morning, the guide who walked drag with me came over to my position with LT Lam. The LT said, "You have Salem cigarettes, Dung here would like to make a trade." Dung then held out a long bayonet in a black leather scabbard.

I inspected the bayonet and asked the LT, "What does he want for it?" The LT and Dung jabbered back and forth and the LT told me all of my Salem's. I had one spare unopened pack and an open pack with about fifteen cigarettes left. Knowing the Vietnamese will bargain and during our briefing, we were told the Cham like to haggle and trade I made my counter offer of just the open pack.

Dung and the LT discussed this at length and then the LT gave me Dungs final offer of just the unopened pack. I handed over the fresh pack of Salem's and the deal was done. Dung seemed to be very happy and shook my hand and said, "cam on ban, cam on ban," (thank you thank you) in Vietnamese. I still have that bayonet today. A little research I did shows that the bayonet was made for a Spanish rifle around the late 1890's. I had no idea of this at the time but I still wondered then how Dung had come to possess it and how it ever got to Vietnam. The Vietnamese had been at war for decades.

Just before noon, we got the word to pull in the claymores and to be ready to move. We would be moving northwest about a click to another mountain where the Cham would lead us to an NVA base camp.

The village chief had informed LT Parker and LT Lam that the NVA used this camp on and off and they were not sure if it was occupied now or not. In addition to the two guides who brought us up the mountain, we had three additional Cham leaving with us. These three guys had been to the camp many times and knew the lay out. We were also told they only went there when the NVA were away. Once we got to the hill the three Cham would check the camp to see if it was occupied or not. LT Lam told us the Cham were very adept at moving around the jungle undetected. Well I can attest to that.

We covered the click in about three hours and we were set up in a defensive position at the base of the hill. Collard was on point with his Cham counterpart and Dung and I brought up the rear. The other three Cham tribesmen went out ahead of us to scout the base camp. We were in the defensive position for about thirty minutes when one of the tribesmen came back, he told LT Le the NVA were not in the camp and that we should climb up the mountain to the camp. The peak was 209 high meters but it was a steep climb. Once on top we were greeted by the two remaining Cham tribesmen.

There were ten bunkers around the camp and there were ropes and carabiners tied to the trees for hammocks. We also found three cooking fire locations in the center of the camp and there was of all things a picnic table.

The Cham told us the NVA basically used the site for resting and it was not used as an operational base. The NVA would occupy the site every few weeks or so and they had not been here for a while. We set up our NDP in the base camp and would spend the night. The LT briefed Sgt. Patchart and he and Sgt. Layden and Peady made their respective rounds and gave us the scoop. The five Cham tribesmen would be leaving us this afternoon and were told not to return to this camp ever again.

LT Parker had some toys with him and if we had no contact with the NVA we would RTB to FSB Mace by mid-day tomorrow at an LZ about 600 meters to our southwest. The toys he had were three sensor devices. They looked like animal droppings and were nick named 'TURDSIDS'. They had a battery life of a few days and we would be leaving them under the picnic table.

If the NVA returned to this base camp the sensors would send out a radio signal and the site would be bombed or fired on by arty. The Cham left no signs of their presence and we were told to leave some litter around the edge of the camp and on our way to the LZ. The NVA when they returned would see the litter and make the assumption their camp had been discovered by US forces but by then it would be too late. It was not the first time Recon used an NVA camp for an NDP but we were all on high alert anyway.

With our claymores deployed and the watch schedule set, we hunkered down for the night. Jack was off to my left again and as we were eating our chow, he started making kissing and snorting sounds as quietly as he could. "I bet you miss that perky little mama-san Ski, she love you long time," he whispered laughing. I gave Jack the one finger salute as my response.

The night passed without any contact with the NVA and we had breakfast and coffee and stayed in the camp until around zero nine hundred. Then we pulled in the claymores and got ready to move out.

We all left some trash behind but nothing the enemy could make use of. Paper packets of coffee, crushed cheese cans, and cigarette butts were left just outside the perimeter. LT Parker called in a marker round right above us so that the FDC had a confirmed target location.

The LT left his 'TURDSIDS' under the picnic table and they went active while we were there and he told the battalion FDC we were leaving. Any signal from the sensors once we were gone would bring down a rain of HE from the 105mm howitzers that were plotted to this site.

We humped down the southwestern side of the mountain and headed for the LZ. The choppers showed up on time and this time we had a Cobra team escort. We mounted the Hueys and took off and were on our way back to FSB Mace.

Once back at Mace we had showers, clean uniforms, chow and of course mail. LT Parker and LT Lam left the fire base together and the speculation was they had to debrief someone higher up on our mission with the Cham. We were assigned our usual bunkers and we settled in to life on the base. Sgt. Patchart informed us we would be here for a few days. This was good news and no one complained.

The next morning after breakfast, we were all sitting around cleaning weapons when Sgt. Patchart came back with those same mimeographed sheets of language translations. We had already had fun with those but now we were suspicious. The translations were of no use to use on our last mission the Cham spoke an entirely different language so why the renewed effort for us to brush up on our Vietnamese.

Sgt. Patchart had no answers just that orders were orders. So we finished cleaning our weapons and then brushed up on our new task. Quickly bored with that we found that sleeping, writing letters and rereading our mail was more interesting. We set our bunker watch schedules and had a quiet restful night.

The next morning just before lunch LT Parker came back from wherever he had been. LT Lam was with him and he had five more Rangers with him. They also brought along a squinty eyed little guy who they watched like a hawk. This short little guy wore regular ARVN OD green fatigues and Ho Chi Minh sandals. The Rangers were all in Tiger fatigues with all of their patches. We also noticed that the Rangers were man handling the little guy. Sgt. Patchart let us know that there was a briefing after lunch and everyone was expected to attend. This could only mean another special mission involving Lt Lam and his new friends.

After chow, we met in the TOC bunker and we were told the next mission would be about twenty-four clicks northwest of our old fire base Nancy. This was way out of our normal AO and we had never been that far north. During the briefing, we were told that the squinty eyed little guy was a recent POW and was part of the 33rd NVA Regiment.

He was to be our guide. LT Lam and his Rangers would be on point with their guide and we would serve as fire support and security for the mission. LT Lam said, "During this mission we will be guided to a field hospital, base camps, training facilities and villages. All of the personnel we encounter will be NVA or NVA supporters.

Our mission is to plot the locations of these facilities and destroy what we can." Then LT Parker told us we would be out for five days and inserted by chopper with a line company.

Then LT Parker added, "Anything we can't destroy ourselves will be pounded by arty or by airstrikes. You will all carry extra C-4 for blowing bunkers and anything else we find. In addition, each man will carry three M34 WP grenades and the M79 gunners will carry WP rounds also." "Remember all personnel are considered hostile so be alert." "Any questions?"

Sgt. Peady asked, "Is the line company going with us?" Lt Parker replied, "Negative, we will all land on the same LZ the choppers will come into the LZ from the south, all Recon members will load up on the port side of the aircraft and when you exit the birds you will move west and we will assemble inside the tree line."

The line company will assemble north, west and east on the LZ and make a great show of moving north and northeast". "We will stay put and move away from the LZ later in the afternoon heading southwest."

"The idea is if the enemy is watching the area he will see a line company land and march north and then northeast, hopefully he will not notice we are there. Anything else?"

Sgt. Patchart asked, LT how do we know this guide is not going to walk us into an ambush?" LT Lam answered, "He has been told that all of my Rangers and I are tasked with killing him should he decide to betray us."

"The men I brought with me are on my personal team and I trust them with my life they are all veterans and highly dedicated." If his team was of the same caliber as LT Lam then I felt comfortable.

Jack Meadon asked, "Lt did you say villages?" LT Parker answered, "Roger we have been told there are NVA villages hidden in the jungle they are inhabited by family members and support personnel. These are the places that Charlie goes to rest up and relax."

"We take off from the LZ in the morning at zero seven hundred so get your supplies and gear together today. "Anything else?"

With no further questions, the briefing was over and we went back to our bunkers. Sgt. Patchart showed up a little later with LRRP rations and the extra C-4 and WP grenades. The M34 is called a WP or 'Willie Pete'.

It burns at an alarming rate of speed and is superhot. Designed to burn through metal it also sucks all of the oxygen around it and as long as it has air, it will continue to burn. Fragments or shrapnel from a WP will burn right through any part of the body from one side to the other so long as it has air. Nasty stuff.

We got our gear together and waited out the night thinking about this new mission. It would seem that LT Parker was a little more than just some line company officer. Some of wondered why our mission strategy had changed and why we had been handpicked by Brigade for this assignment. Some of us were looking at our mimeographed sheets of language translations a little harder. We were all up before dawn checking our gear again and eating breakfast at the mess hall. LT Parker got us LRRP rations but also had given us some C-rations.

This was so we could eat on the run without having to stop. How this was going to work out was unknown because if we had C-rats we ate those first to lighten the load. The choppers were on time and the first sorties of 9 birds were waiting on the pad. The next sortie of 9 Hueys was circling the base. We had two men on each chopper all loading on the port side behind the co-pilot.

As soon as the first sortie took off the second came in and landed and the process was repeated.

Recon was assigned to be on the 1st and 2nd sortie. The rest of the line company from 3rd of the 7th would land on the third and last sortie.

Once we were airborne, we headed northwest for the seventy-five-mile trip that would take forty to fifty minutes. We had two Cobra team escorts and the LZ would be prepped by arty.

Looking back at the twenty-seven Hueys two Loaches and the four Cobras flying in formation at about 3000 feet was like watching a movie. This would look like a major operation from the ground and if the NVA was, where they were supposed to be they would have to know that the Americans were in their back yard. On arrival we approached the LZ from the south and watched as the arty prep finished and one of the Cobra teams started hammering the west side of the LZ with rocket and mini-gun fire. I was hoping this was planned as prep fire. The Cobras were working over the area we were supposed to go to once we landed. If they spotted enemy in that area our LZ was going to be hot. The LZ was large enough to accommodate all eighteen choppers of the 1st and 2nd sorties.

The last sortie would land once the first eighteen cleared the LZ. We hoped off the birds and headed west as planned.

Tony Collard and I were in the eighteenth chopper we had already been assigned to drag duty together. The tree line along the western edge of the LZ was filled with smoke.

The fires started by the rockets and tracers from the mini-guns. The smell of cordite and burning vegetation was making it hard to see or breath.

Tony and I walked into the wood line and saw Sgt. Layden signaling for us to fall in behind him. Recon was already moving off the LZ and heading further south and west. We moved about 300 meters and set up a defensive perimeter.

Mr. Magoo was the nickname we gave to the POW guide brought along by LT Lam and his Rangers. He got the name from his squinty eyed look. Hopefully he would not stumble into bad things like the cartoon character always did. He did indicate we were about one click away from an NVA base camp. That's where we would be heading this afternoon.

Once the line company was fully inserted they made a big show of heading north off the LZ. Hopefully any NVA scouts watching the show would focus their attention on the company and be oblivious to our presence. Orders were to sit tight be quiet, no cooking fires, no coffee. We did not want to reveal our position or even our presence. Sgt. Patchart came around with Sgt. Layden and let us know we would be moving at noon sharp and heading west to an NVA base camp. We had about three hours to kill so we just hunkered down and stayed alert.

I sat with Collard and said, "Something's not right about all this, why are we being super quiet once we hit that base camp if Charlie is there every NVA in the area will know were here." "I know your right if we're gonna be hitting this hospital and villages what's the use of all the noise discipline," he said.

"This is search and destroy plain and simple and why not just take the line company in to do the dirty work this is starting to look like a bad mission," I said.

At noon, we headed west the Rangers and Mr. Magoo had the point so me and Tony pulled the drag duty. We started up a small ninety-meter hill top the terrain was high grass and brush wood. Just before Tony and I hit the top, we heard a long burst of AK-47 fire from up front. This was followed by short bursts of M16 fire. Then everything went quiet. LT Parker then called everyone up to the hill top. We set up a defensive perimeter and searched the area. This was not much of a base camp we found five bunkers at the top of this hill.

The terrain on top was heavy forest but not quite a jungle. The five bunkers were spread out along the top of the hill that was 200 meters across in any direction.

LT Le commented that it looked more like an OP than a base camp. That meant something hotter must be nearby. He had an extended conversation with Mr. Magoo who indicated we were close to a training camp and village.

We humped north for about 400 meters and came across another small hilltop with woods on the southern side and an open high grass and brushwood area on its north side. We had just gotten to the top and started setting up a perimeter when we had another burst of AK-47 fire from below our position. A few of us ran down a small trail and came into the open area on the north side. Some of the Rangers were off to our right and appeared to be chasing an NVA going east along the side of the hill.

When we turned our weapons on his direction they shouted, "Hold fire, hold fire." No one fired their weapon and we waited for the Rangers to come down to our position.

The NVA got away. LT Parker, Sgt. Patchart and LT Lam came up to our spot as well. We wanted to know why we were told not to fire our weapons and the response we got was confusing. The Rangers thought we were going to fire on them and that why they said what they did. At the time, we thought this was baloney the NVA running away was a good thirty meters in front of the Rangers. The lieutenants both agreed that there was to be no shooting unless you had a clear target.

Recon was beginning to understand this mission had some bad vibes and everyone was on edge. We had been on the mission for just twenty-four hours and we have had contact twice today. It was already getting late and we needed to set up an NDP.

We spent the rest of the afternoon checking out the training camp. The area where we were going to fire on the escaping NVA was flat and open. This area was used as a target range and there were heavy canvas bags filled with dirt and jungle debris that were used for bayonet practice. It was small about twenty meters wide and thirty meters deep. On top of the hill there was an open air hut used a class room with a blackboard nailed on one side of the hut. The canopy here was very thick. We found benches made from tree branches inside of the hut.

We found no documents or gear here. Spades and Hearts were tasked with trying to find bunkers or tunnel entrances but we found none.

For all intended purposes, this camp was deserted. It was almost as if the shooting at the OP on the first hilltop we encountered had warned the NVA we were close.

We set up our NDP right on top of the hill and put mechanicals out on the trails leading into the camp. Everyone had an extra claymore as well as C-4 for this mission. We set our watch schedules for the night and Sgt. Layden checked in with me and Collard at our position. He said to us, "We move at first light so have breakfast quick as you can, were gonna torch the classroom and the LT is plotting our position now with FDC. We'll move about a click due south to an NVA village, Charlie is all over the place so you two keep your eyes open walking drag. I don't want any of these slippery bastards sneaking up our rear." "No problem Sarge," Collard said. Layden left and moved on to the next position when a marker round came in right over head. Whatever quirks LT Parker had, the man could read a map.

We had no movement or problems that night and we started moving at first light. Mr. Magoo had the point followed by the Rangers, LT Lam and the CP group.

Hearts fell in behind them followed by Spades. Then we noticed that Binh was walking with Spades team, which was odd he usually moved with the CP group. Tony and I had the drag and we alternated moving back and forth as the last man. We also were spread out as flankers on drag. We moved the click at a good pace and came up on the perimeter of the village around noon on the north side. We spread out with Hearts and Spades on line behind the Rangers. The CP group minus LT Parker was behind the two teams and Collard and I stayed back about twenty-five meters to guard the rear.

The Rangers ran into the village with Spades and Hearts behind them on line. There was no shooting but there was an awful lot of shouting in Vietnamese.

The CP group stayed inside the wood line as Collard and I watched the rear. We heard women screaming and children crying as the Rangers continued to shout at people. Stuck in the wood line we had no idea what was going on. Then we got word over the radio to enter the village but Sgt. Patchart told Collard and I to stay in the woods and watch the rear.

Tony and I watched the rear as the shouting and crying continued. Spades and Hearts had been deployed around the perimeter of the village and Jack Meadon came up on our position.

"You won't get any piggy kisses in this village Ski, these bitches are just plain nasty," he said. I asked Jack, "What's the sit-rep?" Jack replied, "There's four women, three kids and an old man in the vill, the Rangers are tearing all the hooch's apart looking for stuff."
"Any signs of the NVA," I asked. "Nothing so far as I know," he said. Tony added, "What the hell are we going

to do with women, kids and an old man?" Jack replied, "Standby GI you'll find out in tee tee time."

We waited another thirty minutes when Sgt. Patchart came back to us. "Jack go ahead back to your team, Tony, Ski when we move out I want you two guys to burn all the huts there's seven of them we'll be moving southwest along a trail out of the village, clear," he said.
"Patch what about the women and kids?" I asked.
"They're going with us," he said. "Keep your shit together this starting to get out of hand," he added and left.

Recon started moving out and Tony and I got our first real look at the village. It was just seven hooch's close together the village was smaller than the Cham village we had been in there was no live stock or other animals and now it was deserted.

We followed orders Tony kept an eye out to the rear, he did not smoke. I took out my zippo and started lighting the hooch's. As Tony and I left, the heat from the burning village could be felt as we picked up the trail and caught up to Recon.

We moved about 200 meters out of the village after crossing a creek and stopped. A quick defensive position had been set and the LT called Tony and I up to the front. "LT Le says there were signs of NVA in the village and from the conversations overheard from the women there were three of them. They left along this trail so you two keep your eyes open they may try to follow us," he told us. "OK LT no sweat," I said.

Then there were three quick bursts of AK-47 fire. The Rangers got up with the women and kids and started down the trail. "Shit, let's move now," the LT said.

The LT and Sgt. Patchart were right behind the Rangers and Tony and I ran right after them.

I could hear the rest of Recon getting together to join the chase. We ran at full speed down the trail into an open brush area with high grass and brushwood. We had run about 100 meters when the trail took a slight turn to the right. Another burst of AK-47 fire was heard and I could see green tracers going by to my right.

Then I saw the three NVA running about 100 meters away from my right to left into some high grass. I stepped off the trail to my left and leading the first NVA I fired a magazine going left to right. I could see the tracers going through the high grass into the three fleeing NVA.

We continued to run down the trail and when it turned to the left, the rangers were gathered together with the women children and the old man.

One of the other Rangers was with LT Lam further down the trail standing over two bodies. Lt Lam said the third NVA got away in the grass. Neither of the two bodies on the trail had weapons. One of the fleeing NVA lying on the trail was an old man, the other was a young man about twenty years old, he had a military style haircut and was wearing a khaki uniform. The rest of Recon arrived and 'Chief' Howard had his M60 in a prone position. I told him to fire his weapon into the grass in front of us. "What for," he said. "The one with the AK-47 is in the grass now fire that weapon," I said. The LT came up and ordered everyone to cease fire.

The LT had us set up a defensive position. Checking around the grass growing at the edge of the trail I found a bunker about twenty meters from the two dead NVA. I alerted Sgt. Peady who was close by and he indicated I should use a frag on the bunker. I released the safety catch pulled the pin and called out, "Fire in the hole," and then tossed the live grenade into the bunker. The grenade went off a few seconds later; anyone who was inside was surely dead. The LT was on the horn with TOC and told Sgt. Patchart to have us eat a quick lunch. I sat on my pack after pulling out a can of spaghetti and meatballs.

Sitting there eating from the can I remembered the door gunner at FSB Nancy eating from a can as his chopper took off with the bodies of dead Americans on board.

I looked down at the young NVA soldier continuing to eat and thought to myself, I had come full circle. Death was just another part of the day. In Vietnam, the GI's used to say "Don't mean nothing." But it did. I was responsible for the two dead men on the trail. The hardened soldier in me was not showing any signs of emotion or regret. Deep down inside me though the magma of guilt was churning like lava in a volcano. Years later, the pressure would build and the guilt would erupt.

The LT got his orders from TOC and we moved west to a small hilltop about 600 meters away. Once on the hill top we set up an NDP and used all of the claymores we had. The Rangers stayed inside the center of the perimeter with the people from the village. Our CP group was in the same location. Binh was just inside the perimeter over by

Spades. This was odd like I said earlier he usually stayed with the CP group. Sgt. Layden came over to check with me and Collard and I asked him, "What's the deal with Binh, why is hanging out with Spades?"

Layden answered, "Rangers don't like him, you would think being countrymen and all they would all get along with one another."
Collard said, "Like Woung used to say numba ten asshole."
Layden added, "Two men at each position stand the same watch schedule, stay alert." Then he left.

Collard said, "Maybe Binh tried something with one of the women, I wouldn't put it past him he's a sleaze ball."

I replied, "Christ have you seen those women they are truly fugly." Collard laughed.

We spent the night and started the third day of this mission at the crack of dawn. Sgt. Patchart and Layden came to everyone to brief them on the plan of the day. Mr. Magoo told the LT and LT Lam that there was a hospital about 700 meters' northwest of us. We were heading that way. They also stressed that the LT is concerned about the NVA following us so Tony and I should be alert. With the women and kids up front on point, any attacks might come from the rear.

After breakfast, we moved out and started moving northwest. The forest here had thick canopy overhead but was fairly open on the ground. We had good lines of sight and Tony and I hung back fifty meters at times from the main column of Recon. We crossed another small creek and stayed in the forest. The terrain opened up for a time on our left and right to high grass and brushwood.

We made the climb up to the top of the hill where the hospital was located. The LT had Spades and Hearts set up a perimeter after going into the unoccupied camp. Just before we reached the top, the terrain opened up with high grass and some bamboo. Then stepping back into the wood line we were in the hospital complex. Thick canopy overhead made sighting this complex by helicopter impossible. The enemy had strung cargo nets and heavy ropes from tree to tree in the upper canopy and the vegetation just clung to it and used it to almost completely block out the day light. Down on the ground it was like the Cham village. The ground was hard packed and devoid of any plant life. The huts were all constructed using material from the jungle.

We found cots and hammock locations inside the huts. Other furniture was present inside, including desks, chairs and cabinets, all constructed from raw materials found in the jungle. In the center of the complex was a triage area with some cabinets and tables used to evaluate the wounded. This was a real find and the craftsmanship of the work was amazing. There were no bunkers in or around the complex, which we felt, was odd but I guess the NVA used it strictly as a field hospital. We also searched for tunnels and found none. Despite its primitive beauty, we would destroy what we could. Burn everything else and when we left, artillery would finish the destruction. The enemy would have to re-build what must have taken months if not a year to accomplish.

The LT ordered us to break up all of the furniture and pile it all into the largest hut. Then we took out or lighters and set everything else on fire. The final destruction was left to a M34 WP grenade tossed into the largest hut with all the broken furniture. The WP would insure that everything was burnt and transformed into ashes.

Before leaving, the LT called in another marker round on top of the hospital. It never ceased to amaze me his accuracy with map reading and plotting arty fire. We moved southwest and told we would be going to another village about 600 meters away. Tony and I were the last to leave the heat and smoke from the burning hospital complex was getting to us. The flames from the large hut reached up into the canopy and the jungle was burning as well. I had no doubt the entire complex would be burned down to cinders.

We moved about 300 meters when we heard the incoming arty rounds hitting the hospital hilltop. To add insult to injury the LT had arty fire WP rounds. By the end of the day, the smoke from the burning hill top would fill the air.

We followed the same plan as the last village, we stayed in the wood line and Hearts and Spades got on line in front of the CP group and the Rangers would go into the village. The seven people from the last village stayed with the CP group. Charlie was home today and before the two teams could get fully on line, we got AK-47 fire from multiple locations inside the village. Tony and I hit the ground as green tracers buzzed over our heads. The enemy fled from the village after they fired their weapons and were on the run out of the back end of the village. There was a lot a screaming in Vietnamese again and the children were crying hysterically.

Rangers got everyone rounded up after the situation calmed down and to my surprise, there were only two children and four teenage girls.

The four girls were downright hostile even to the point of attempting to punch and kick not only the Rangers but some of Spades as well. They were in their mid-teens and full of hatred for us. The two teams searched the village and anything they found that the LT thought would be of use to the enemy was broken up and piled into one of the four hooch's in this village. There were also some sacks of rice that we found in a storage shed. Each hooch had its own bunker but we found no weapons or ammo. We now had fourteen people with us and this was a concern especially with the aggressiveness of the four girls.

The children were all small and under five years old. They had to be carried by the women and that was going to slow us down. Our ability to maneuver as a combat unit was compromised and we had to think about security during our NDP that night.

We set up a defensive position and had lunch. The LT spent a lot of time talking with LT Lam and TOC on the radio. I'm sure he was concerned with the number of people that we had and was looking for a solution. Mr. Magoo said there was another village 700 meters south of us. So far, he had been true to his word and the mission was developing as promised with the exception of all the civilians we had with us.

The LT informed Tony and I to burn the village after they left to pursue the NVA that fired on us. The NVA left the village on a trail heading south.

The Rangers and the CP group had the point with all of the people we had rounded up and followed by Spades and Hearts. Binh must have thought he had a chance at one of the teen age girls he was now at the back of the CP group.

Tony and I waited until Recon cleared the village and I started setting the hooch's on fire.

We left and with the burning village and the torched hilltop, the air was full of smoke. As much as we did not like it, we walked the trail heading south. There was just no way to break jungle with all the so called civilians we had. We covered the 700 meters in just about an hour and we also crossed a small creek.

Attempting the same maneuver tactic on this village was just not going to happen. Aside from all the extra people, we had with us this village was well aware we were coming. Everyone was outside and there were a lot of people this time.

We came out of the wood line into a high grass and brushwood area with some bamboo. There were also a few tall trees. The Rangers were the first ones to enter the village and the shouting back and forth in Vietnamese started up again. Now we had a real problem there were nine more people to add to our group one man, three women and five children. The civilians we collected now totaled twenty-three.

The LT had the teams set up a defensive position around the small village of five hooch's. Then he had me and Tony cloverleaf to our east to check out a wooded area for a possible NDP. The area we found was about 150 meters north to south and 100 meters east to west. The eastern side had the small creek we crossed and the western side had the trail. We reported back to the LT and we moved everyone to the site. We set up mechanicals on the trail to the north and south of our position. Spades took the creek side of the NDP and Hearts was on the trail side.

The two teams met on the northern side of the NDP and the CP group covered the southern end. It was late in the afternoon and we had some time before darkness set in. In the center of the NDP, the Rangers and the twenty-three people we had collected were settling in for the night. The two men were older but some of the younger women had already demonstrated their hatred for us. The other stark contrast was the children. They were all ranged in age of two years to seven years.

The difference with them was they were terrified of us. Unlike the kids in the Cham village who were curious, outgoing and friendly, these kids were just plain terrified of us.

Making eye contact with any of them and they would turn away or start crying. One can only imagine what their parents were telling them about us. It was a sickening feeling to have a child look at you like that. It was not going to improve in fact the next day it would be worse.

The perimeter was not quiet like our usual NDP's. The females would talk out loud the kids sometimes cried noise discipline was gone all night. Not that it mattered the NVA most likely knew just where we were. It was starting to dawn on all of us the only reason we were not getting hit was the NVA was afraid to engage us due to the presence of their relatives.

It was a restless night but at dawn, we had breakfast and coffee. Feeding all of the people we had was the responsibility of the Rangers. The Rangers had adequate amounts of rice but the adults refused to be fed by them anyway. Only the children seemed to eat and drink. The LT wanted to move east even though Mr. Magoo was telling us there were two more villages to the south if we followed the trail. The LT wanted to get into a more terrain friendly environment for a defensive position so he was looking at a heavily wooded area with some open ground around it. The place he picked was 700 meters to our east. There was a trail that cut through an open area with high grass and the jungle stuck out like a bulge to the west. The area we moved trough was high thick canopy and grass and brushwood on the ground. We found a trail going east and we were making good time.

Tony and I had drag again and he was bringing up the rear. One of the men we captured was walking in front of me and then there was Sgt. Layden.

We had so many people with us they were strung out through our entire column. The other man was at the front and we separated the 4 female trouble makers. Occasionally I looked back at Tony and saw he was getting further away from us but the area was open with site lines extending to fifty and seventy-five meters. The old guy in front of me was having a hard time keeping up with Layden and I kept looking back for Tony.

Layden was widening the gap between him and the old guy and Tony was nowhere to be seen. This at first did not concern me we did this often when walking drag but now it seemed like Tony was out of site for too long. Layden was too far ahead for me to make any contact with him so I jogged up the trail catching up to the old man. I stopped him and gestured towards a high tree with a thick trunk. He complied but was concerned about my actions. I placed his back against the tree and put the barrel of my M16 against his chest right over his heart. I gestured with my finger to my lips that he was to be quiet.

Then I tilted my weapon to the right and let him see that I moved the selector switch of my rifle to full auto. Any movement on his part would mean twenty rounds of 5.56mm ammo would cut through him in the flash of an eye. He was wide eyed and was scared out of his mind. I looked down the trail for Tony and he was still not there. I looked up the trail and Layden was fifty meters away and turning to his left following the trail. Then I looked back down the trail and saw Tony.

I stepped away from the old man pulling him back on the trail and gestured to Tony with a double fist pump indicating he was to double time to me. Once he reached me he was out of breath but was able to report, "We're being followed by a large group."

"How big and how far back," I asked. "Not sure maybe a platoon or bigger 200 maybe 250 meters," he said. "OK, you take papa-san here and follow the trail and tell Layden so he can tell the LT, I'll hang back here and watch the rear." Tony took the old guy and was gone. I was still in the same spot squatting behind a bush. I was watching the trail for the NVA. A few minutes passed and I looked back towards where Tony had taken the old man and saw Layden kneeling on the trail.

He was where the trail turned to the left and was fifty to seventy-five meters away. I made hand signals to maybe get Hearts on line and wait for the NVA. He had his RTO with him and was on the horn and gave me one finger to indicate wait one. I turned my back to him and was watching for the approaching NVA. I could see movement in the brush 100 meters out. Layden was trying to get my attention without shouting and was not having any luck. I was so intent on the movement I forgot about Layden.

Finally, a small rock went skipping down the trail past me and I turned to see Layden signaling me to double time to his position. I was a little surprised by his order but the reason came screaming over my head a second later. I ran up the trail and then the three artillery rounds started breaking through the canopy above me causing branches and leaves to rain down on me. This was followed by the impact of the rounds one after the other. Whoump, Whoump, Whoump.!

I could feel the shock wave of the explosions pushing me along and I could hear the shrapnel cutting through the tree branches and smacking into the trunks of the trees. I went into high gear and fell down in front of Sgt. Layden and his RTO.

Then 3 more rounds came in and exploded 50 meters further down the trail. "Do drop in GI you want chop chop or boom boom," Layden asked. "Very funny," I said. "Let's get back to Recon," Layden said. Then we went back up the trail about 100 meters and found Recon. The LT continued his arty mission to try and discourage the NVA following us too closely. We had another 500 meters to cover before we could get to our destination and we made quick time getting there. The last 300 meters was all open ground but we hit the wood line without any trouble.

We set up a defensive position and the LT was on the horn with battalion. We had to get rid of these people even though they were a shield against enemy attack. We were also running low on water and rations. Mr. Magoo informed us there were two more villages for us to get to and that added to the anxiety. The people we had were now referred to as POW's. That meant the Geneva Convention governed how they were to be treated.

Not that any of us were mistreating anyone. I'm not too sure about the Rangers they seemed to treat these people as trash.

Word was passed around the perimeter that arty was going to be firing missions around us as Delta Tangos were set up. We would NDP here the rest of the day and night and go into the final two villages in the morning. Once the Delta tangos were set up, the LT had arty fire a mission to our east just outside our perimeter.

If the NVA were thinking about any kind of assault, it would come from this direction. It was the only side of our position that was wooded. The other three compass points were all open ground for several hundred meters. Claymores and AW fire would decimate anything that came from those sides.

We got some much needed rest during the afternoon once arty finished its job. The LT and LT Lam were on the horn with battalion sending and receiving coded messages. Just before evening chow all, the team Sergeants were called into the CP group for a briefing. Sgt. Layden found Tony and I first and filled us in on the plan.

"OK guys listen up, in the morning just after first light we would move west out to the trail and then follow it southwest into the next village. You two will have the drag again.

All of the POW's will be together behind the Rangers with the CP group followed by Hearts and then Spades", he said.
He continued, "Sgt. Peady and his RTO would be in front of you. Any movement behind us is to be reported and like

yesterday the LT will use arty to keep, them back so don't drift too far away from the main group. Once we get into the first village, the Rangers will round up whoever is in the village. The second village is supposed to be 500 meters away from the first. There is a large open field of sugar cane and high grass between the two. Once we round up the people in the second village the LT will call for a CH-47 and some Hunter Killer Teams.

The Rangers and the POW's will extract and then we will haul ass about a click southeast to set our NDP. We will RTB at first light the next morning, any questions".

"Sarge how many more people can we expect to pick up in these two villages?" I asked. Layden answered me, "Mr. Magoo says maybe a dozen all total." Tony asked, "What about the NVA how do we know they're not gonna ambush us as we get to either village."
"So far Charlie has been holding back maybe he's afraid of killing his own people, then again once that shithook sets down the situation could change so keep your shit together," Layden answered. With nothing left to say he left to brief the rest of Hearts.

Later LT Parker and Sgt. Patchart came over to talk with us. The LT said, "Collard, Ski you guys are doing an outstanding job on this mission, tomorrow I need the two of you to be on your toes. Maintain site with each other at all times, I don't want a repeat of yesterday to happen again, clear." "Yes sir," we both chimed in.

He continued, "I'm going to use arty as much as I can if the NVA get to close to us, Ski, Sgt Layden told me he couldn't tell the difference from the smoke of the arty rounds and the smoke coming off your ass yesterday."

"For sure LT I was haulin ass," I answered. He laughed and then he and Patchart got up to leave. "OK get some rest we have a big day tomorrow," Patchart said.

The night passed without any problems other than the noise from the newly designated POW group. We had a quick breakfast and started moving as the sun just started coming up. We made it to the trail in no time and started following it towards the village.

We moved about 600 meters and the trail turned west then we humped another 500 meters and the trail turned south. We were moving as fast as we could with our extra people and had been humping a good hour and a half.

We passed into a wooded area and there was a small gulley to our west. The gulley itself was about fifteen meters deep and forty meters long but only ten meters across. To our east was the open field we had been walking in. The morning calm was disturbed by a thirty round burst of AK-47 fire from the bottom of the gulley. All of the rounds were fired at too high of an angle and went over the heads of Spades. Spades reacted instantly as they had been trained and seven M16's and Chiefs M60 responded with 190 rounds of return fire into the gulley. The column was halted while Sgt. Peady, Waller and Savicci went into the gulley to access the damage. The three men were in the gulley for five minutes and returned to the trail. They found the bullet riddled body of a single NVA soldier and retrieved his weapon. When Sgt. Peady reached the trail there were tears in his eyes. Along with the NVA, they also found the bullet riddled body of a three-year-old girl.

The news of this tragedy spread through Recon like a violent summer storm. Everyone was sickened by the news. As Tony and I came up to the scene, I asked Peady, "Where is she?" He gestured and pointed into the gulley and told me, "Down there next to that tree stump." I looked at the spot that he indicated but I still didn't see her. I'm glad I didn't and I let it go. To this day, I'm glad I never saw her body. It would only add to the pile of bricks I would carry for the rest of my life.

The LT got us moving again and we were about 300 meters outside of the first and largest village so far. Once again, there was no element of surprise and everyone in the village was waiting for us.

There were ten people in the village five men and five women. None of them were armed but the village itself had bunkers in each of the eight hooch's.

Tony and I stayed back on the trail about fifty meters or so to watch our rear while the Rangers and Recon searched through the village. We saw no sign of the enemy. We sat on the edge of the trail and were silent. Each of us buried in our own thoughts about the fire fight that morning.

Once a sweep of the village was complete, Sgt. Peady came up the trail to let us know we were moving to the second village. We were told not to torch the hooch's and we moved through the village out into the field of sugar cane and grass towards the last village. We covered the 500 meters to the next village in under an hour. The village itself was in a wooded area with very thick canopy. It was located almost in the middle of the sugar cane field that covered a full click running north and south and 500 meters east and west.

The woods were shaped like a fish hook with the village located on the northern tip of the hook.

No one was home in the seven-hooch village but stacks of rice bags and small baskets of produce were in the all of the hooch's. It was almost dark in the village due to the heavy canopy. The LT called battalion and made arrangements to extract the now thirty-three POW's in our custody.

The Pink Teams and the Chinook were already on call and arrived about thirty minutes later. Once the choppers came, on net, we popped smoke to indicate they LZ and the big clumsy bird came in to land. The Loach's from the two Pink Teams were buzzing around the first village and the wood line to our west. The four Cobras circled around like slithering snakes waiting to pounce on their prey. The big bird finally set down and the back ramp was lowered.

The Rangers moved all thirty-three POW's and Mr. Magoo on the big bird and then it lumbered up into the air and was on its way to who knows were.

None of the after action reports or newsletters mention anything about this mission except a one line notation in the 'Keystone Robin' operation report that an element from the 4th of the 12th medevac'd thirty-three people from Dinh Quan. The Battalion ceased operations in the Dinh Quan area in June when they moved their HQ from FSB Nancy to FSB Eagle. The only explanation is that Recon was OPCON to another command for this mission.

We set up a defensive perimeter to secure the last village and prepare it for destruction. Hearts was sent back into the sugar cane field to protect the northwestern flank looking back towards the first village and the wood line. The Pink Teams stayed on our net and continued their operations looking for targets. They found nothing to fire at so they left for their CAP.

The LT brought Tony and I back into the main perimeter and thanked us again for a job well done. We reported we saw no signs of the enemy following us this morning.

Spades was busy rigging the last village with C-4 and the WP grenades. Once we completed this, we called Hearts on the radio to return to the main perimeter.

First, there was a burst of a single AK-47 firing from the wood line to our northwest. Then it seemed the entire wood line opened up with AW fire that was concentrated just to the right of Hearts position. They had been spotted by the NVA as they started moving back towards our main perimeter.

The high grass and sugar cane was concealing the true position of Hearts who immediately began returning fire into the wood line some 150 meters away. The LT was on the horn right away and reported he was in heavy contact with a large enemy force.

He sent Spades up to reinforce hearts and we were all on line exchanging fire with the NVA. Green and red tracers were passing each other through the high grass. I found an old tree that had been cut down and left to rot. The thick trunk was perfect cover and I joined in with the rest of Recon now firing single rounds back at the wood line.

The Pink Teams were the first to join in the fight. I was wondering when the LT was going to start his artillery magic and now knew why. With the choppers in the air arty was on hold. The Loach's buzzed around the wood line drew fire and banked back over the cover of the tree line so the Cobras could do their thing. They came up behind us and fired rockets and mini-guns into the enemy positions. The only thing missing was the sound of a bugle playing charge. The four Cobras made two passes each and the enemy fire subsided. The Loach's then returned buzzing around the enemy positions and still drew fire. Green tracer rounds were now streaking into the sky after the little helicopters.

The Cobras returned and with all the anger they could muster pulverized the enemy positions with the last of their rocket and mini-gun ordinance. Then they formed up and left the AO. Their replacements were going to be much harder to deal with. Word was passed down our line to keep our heads down fast movers were inbound. We could see the sun glistening of the wings of the two Fox Fours coming in fast from the northeast.

They were flying low and fast at about 500 feet and were on the gun target line in just a second. Each dropped a 500 pound HE bomb from under their bellies. The bombs flew through the air and tumbled toward the wood line were the enemy was suspected to be.

As the bombs tumbled toward their target, the two jets banked over us and climbed back up into the air, the sound of their engines was deafening and the jet blast from the engines could be felt on the ground where we were. The bombs continued their deadly dance and impacted into the trees breaking off and sending branches and the tops of trees flying into the air. Then they exploded one right after the other. Whoump, Whoump!! The shock wave of the two explosions washed over us like the wind of a tornado. Then we saw huge whole trees root ball and all flying up into the air, the sound of the explosions adding to the din of the jet engines and I swear lying there behind the dead tree trunk I actually bounced twice as the shock wave travelled through the ground. Then another dimension was added as the fire ball and smoke rose into the air. We were confident that no one was going to survive that assault.

The LT had us get on line to do a BDA. Sgt. Patchart led the two teams of Recon into the divested wood line. We found two huge craters amid the smoke and fires that were still burning.

The jungle here in the blast zone was totally destroyed. Entire trees had been blown to splinters and there was broken leafless branches and tree trunks all around the edges of the two craters. We also found pieces of bodies and broken bits of rifle stocks and web gear.

There were small piles of blackened goo in various spots the obvious remains of the NVA that suffered the impact of the bombs. A body count was impossible. We were ordered back to the last village where we got ready to move out to the southeast. Sgt. Layden stayed behind with Tony and I to blow the C-4 charges and WP grenades left in the hooch's with the rice and produce. He used a claymore clacker to blow the charges.

Each hooch had a WP grenade and a one-pound block of C-4 wired together by detcord. We waited until Recon reached the next tree line some 700 meters away and then blew the charges. We were about 100 meters away from the village in a small depression in the ground. Layden said, "Fire in the hole," and blew the charges.

Whoump!

The village went up in a blast of WP and HE and was totally ablaze in fire. Debris from the blast rained down on us and it was a little messy. We had rice and bits and pieces of vegetables and fruit all over us. The two Fox Fours were back this time they each dropped two napalm bombs on the first village we came into this morning.

The heat wave from the blast was felt by us even though we were a good 500 meters away. Then we hauled ass to the tree line to rejoin Recon.

As we came back into their perimeter brushing off the stuff that landed all over us, Sgt. Patchart commented, "LT I think we've just been resupplied with fresh veggies and other stuff." Everyone laughed but the light hearted feeling was not to last.

We had a one click hump in front of us before we would NDP. We reached our destination by the end of the afternoon in the elbow of a wide fast moving stream. The elbow of water was on our west, south and eastern sides. Anyone crossing the fast moving stream would make a lot of noise.

The stream itself was about thirty to forty meters wide. We deployed our claymores and settled in for evening chow on the last of our rations. We were all hungry we had not eaten all day. Exhausted we still had to maintain our noise discipline again and our watch schedules.

Hopefully the last of the NVA in the area had been either killed today or discouraged from any more contact. Walking drag to this position Tony and I saw no signs we were being followed.

The night passed quietly and we were up at the crack of dawn. We moved northeast towards our extraction LZ. Once on the LZ, we checked it for signs of the enemy and satisfied we were finally alone the LT called for the extraction birds. An hour later, we pooped smoke and the four Hueys landed at the same time and we ran to the choppers.

Cobra gunships were flying around waiting for any NVA who was looking for a fight. The morning would remain calm disturbed only by the sounds of the departing helicopters and our collective sigh of relief. The choppers took us back to FSB Mace. Everyone needed to wind down from our stressful mission.

We spent six days in the bush and made contact with the enemy every one of those days. During that six-day mission besides collecting thirty-three POW's Recon was in eight fire fights, killed three confirmed NVA, plus an undetermined number of NVA from the airstrikes, and destroyed an enemy hospital, a training camp and five hamlets hidden in the jungle for the NVA.

We all had our own thoughts on the death of the little girl. It wasn't intentional. Despite any way you can rationalize this terrible incident it was something every one of us would have to live with. Recon kept it all to themselves no one would speak of it. We deserved an R&R. Recon was a good unit and it would leave Vietnam with a big mission to its credit. We had no idea yet but Recon had completed its last mission. The brigade was in full pack up and get ready to go home mode. By the 7th of October, the Brigade's Advance Party would depart Bien Hoa Airbase. Soon it would return to Ft. Benning Ga. Not yet known to us the 4th of the 12th would motor march back to BMB on

15 September right on schedule. For now, we were informed that for the next three days we should rest up and relax and so we did.

Lounging around for three days with nothing to do other than shower, eat, sleep, and drink beer may sound boring, but it was a challenge we were all ready for.

Sgt. Patchart informed us that LT Parker had gone back to BMB for a debriefing. That meant he was in charge of Recon. Patchart was a good NCO and considered himself one of the guys. Once he let it be known he was in command, the guys assaulted him with requests for R&R, promotions and pay raises.

It was all good natured fun and Patchart took it all in stride. Recon was coming back to be the close knit unit we had become.

We passed the time reading and writing letters home cleaning up our gear and just hanging out. The rumor mill was working full steam ahead and we heard everything from returning to BMB, staying here at FSB Mace for the duration of the Brigades time left in Vietnam to being sent into North Vietnam on a special commando mission to kidnap Ho Chi Minh.

After our three day rest, Sgt. Patchart came around with more news. "OK listen up, as of now Recon will no longer be field operational, no more humping the boonies," he said. We were of course elated there were cheers and back slapping, handshakes and hugging. Patchart let the celebration continue and when it started to die down, he spoke again, "Recon will maintain its two teams of Hearts and Spades. On alternating days each team will be assigned to bunker duty as part of base security and they will also be used as additional fire power for D Troop 17th Cav as they make their daily runs off base." That last piece of information got the group quiet fast. Now we were all looking at Patchart as he stood there grinning. "You mean to say were gonna be riding on tracks?" Woodard asked.

"Affirmative, those are the orders, Sgt Layden you and your team will report to the TOC at zero nine hundred tomorrow and will hook up with SFC Maretti, and he will brief you and your team."

Then he added the last bit of information, "LT Parker will remain at BMB, he will not return."

In a couple of weeks, we will motor march with the 17th Cav back to Brigade BMB and begin the processing of sending people home or transferring to new units."
"Sarge, any idea if we get to go home early is there some kind of a cut off, you know like guys with less than sixty days go home?" Jack Meadon asked.

"So far that is just a rumor, which gets transferred and who gets to go home will be decided when we get to BMB, that's all I know at this time," Patchart said.
"Sgt Peady you and your team will report to the TOC at zero nine hundred day after tomorrow, you may want to go with Lyle in the morning just to get meet SFC Maretti. Spancer you're on Hearts and White you're on Spades, leave your radios here in the bunkers you won't need them anymore. Lawder you will also be on Hearts team, Howard you're on Spades, Doc Keiller you report to the base aid station tomorrow, any questions?" Patchart said.

"Patch what time does my freedom bird leave?" I asked. "Day after next year," he grinned.

So that was it. No one knew what our fate was to be but we find out soon enough when we got back to BMB. For now, we were riding on tracks.

We all had training in AIT on how to deploy from the M113 tracks but those type of tactics were not used here. We would find out tomorrow.

The next morning Hearts went to the TOC with Lyle and we all got to meet SFC Maretti. He informed us that we were going out on convoy escort today from FSB Mace to Xuan Loc.

We mounted up on the tracks met the crews and got ready to move out. I remembered my days with the 'Tiger Patrol' and here I was again. There were ten of us now on hearts team so we split up and we had two men on a track. Leaving the base on RD 333, we headed south to pick up QL 1 the main highway that ran all the way from South Vietnam to the DMZ. We were escorting trucks coming from FSB Den that had stopped here yesterday and loaded up supplies to go back to BMB.

QL 1 is all black top road so the ride today was relatively smooth. I say relatively because each time the track started up or stopped it rocked like carnival ride. The trip to the western edge of Xuan Loc was about thirty-five clicks or approximately sixty-five miles. We would meet up with elements of the 11th ACR who would escort the trucks the rest of the way to BMB. Each track had a .50 caliber machine gun mounted in the front turret and an M60 machine gun mounted behind a shield plate on either side. We sat on top as instructed by the crew of three. The driver sat in a spot to the left of the center mounted .50 caliber where the track commander sat and the third crew member manned one of the M60's mounted on the left and right side.

Normally there would be a crew of four but with the brigade getting ready to deploy back to the States man power was not up to the usual TOE. That's where we came in, we were the extra men and guns.

The convoy started out off the base by zero nine thirty and headed south to pick up QL 1. It would take about an hour and a half to get to the rendezvous point with the 11th ACR and the trip was made without incident. The enemy knew we were leaving so like an unwanted guest at a party it was just easier to let us leave.

This and bunker duty at night would be our life for the next two weeks then everything would change.

Chapter Nine, Stand-down Begins;

The next two weeks were pretty much the same. Every other day we left with the 17th Cav and either escorted convoys or ran operations along the main roads back in the fields and woods to keep the roads open and to deny the enemy the opportunity to set ambushes. Enemy activity in the area dropped off and during the entire month of September, not one 'Redcatcher' lost his life. This was the first and only month since the Brigade arrived in November of 1966 that no one was killed. At night on those days we did not go out with the tracks, we sat our bunker duty guarding the berm and the base.

We had three bunkers assigned to us and usually there were seven men to a bunker. This is where we slept, hung out and ate our chow the battalion was in the process of shutting down the mess hall. We were living on C-Rats and LRRP rations.

Patrolling the roads was not bad but once the tracks went off road the day became a bone jarring gut tossing ride. Sitting on top of the track, you held on for dear life when in the fields. There was space to ride inside the track but the M113 APC armor was not enough to stop a well-placed RPG around. Better to be blown off the track then be trapped inside with flying shrapnel bouncing off the walls.

I'm sure that every vet who served in these type units when buying a new car would order air conditioning, independent suspension and heavy duty shocks before anything else.

During the two-week period of serving with the 17th Cav, there were no problems. We had no contact with the enemy and our days became redundant and boring. FSB Mace also was to be occupied by elements of the 11th ACR (Armored Combat Regiment) 'Blackhorse'. They would be building a new FSB along QL 1. Sometimes the 11th ACR and D Troop would combine their operations around the base.

We did an awful lot of convoy escorts as the units of the Brigade came through FSB Mace to be motor marched back to BMB. At night when assigned, we pulled our bunker duty and actually just split the watch schedules up between us so that everyone was catching up on lost sleep. We found out that other units in the Brigade had already been re-assigned or were designated to be re-assigned.

Our sister battalion the 5th of the 12th would be the first combat unit to stand-down and return to BMB during segment one of Operation Keystone Robin. During segment two, the 2nd of the 3rd was re-assigned to the 25th Infantry Division 'Tropical Lightning'. They were sent back to BMB to complete the process and equipment had to be returned before they re-deployed to the 25th Infantry Division. Then during segment three, the 4th of the 12th and D troop 17th Cav would motor march back to BMB and then D Troop would be picked up by the 1st Air Calvary Airmobile Division.

D Troop 17th Cav would be involved with escort duties of other Brigade units moved to FSB Mace to motor march back to BMB. Recon had very little to pack up everything we had was carried in our ruck sacks so when the day of departure arrived we were ready to go.

We rode back to BMB in the back of two deuce and a half trucks and was of course escorted by our friends in the 17th Cav and the 152nd MP Platoon. We left early on the morning of the 15th and arrived at BMB just in time for lunch. Top of course had burgers and hot dogs cooking on the grill and there was cold beer and soda. Today was a day to relax and take it easy. Some of us would be rotated back to "The World" and the rest would be assigned to new units. Top instructed us we were to report into the CP every morning by ten hundred to check on the status of our individual orders. No exceptions but other than that after we cleaned our weapons and turned them into the company armory we were free to go to the PX or the EM club.

The next morning, we all assembled at the picnic tables outside the CP and cleaned our weapons. After all the weapons were cleaned, we turned in all of our ammo, magazines, grenades and claymores and anything else that could go boom. Then everyone just hung out hit the PX, read our mail and sent letters home. After two nights at the EM club most of us were too hung over to keep up the pace so we caught up on some much needed sleep.

On the fourth day at BMB, I got up and had breakfast early. I went back to the CP around nine and saw Top. "Just the man I need I hear you like driving jeeps," he said. I used to kill time at FSB Nancy between missions by driving the company jeep around the base.

"Go over to the motor pool and see Sergeant Washington he's expecting you, he'll sign you out a jeep. Then report over to Headquarters Company some Hershey bar needs a driver to take him on his errands," Top said.

"OK Top," I said sullenly. "Hey you're doing me a favor I won't forget it and it's an easy detail," he replied.

I went over to the motor pool found Sergeant Washington and he signed out a jeep to me. Then I drove over to HQ saw the clerk at the desk and let him know why I was there. A few minutes later a fresh in from the world 2nd Louie with a small pack indicated it was time to go. He never introduced himself he just hopped in the jeep and said, "Let's go." "Where are we going? I asked. "Go up to the main road hang a left and I'll direct you from there," he said.

I followed his instructions and noticed we were leaving BMB. We passed through the gate and the MP's saluted him and we started down the road towards Bien Hoa. "LT if were going off base maybe we should have our weapons" I asked.

"Nope where were going everything is secure no need for any guns. I've made this trip before we won't have any problems," he said.

I noticed his fresh new green starched fatigues baseball cap and spit shined jungle boots. I'm sitting next to him in faded strikers and a boonie hat. My jungle boots had no shine in them at all in fact the leather had been so beaten by walking in the jungle the leather parts of my boots were like suede. He was probably in country as long as I had to go. 110 days and a wake up, I was short!

We continued driving into Bien Hoa on QL 15 and eventually crossed the Song Nha Be River. Then we started heading northwest.

We drove for about an hour and ended up just south of TX Ben Cat. We passed through several small hamlets on our way.

The route had taken us north of Saigon and we were about twenty miles from BMB. I was still concerned over the fact we had no weapons but there was a lot of ARVN and US Army MP traffic on the roads.

Just south of Tx Ben Cat the LT told me to pull into a driveway on my right. There was a two story building set back from the road about thirty meters and we pulled around to the back. In the back of the building was a fifty meter by 100-meter open field that was covered by cut grass. The parking area in the back had no other vehicles. I stopped the jeep and we both went inside. The first floor was a large open room with a bar to the left as you came in the back and offices along the back wall. There was a staircase on the front wall that led up to the second floor and then there was a cat walk around the second floor where more offices were on the back wall. No one was home. The place was deserted.

A variety of Army unit insignias were hanging all around the main room, it looked like some type of meeting hall. The LT told me, "There's a latrine upstairs along the back wall if you need it." Then we heard the wop wop of helicopter blades and the LT said, "OK there's my ride you stay here until I get back I won't be long so just relax while I'm gone." The chopper landed out back on the field and the LT ran to get on the Huey.

Based on the way the co-pilot was waving at me and the reception the LT got from the other man in back this was not a business pickup.

I got the impression these guys were going out to lunch. I checked my watch it was ten forty-five. The chopper lifted off and there I was all by myself. I had nothing to do but to look around the building. There was fridge behind the bar but it was empty. Likewise, there were no other supplies behind the bar. I checked the sink at the bar and the water was working. Then I checked out the latrine. It had a real flush and working toilet so that was a plus but after going through all the offices the only thing I found was two cans of pimento cheese and a stale box of crackers.

I went outside and sat in the jeep it was still shady out back so I just sat there and smoked a cigarette. The hours passed and the sun came over the building so the back of the building was now bathed in sunlight. It was too hot sitting in the sun so I went back inside the building. I looked up at the ceiling and noticed ceiling fans so I started liking for the switch that controlled them. Once I found it, I activated the fans and that helped a bit. Now I was getting anxious. I kept checking my watch and the day just dragged on and on.

It was just past fourteen hundred when some Vietnamese men most likely farmers or loggers cut through the field out back heading towards the town. They paid no attention to the building or the jeep and I got the impression they had been through here before but with their presence and my lack of a weapon, the anxiety and my anger were mounting. I went back upstairs to where I found the crackers and cheese. Fortunately, the chain that held my dog tags also had a P38 on it. I opened the cheese and with the three stale crackers, I had the only food since breakfast.

More time passed and I started thinking about where the hell this asshole was. For all I knew he and his buddies were shot down. I was in a dilemma. An Officer had given me a verbal order to stay here until he returned. Officially, this was my post. Leaving it would be a court martial offense.

Then again, it would come out in the court martial that this moron had left me there with no food no water and worst no weapon. All his little buddies would be in trouble as well for using the chopper for their personal little joy ride. The UCMJ would make mincemeat of their Army careers. I checked my watch again, it was seventeen hundred. I knew it would be dark soon and at that point, I needed to leave court martial or not. I came to decision if the LT did not return by eighteen hundred I would try to make my way back to BMB or try to catch an MP patrol.

Then at seventeen forty hours, I heard the wop wop of the Huey and looked up and saw the inbound bird approaching from the north. This goober actually turned on his landing lights and set down in the field. I fired up the jeep and saw the LT walking not very steadily towards me. It was not dark yet but it would be in the next half hour so I knew part of this trip would take place at night. He climbed into the passenger seat and before he was fully settled I popped the clutch and headed towards the road. He almost fell out and then I stopped at the end of the driveway and then tore out unto the road with my tires squealing on the hard top.

"Slow down what the hell are you doing?" he yelled. I ignored his question and asked my own, "Where the hell have you been all day shithead you left me here all day with no food or water," I yelled back at him.

"I don't like your tone soldier you are addressing an officer," he slurred. "Listen up asshole you better pray we don't get ambushed on the way back but if we do I'm gonna kill you myself before the VC get me," I said. "We are not getting ambushed we'll be fine now slow down," he said. "Fuck you," I answered and stomped on the gas.

He had nothing else to say he was holding on as I was driving very fast through the hamlets and villages. He looked like he might puke but I was not in a sympathetic mood. He stayed alert enough to give directions and we flew through the gates of BMB forty minutes later. The MP's yelled but my thinking was screw them too. I blew right through the gate. I slide to a stop in front of HQ and said, "Get the hell out of my jeep asshole."
"Take me to my quarters that's an order troop," he slurred.
I replied as I pushed him out, "Get out and walk you REMF asshole." I gave him a shove and he stumbled out of the jeep just as I popped the clutch and tore away from the front of HQ.
I went straight to the motor pool. MP jeeps were now running around the base looking for the vehicle that ran past the gate but I was on foot now. I grabbed the paperwork from my pocket and turned the jeep in and walked back to the Echo Company CP.

I had missed evening chow at the mess hall so I went to the PX to get something to eat. Some of the Recon guys were up playing cards and I told them of my ordeal. Sgt. Patchart told me to go see Top first thing in the morning.

I got up early had breakfast at the mess hall and checked into the CP. Top saw me and called me into his office.

"Ski that lieutenant you drove yesterday says you were insubordinate and you assaulted him, is that true?" He asked. Then I told Top my story and even admitted to the charges but as I told him what happened the madder he got. "Let me get this straight, this asshole had you drive him off post out to the boonies got on a Huey at ten forty-five in the morning and left you there for 5 hours by yourself with no food no water no weapon and no means of commo. Then when he does return he's drunk, have I got this right? He asked.
"That's affirmative," I said.

He picked up the phone on his desk and dialed a number. When it was answered at the far end he spoke, "This is First Sergeant Haskill Echo 4th of the 12th give me the Sergeant Major". He waited a second covered the mouth piece and said, "Wait outside with Tom." I walked out of his office and sat at Tom Phillips desk, he was the clerk. I could hear bits and pieces of the phone call from where I was sitting. "Mike it's Frank, your Hershey bar left some details out of his story," Top said to the Sergeant Major. Then he explained my side of the story. When the call was, done Top came out to Tom's desk.

"OK, listen up there will be no charges the Sergeant Major will enlighten the Lieutenant as to his unbecoming behavior and get him squared away," Top said. "I'm sorry this happened to you that detail was supposed to be on BMB only, my best advice to you is to forget it and move on."

Top was telling me that if I pursued this matter the LT would be in deep shit but so would I. The Army was not kind to enlisted men who ruined the careers of their officers.

But like I said earlier, the sergeants run the Army anyway. I could just imagine the conversation with the Lieutenant and the Sergeant Major. Top told me to carry on relax and check in each day for my orders.

I was not going to miss lunch today so I walked over to the mess hall and waited for the lunch hour to begin. Tony Collard had the same idea and asked me how I made out with Top. "No sweat we're all good, don't mean nothing," I told him.

Another week went by and we all enjoyed the time off from the war. This was still Vietnam however and it's not like you can just pick up and go somewhere. There was nothing left at the PX that attracted our interest and even the allure of cold beer bad rock and roll and scantily clad dancing Filipinos in revealing tops and mini-skirts at the EM club no longer entertained us.

We were bored out of skulls and needed to desperately get moving again. Then like magic, the word spread that orders were at hand. When I got to the CP, I found out I was heading to the 5th Infantry Division on the DMZ. My orders authorized me in country travel from Bien Hoa Airbase to Quang Tri Airbase in I Corps and they were dated for 30 September. My reporting date was 5 October. The Army was giving five days to travel a distance that could be completed with a single three-hour flight.

I saw Top and he asked me if there was anything in my personal duffle bag that I would need during my five-day trip. I told him no. Then I found out why. "I got your orders processed now listen up. You did me a favor and got in a jam so I'm taking care of you.

Take this ruck sack when you leave on Wednesday. I put some C-rats in it for you and a canteen make sure you keep your poncho liner. Don't check into a BOQ on your trip they'll make you lock up your SKS and it will be gone. Stay in the terminals. You got five days to get to your unit take them and good luck," he said. "Thanks Top," I said. Then he added, "I'll have your duffle shipped up to Quang Tri terminal see me the day you leave and I'll give you the claim ticket, this way you can travel light."

Well that was it I had five additional days of leisure time and as any grunt will tell you any day not in the boonies is a good day. There were still a few more days to kill in BMB but at least now, I knew where I was headed. The day of departure came and I found out the shuttle to Bien Hoa Airbase would pick me up at ten hundred hours.

I saw top at zero nine hundred and he gave me a claim ticket for my duffle bag. All I had to do once I got to Quang Tri was take the ticket to baggage claim and pick up my duffle. I said my goodbyes to the guys who were left some of Recon had already shipped out to 90th replacement and others had gone home. I was one of the last to leave. Everyone promised to write but deep down I believe we all knew it would never happen. There is some remorse leaving people like this knowing you will never see each other again after having been through so much together. There was a conflict you wanted to leave and at the same time, you wanted to stay. I got on the shuttle bus and my five-day trip of leisure began.

Once I got to the terminal, I went to the flight desk and showed my orders. The airman at the desk noted I was not needed in Quang Tri until the 5th of October and he asked me, "Taking the tourist route?"

"Sure why not," I replied. He booked me on a C-130 for Camh Ran Bay that afternoon at thirteen hundred. Now all I had to do was wait for the flight to be announced. I found a seat in the waiting area and settled in. I got a lot of stares from new guys who had just come into the country and were headed out to their units up north.

I was dressed in my faded strikers and a new black beret I bought at the PX. I had my SKS slung on my shoulder and my .38 was on my hip. There was a coffee shop in the terminal and I got a sandwich and a Coke. I waited for the flight and when it was announced, I walked out the gate onto the tarmac and boarded the C-130. There was no first class or coach seating just a bench along either side of the aircraft. I strapped in and the noisy flight took just under an hour. Aside from me, there were some other passengers and pallets of supplies making the trip.

It was a short but noisy flight to Camh Ran Airbase. I can't say much for the stewardess on the flight she wore a baggy flight suit and helmet with large bug eyed sun glasses. Her moustache was to long but hey, the Air Force will sign up anyone. Once I got into the terminal, I found it had a Red Cross stand and a USO spot. There was also a lunch counter so I would be able to get some food even though I had some C-Rats from Top. I have to say Top stocked me up with the best he gave me turkey, beef and chicken as well as several cans of pears and peaches. My only problem was what to do.

There was also a news stand so I was able to get some reading material. Spending five days in this or any other airbase terminals was going to be boring but it was not beating the bushes in the boonies.

Another problem I had was the attention of the MP's in the terminal. It seemed that every new shift that came and went checked my orders that I kept handy in my breast pocket. Looking around I was the only guy in striker fatigues and carrying weapons.

Everyone else had their luggage some officers had side arms but my ruck sack rifle and overall grungy appearance made me look like I just dropped in from the bush. Maybe I made people nervous.

The next day I managed a flight to Da Nang on another C-130. The air force crew chief or stewardess was no improvement over the last one. Once inside the terminal I found a comfy spot and waited for the obligatory MP check.

I took a nap and woke to find three young Marines sitting across from me. They were waiting for the shuttle bus to take them out to their base they had just arrived in the Nam. All three were in brand new plain green jungle fatigues with boots that still held a factory shine. And there I was in my dingy attire and brandishing weapons. The SKS was on top of my rucksack that I was using as a hassock with my legs stretched out across it.
I was not wearing any rank insignia but one of the Marines gathered up enough courage to speak to me as I lit a cigarette. " Is that an SKS? He asked. I blew smoke out from the cigarette and responded, "Affirmative."
Then another of the three asked, "Did you take it off a dead VC?"
"Nope bought it off him," I said.
Then the first one spoke again, "Wait you bought that off a Viet Cong soldier?"

I looked up and replied in a calm matter of fact manner, "Sure happens all the time, they come in from the jungle and sell their weapons; cheap too only ten bucks". The first one leaned forward in his seat and got a little confrontational, "No way man you're just messing with our heads."
I sat up looked him in the eye and said, "Watch your tone Marine."
"Yes Sir, sorry," he replied and sat back up straight.

Then the third chimed in with his own question, "So you're saying the VC come in here and sell their weapons and nobody stops them."
"Yup the guys coming back later can't miss him short black hair obviously Vietnamese he's got on black pajamas sandals and a faded out green boonie hat," I told them. I was also describing most of the male population of the country. Then the second one laughed, "Oh man you really had us going where you headed?" He asked.
I smiled and told them I was on my way to the DMZ. They introduced themselves the first one's name was Dennis, the second Marine was Tom and the last guy was Fred. We chatted for a bit, they had the usual questions and then the PA announced the arrival of their shuttle bus. We all shook hands and wished each other good luck. There were two busses that the Air Force used a regular sized bus for normal people and the little bus for the Leathernecks.

I got a flight up to Quang Tri the next day I still had one more day before I needed to check in. hanging out and sleeping in terminals was getting old so I caught the shuttle bus to Camp Red Devil and presented my orders.

It was late afternoon and the clerk told me they would get me assigned the next day. He showed me where the BOQ was and I checked in. No one seemed interested in checking my weapons so I found myself sleeping on a real bunk with a thin mattress for the first time in days. The next morning, I got chow and went back to HQ to be assigned. I was ninety days short.

Story Two 5th Infantry Division

Chapter Ten New Unit, New Friends;

Arriving at personnel for the 1st Brigade, 5th Infantry Division, I sat with the clerk and asked if there were any 'rear' jobs available. I was eighty-nine days short, and humping the boonies along the DMZ was not something I wanted to do. He let me know that any rear jobs would go to existing 'Red Devils' no matter how short I was. He looked at my Recon tab over the 199th patch and gave me two options. I could go to Papa Company 75th Rangers or Recon 1st of the 11th.

Both units did LRRP operations and operated in five and six man teams. I noted he was wearing a CIB on his fatigue shirt and asked him to be straight with me, which was the better unit. "Rangers get into some nasty shit, they are not a good spot for a guy as short as you, Recon is a very tight group, and you would be a better fit there."
"Where are they based, at the 199th I had my own hooch." I did not want to be living out of a bunker on a fire base. "Recons base is at Camp Red Devil, I was in Delta 1st of the 11th, and they have their own CP and hooch's." I had found a home, Recon 1st of the 11th it was.

I reported in on 5 October to the E Company CP, at Camp Red Devil and was assigned to Team One. The team leader was Ron Zakrin from Indiana. He was a graduate of Ft. Benning's NCO school and had been in country since June.

My other team members were SFC Doc Byler the team medic, PFC Don Medley, PFC Alvin Edison the team RTO and Larry Morganni a sniper.

In another week, we also had PFC Johnny Rickets. I was the shortest man on the team.

'Doc' Byler was regular army, and on his second tour. He was a Staff Sergeant and knew his stuff. Don Medley was tall with reddish brown hair. He wore it as long as he could and kept it tucked up inside his boonie hat. Without his hat and with his hair and moustache he looked as if he came right from Woodstock. Al Edison was a new guy who arrived a week or two before me. He was the assigned RTO. Having done some duty as an RTO, we got along right away. He had a multitude of questions and I was able to help him with the setup of his gear. We went over map reading and the code books. Larry Morganni was another real tall guy. He came in country around the same time as Al.

I had to turn in my SKS and .38 Special to the company armory room, battalion policy did not allow for personal weapons. I was assigned to a bunk in one of the hooch's, which was really a smaller version of the barracks at BMB at Camp Frenzell-Jones. My bunk was in the back of the barracks in a small room off to one side. I had enough room for a real bunk and a mattress and not much else. I did have a small record player that I used. Most of the time I listened to the armed forces radio but if I needed to just mellow out I listened to this Henry Mancini record I had.

It was all instrumental but the slow tunes were calming. There was a hooch girl to keep the place clean and do laundry.

The 5th Division patch was a simple red diamond. We wore a scroll tab over the patch that had E Co on the left,

1-11 INF on the right, and the main scroll had Long Range Recon Patrol. This was all black with white lettering and red trim. Barnie Jackson was on team two, and he was working on a new pocket patch, and a new scroll.

The M16 I was issued was standard except for the silencer on the end of the barrel. It extended the length of the weapon by about nine inches and also came with two 30 round magazines. Some of the M16's the other guys carried had M203 grenade launcher attachments. My impressions were these guys had their act together, and Ron asked me about our operations in the 199th. Instead of starting out on a mission in platoon strength and then breaking up into smaller teams, these guys just started out that way. Otherwise, the work was the same. The terrain was different in their AO as well. There was very little dense jungle, lots of hills, open plains and swamp areas.

In the mountainous areas, the terrain was just forest or dense forest. My first mission was just five days out on the 10th, and I learned I was the assistant team leader.

Saturday the 10th came around and the slicks arrived and we hopped on for the eight click ride to a hilly area around the Song Vinh Phdoc River. The area was open with tall grass steep ridges and lots of trails. We had a 'Pink Team' escort us in. Once we were on the ground one of the Cobra pilots decided to test his M28 mini gun.

He dove straight at us and when I saw the muzzle flash of the M28 I thought the cobra was going to strafe us. Being in an open area like this was different from chopper inserts with the 199th.

We often had these 'Pink Teams' but due to the jungle and heavy forest we never saw the cobras out in the open sky like this.

The M28 was on a turret and he was actually firing off to our left, even though he was coming straight at us. I could see the pilot laughing as he went by us.

I looked around from my vantage point on the crest of a ridge line and could see a long way in any direction. This was going to take some getting used too. I was used to hiding in the jungle, being out in the open was unnerving. We humped along the trails on these open ridge lines to get to the area we would set up our NDP. From the top of the small hill, we had a commanding view of the area including the Song Vinh Phdoc River a tributary of the Song Hatch Han River. We were supposed to keep a watch on the river, Intel during the briefing indicated that the NVA was moving weapons and supplies down the river.

We moved into the chest high grass and basically stamped out an area for each of us to be able to lie down to sleep. We also stamped out pathways to each other's positions. We checked to see if our positions could be detected from any of the other ridge lines around us and satisfied ourselves that we would be OK.

Morganni found a spot next to small tree and some brush to be able to pick up any targets that might pop up. He had the XM21 modified M14 rifle with scope.

I thought back to my old 'Tiger Patrol' days and thought how great it would be to have a starlight scope with us.

The mission was set for five days. We set up a mechanical ambush over on one of the ridge line trails and placed the rest of our claymores in other areas that could be used to approach our position. Morganni and Ron kept an eye on the river that was about 150 meters away at any point and below us. We had an elevated position but it was only about seventy-five meters above the river itself. Our NDP was on the northern most tip of a bend in the river. It came down stream towards us from the southeast flowed around our NDP and then cut back southwest from us. Any river traffic would be under Larry's scope no matter what direction it came from.

My days were filled by checking the claymores around our position as well as the mechanical we set up. Don Medley and I also checked the area for any signs of enemy and civilian activity. We were alone and isolated. There was some small boat traffic but really just little one or two man dingy type boats with local fisherman just trying to get a meal.

One thing I did notice about this unit was that Ron made sure everyone understood the mission, where our exact position was and the call signs we used to communicate with battalion. He made sure we all could read the map and use the code book that Al carried as the RTO. Each man had to know what every other man's job was as part of the team. We took turns using the radio to call in traffic and sitreps as well as changing the delta tango arty missions around our position. Having been an RTO myself using the code book and reading the map was easy stuff.

Except for the clover leafs and checking the claymores, the five days passed without any action and we were pretty bored. On the 14th, we were picked up by the slicks and we were RTB.

Back at Camp Red Devil, my mail had caught up to me again and I had a stack waiting for me. I had letters from Susie, Mary, 'Mom Peggy' my brother and my Mom and Dad. I read each letter twice knowing it wasn't too much longer and I would be home.

I cleaned up my gear and weapon. I was really curious to see how loud or quiet the M16 was with the silencer. I was not looking forward to contact but maybe I could get to a range and try it out. We had clean uniforms, hot food and cold beer at the club. We had a briefing on the 17th we would return to our river overlook spot the next day.

The insertion was pretty much the same except this time the 'Pink Team' just flew overhead. We found our old position and checked it and the surrounding area for any signs someone else had been there. It had been undisturbed and the surrounding area was clean as well. We set out our mechanical in a different location and tried to change our claymore positions as best we could from our last visit.

The weather was overcast and rain was on its way. Being out in the open in the rain was not going to be fun. Sometime around midnight the rain started. Not too hard at first but an hour or so later it poured. With no overhead protection from trees or bushes, there was nowhere to hide and we all got soaked. Everyone was up all night anyway so we double up and tried to sit it out.

By the time, the sun came up at dawn we were soaked and sore. We moved around checked the claymores and the mechanical and watched the sun poke in and out of the clouds all day. We did have radio traffic to alert us that an ARVN patrol boat was going to be running up and down the river. They would not know our position so if we spotted it we were to lay low. Telling the ARVN we were there was a bad risk. Some one's cousin may find that info useful. They were supported by our 5th Battalion 4th Artillery.

They knew where we were so we would not be getting any incoming arty fire called in from the boat. We would keep a low profile just the same if we saw the boat. No boat ever showed itself so I guess the ARVN were on their typical search and avoid mission and the rain started again in the afternoon. There was no other traffic on the river that day at all. It's as if the local population and the enemy had enough sense to stay in out of the rain. Because everything was wet including us we were miserable all night. Battalion called us every hour for a sitrep and we counted the hours until day light.

The next day was clear and we took everything out that we could spread it all out across the top of the high grass to dry out. We ran more clover leafs and even went down to the river bank.

Morganni and Ron stayed in their little snipers' perch and the rest of us took turns moving around to check the area. We were the only ones there.

Intel got it all wrong again.

We slept better that night and the rain did not return, but the temperature got down in the low sixties. The cooler temps and the lack of sleep the last two nights had us bundled up in our poncho liners and we were out like lights. Standing watch and answering sitreps from battalion was tough. Sometime around zero three hundred, the mechanical went off.

We had already responded to our sitrep by breaking squelch twice so when Ron called battalion they responded right away. "Red Roamer 3 this is Reaper One 6, over"

"Reaper One 6, this is Red Roamer 3 over."

"Red Roamer 3 we have a Mike Alpha at Yankee Delta 565236, over."

"Copy Reaper One 6, mike alpha at Yankee Delta 565236, any other contact, over."

"Negative contact, request hotel india (H&I) at Charlie Brown, over."

"Roger Reaper One 6, Rein Fire 3 is on net standby for shot, over."

The battery of 155mm howitzers were now notified to fire a three round high explosive H&I mission to the delta tango's pre-plotted co-ordinates known as Charlie Brown.

"Reaper One 6, this is Rein Fire 3, shot out."

A few seconds later, the arty rounds could be heard coming in and exploding at the pre-designated position.

"Rein fire 3, this is Reaper One 6, drop 5 zero, right 5 zero, & repeat over."

Now we were telling arty to fire the mission again but to adjust fire 50 meters south and east.

"Reaper One 6, rein fire 3, copy drop 5 zero, right 5 zero, repeat, shot out, over."

Once more, the arty rounds came in with the new co-ordinates.

"Rein fire 3, red roamer 3, this is Reaper One 6, fire mission complete, stand down, Reaper One 6 out."

Now all we could do was wait for dawn, and then go out and check out the area, to see what had tripped the claymores. There were three claymores daisy chained on this mechanical we left on a trail at the bottom of a ravine to our southeast.

Everyone was wide awake now and the only thing to do was to sit tight and wait for morning. Just to throw any suspicions off the enemy might have Ron had called in the arty to our south and southeast.

The NVA knew we used mechanicals and that when one went off it meant an American unit was close by. The incoming arty was supposed to make the NVA think this was nothing more than an H&I mission.

The next morning at first light, we hunkered down and watched the area to our southeast. We did not detect any movement. Because we had the high ground, any movement from us would be silhouetted against the morning sky.

We decided to move off our high position by going north and then west using the ridges as cover and worked our way back south towards the ravine. We came up on the ravine from the west and saw no movement or enemy activity.

Now we just needed to figure out what tripped the mechanical. Finding the area that was impacted by the claymores was easy. We found no bodies of enemy troops but there was blood around. We also found some guts and some fur. Whatever tripped the claymores must have been right in front of one, there was not much left.

We made our way back to our position and called battalion. "Red roamer 3 this is Reaper One 6, negative contact for mike alpha at Yankee delta 565236, over."

"Copy negative contact Reaper One 6 prepare to RTB, over."

We just got orders to prepare to return to base so we waited for additional orders for the choppers to take us back to Camp Red Devil.

The choppers showed up around noon with the usual 'Hunter Killer Escort' and we were on our way back to base.

We had come back a few days early and no one complained. We got a new man on the team his name was Johnny Rickets from New York City. He would join our team on our next mission. He was quite a character. His hair was longer than military standards and he also had a mustache that he was growing Fu Manchu style. He had lots of questions and seemed eager to get into the bush.

Learning that I was as short as I was and had served with another unit seemed to fascinate him. We became friends quickly. Johnny was also a martial arts expert. He told us one night he had a black belt in karate. We were all a little skeptical and he soon saw this.

One night after evening chow and a few beers, he decided to put the skepticism to rest. I was his volunteer dummy for his demonstration. He claimed to be able to kick a C-ration can off the top of my head while standing just two feet away from me and standing face to face. Medley said, "You can't use him he's too short."
This drew a few laughs but I'm not sure Medley was talking about my height. Johnny and I were about the same height and Al Edison checked the distance between us. I put the can on my head and Johnny said, "Stand like you're at attention and whatever you do don't move, in fact close your eyes."
I complied with the request, and the next thing I knew the can was gone from the top of my head. Everyone was hooting and hollering at this great feat.
Johnny while standing face to face in front of me, jumped straight up into the air did a 360 degree turn in midair and kicked the can right off my head. Everyone was impressed. We all decided we would no longer fight the enemy using our weapons, we would just send Johnny to kick Charlie's ass.

We cleaned gear wrote letters home and just tried to relax, we were going back out in a few days. Rickets, despite the ban on personal weapons had somehow got a hold of an old M3 .45 caliber grease gun. This is a small WWII, vintage weapon that got its name because it looks just like a grease gun used in a garage. It is tubular in shape with a 30 round extended magazine.

The .45 caliber rounds would knock down anyone they came in contact with, and at close range, it was lethal.

The next mission would take us into the mountains just south west of Dong Ha. The Team was comprised of me, Ron, Doc Byler, Morganni, Rickets and Edison. The chopper insert was uneventful. When we boarded the door gunner asked, "Are you guys Rangers?" We were in our usual cammo fatigues, boonie hats and silenced M16's. Rickets new grease gun toy added to our mystique.

"Nope we are not Rangers," Rickets said.

The door gunner replied "Oh good, those guys have been getting into some real bad shit in the area were going into."

This was not the greatest of news, but we already had heard some rumors about the previous Ranger missions. That's why we were going. During our battalion, briefing it was noted that there was some heavy NVA activity in the mountains south west of Dong Ha around the Khe Long La River south of the QL 9 highway.

We set up our NDP position on a hill top south of an old ARVN base camp that was situated on another hill top about 100 meters away. After the insert, we humped to the ARVN location to check it out. The hill top was clear of brush and heavy vegetation and there was a lot of tall calf high grass. Some of the old fighting positions and fox holes were still there.

The ground in and around these areas were barren of any vegetation and the fields of fire looking to the east were open and clear as well. Off to the north was another hill top that was covered with low trees and heavy brush.

All three of these hill tops lined up north to south and looked north and east down into a jungle covered valley with more mountains running from our southern NDP east and then turning north to form the valley below. This was the area we would be doing our clover leafs in. Ron set up three delta tango's, pre-plotted arty missions designated as python, cobra and rattlesnake.

We set up our NDP, placed our claymores, and checked the hill we were on for any signs of the NVA. Satisfied of our defensive perimeter we settled down and discussed the next day's operations. The hill we were on was steep. We had trees and heavy brush from top to bottom, the only exposed area was an old overgrown road lined with high grass just to our north going into a saddle between the two hill tops.

This was the easiest approach to our position so we had most of our claymores deployed to that side. We had our evening chow and decided on our watch schedule for the night. The night went by without incident and Ron took Morganni and Edison on a cloverleaf. Doc Byler, Rickets and I stayed at the NDP.

We sat around while the rest of the team was gone when Rickets thought he heard something on the west side of our NDP just below our position. Doc Byler stayed by the radio and Rickets and I went to check things out from my sleeping position. We watched the area but saw and heard nothing.

Rickets took his grease gun and went down the hill in front of my position against my protest. He was about 30 meters below me and sat in front of a fallen log and was watching the area.

I was snapping my fingers to get his attention. I did not want to call out. Finally, I got his attention and hand signaled for him to return to me, and when he came back he reported, "Nothing, but I could have sworn there was some one there."

"See that log down there?" I whispered as I pointed to the log.

"Yea, I see it that's where I was.'

"That's where my claymore is, you sat right in front of it." I said. "You also went off on your own with that dopey pop gun, don't ever do that again. We stay together, no matter what, and if you have to move with a weapon take your 16, is that clear?"

He looked at me and I could see he was hurt by my rebuke. "OK, I got it." We went back over to the radio.

Doc Byler was still by the radio and asked what we saw. "Negative contact," I said.

We sat back down and stayed alert, Rickets asked "Ski you going to say anything to Ron?"

"No", I replied, "live and learn."

"That was pretty dumb, me sitting right in front of your claymore."

"No sweat GI, next time you'll know better." "What's going on?" Doc, asked.

"Ti Ti shit, don't mean nothing," I said.

The rest of the team signaled us that they were coming back in. They were gone most of the morning and came back from the north using the road. We had noon day chow and Ron told us what they had found in the valley to our northeast.

"We saw lots of trails around the river most heading north." Ron said. "We followed some of the trails along the west side of the river going north; all of these trails have been used recently."

We decided to patrol our hilltop and the base of it that afternoon. We did not see any enemy activity so we made the decision to stay at our NDP one more night. During evening chow, we heard people in the valley to our northeast. There were also heavy chopping noises as they were clearing brush and a lot of hollering in the same area.

It sounded like a large group of people all speaking Vietnamese and making a lot of noise. It was getting dark so Ron called battalion to give them a sitrep.

"Red roamer 3, this is Reaper One 6 over."

"Reaper One 6, this is red roamer 3, send traffic, over."

"Red roamer 3, we have heavy enemy activity at grid Yankee delta 5821, over." Ron was telling battalion we did not have a hard fix on the enemy position but that the grid we gave was active.

"Copy Reaper One 6, say your status, over."

"Reaper One 6, we are NDP and secure, will recon at dawn, over."

"Copy, Reaper One 6, any change in delta tango's, over?" Battalion wanted to know if the three pre-plotted arty support missions we had were to be changed.

"Red roamer 3, negative change, maintain python, cobra and rattlesnake, Reaper One 6 out."

We settled into our positions and listened to the activity in the valley below us. The NVA were acting as if they owned the place, they had no idea we were there.

Once it got dark, the noise subsided and we were on high alert all night. Battalion had us as the first call for hourly sitreps and we responded each time with two broken squelches.

We were all up at first light and Ron wanted to check the valley below us. The valley below us started up with all the same noises as the previous day. He left me with Rickets at the NDP and took the rest of the team on a cloverleaf. They were gone for about two hours and then Ron and Morganni, came back. Ron filled me and Rickets as to what they did.

"I took everyone over to the ARVN position when we left," he said, and then Morganni and I went down into the valley". "We saw all kinds of activity and at one point a platoon of NVA walked right past us, as we hid in the bushes." We were definitely in deep shit.

"I want you two to stay here with the radio, this will be our fallback position if shit gets out of hand, Larry and I will go back to the ARVN position with Al and Doc," he said. We packed up some of the gear for Larry and Ron to take over to the ARVN position. Ron also noted that we should stay on high alert.

They left and Rickets and I waited by the radio. No more than an hour went by, when Ron returned.

"Pack up all the gear and pull in the claymores, were moving over to the ARVN hill," he said. We packed up any of the remaining gear and we were just getting ready to leave when we heard an explosion in the valley. The explosion sounded muffled. Whoummp!

"What the hell was that?" I asked. Ron said, "I don't know, something small maybe a grenade."

The ARVN hill was 250 to 300 meters high off the valley floor so we did not think one of our guys tossed a grenade. As we started to move out, we heard another one. Whoummp! A few minutes later, we heard another one. Whoummp!

Then we heard Morganni's XM21. First one shot then a few seconds later a second. "Oh shit," Ron said, "Larry got one."

We hauled ass over to the ARVN hill, Edison took his radio back, and Doc and Larry were standing back in the tree line looking into the valley below. "I got one of those bastards, Ron the son of a bitch was fishing in the river using grenades," Larry said.
"Right, and now every NVA son of a bitch knows were here," Ron said. He grabbed the handset from Al and called battalion. Rickets and I dropped into a fighting hole and waited.
"Red roamer 3, this is Reaper One 6 contact fire mission, adjust fire 100 mikes north of rattlesnake over."

"Copy, Reaper One 6, standby."

I asked Morganni, "Larry what happened?"

Larry said, "Ski this NVA comes out to the river bank shouts something and throws a grenade into the river. Some of his buddies then go into the river and throw the fish up on the bank. A few minutes later he did it again so I took my shot and missed, Ski he looked up the hill at me and I swear he was looking right at me, I could see him in the scope, so I made an adjustment and fired another round and took him out."

"I told you all to lay low, now we have a shit storm at our feet," said Ron.

"Reaper One 6, this is rein fire 3 on net with your fire mission, say when ready, over."

"Rein fire 3, this is Reaper One 6, ready fire HE on the deck over."

"Copy Reaper One 6, shot out." A few seconds later we heard the arty mission but it was way north of where it was needed. Ron gave the wrong instructions, and quickly corrected the mission. "Rein fire 3, this is talon one 6, check your fire, adjust 100 mikes south of rattlesnake and repeat, over," he said.

"Copy, Reaper One 6 adjust fire 100 mikes south, shot out."

Now the arty rounds were coming into the valley below us just where we needed them. At that point, we had more traffic on net. Being so close to Dong Ha airbase, we got a call from a 'Pink Team' that had just left base for its daily CAP.

"Reaper One 6, this is Snoopy Two 6, we are one click from your pos need any help, over?"

"Snoopy two 6, roger, standby, rein fire 3 check your fire I have air traffic at my POS, standby, over." Ron said.

"Copy air traffic Reaper One 6, rein fire 3 standing by."

"Snoopy two 6, this is Reaper One 6, what have you got, over?"

"Reaper One 6, I got some hostile snakes loaded with fire and venom need your exact POS, can you pop smoke, over?"

The 'Pink Team' had a general idea where we were, popping smoke on our position would let them know where we were but the NVA would also know. Actually, they did know we would just be confirming any doubts they had.

Ron popped a green smoke grenade just in front of us in the open area to our south. "Snoopy two 6, this is Reaper One 6, smoke out, over."

"Roger, Reaper One 6, I have oscar delta, standby."

The OH-6 Loach came in from behind us and flew along the mountain side to our east and started to dip north into the valley, then suddenly shot straight up and turned back towards us.

"Christ, Reaper One 6, you've got the whole NVA army coming up the hill for you, red baron two 5 and 7 hustle your ass over here and give me gun runs north to south and east of oscar delta smoke at the top of the hill".

I watched from my hole as the two cobras came in from the north flying low on the tree line, the first cobra firing his M28 mini guns, spitting out 2000 rounds per minute.

Each cobra held 4000 rounds of 7.62 NATO for each mini gun. The first cobra made his gun run and flew right past us as he climbed over the hill and turned west.

The second cobra was right behind him and made the same gun run. After the cobras made their runs, the Loach that was flying on the other side of the valley came back down into the area that was right below us. He buzzed around at tree top level like an angry bee looking for something to sting. He got some small arms fire and fired a marking rocket into the jungle below him then he climbed back out and called his angry friends in again.

"Red baron two 5, red baron two 7, bring in the big bang party poppers, over."

"Snoopy two 6, roger wilco, time to party."

The cobras repeated the same runs this time firing their 70mm rockets, each cobra was loaded with a pair of M158 and M200 rocket launchers, and this meant each cobra could fire 52rockets. The valley below us was now filled with smoke from the mini gun and rocket fire. Another helicopter was over our position circling at about 3000 feet. This was Lt. Colonel Davidson's C&C bird. He was now on net coordinating all the resources at his disposal.

"All stations, this is Red Roamer 6 on net, standby for traffic over."

"Snoopy two 6, standing by, over."

"Rein fire 3, standing by, over."

"Reaper One 6, standing by, over."

"All stations this Red Roamer 6, Reaper One 6, hold your POS, Snoopy two 6 maintain CAP at yankee delta 586211, how copy over?"

"Reaper One 6, copy over."

"Snoopy two 6, copy over."

The old man now had control, we were to hold our position and the 'hunter killer team' was to fly and maintain his position to our west behind us.

"Rein Fire 3, this is Red Roamer 6, repeat your last fire mission over."

From 3000 feet above the valley the arty fire would not affect the C&C bird, the old man wanted to get a fix on his inbound artillery support so he could adjust their fire as needed.

"Red Roamer 6, this is Rein Fire 3, shot out over."

The arty rounds started impacting in the valley below us. The arty rounds were coming in from Dong Ha to our northeast at an angle that allowed the rounds to drop into the valley below us.

The second 'pink team came on net and joined up with the first team at their CAP position. "Red Roamer 6, this is Snoopy One 6 on net flying CAP with Snoopy Two 6, over."

"Roger Snoopy One 6, maintain CAP, Snoopy two 6, RTB, refuel and reload, report back to CAP and call in, over."

"Snoopy Two 6, roger, RTB, out."

"Rein fire 3, this is Red Roamer 6, check your fire, over."

"Rein fire 3, copy check fire, standing by over."

"Snoopy one 6, this Red Roamer 6, recon the valley, over."

"Roger, Red Roamer 6."

The new Loach came over us at tree top level and dived into the valley the NVA was well aware of what he was up to and held their fire. Despite the enemy's discipline not to fire on the Loach the pilot and the gunner were still able to see lots of NVA troops running around, and that's what they reported. "Red Roamer 6, this is Snoopy One 6, boss you have hundreds of NVA running around down here, this must be a major base camp, over."

Ron was the only one able to hear the radio traffic and he was relaying what was being said, when he passed this news about the size of the enemy force, he was glaring at Larry.

Rickets and I started to pile up our magazines and grenades on the edge of our fighting hole. We fully expected to be attacked. I took the last grenade off my belt and tapped Johnny on the shoulder, "this one's for us," I said. I placed the grenade into my jacket pocket; Rickets just looked at me and nodded. We were not going to be captured.

"Roger Snoopy One 6, R T your CAP, Rein Fire 3, this is Red Roamer 6 repeat fire mission and repeat every minute, over."

"Roger Red Roamer 6, repeat every minute, shot out."

The arty rounds started hitting the valley again. The old man made arrangements to have Bravo Company come in and reinforce or position. Snoopy One 6 was at their CAP position & Snoopy Two 6 came back with fuel and ammo. When they came back on station, the old man had them CAP further north up the valley. The arty fire continued once each minute and then the battalion commander unhatched his plan.

Fifteen sorties of slicks would bring in Bravo Company they would approach from the southwest between our hilltop position and the original NDP hilltop position. They would land or hover into the open area in front of our position and drop their troops. Arty would suspend their fire mission and the two 'pink teams' would be used as fire support during the landings.

The only problem was the landing area in front of us dropped off at a thirty-degree angle, which means the tail rotors of the inbound choppers were at risk of hitting the ground. They could not land, they would have to hover and the troops would have to jump out of the birds.

As soon as the first bird came in it was now evident to everyone they could not land. The first chopper made the attempt then flew down the slope towards the valley aborting his drop off. The NVA with a nice juicy target forgot their discipline and opened up on the helicopter that made it out by flying north as soon as the bird leveled out over the valley.

I ran out onto the landing zone and down the hill, about fifty meters and turned my back to the valley and started using pathfinder signals as the second bird came in.

I was holding my arms straight up like a referee signaling a touchdown. I waved the chopper in watching his rear rotor. As the rotor got closer to the ground, I would then move my arms straight out at the sides and making small up and down motions with my hands and my palms facing the pilot. When I wanted the pilot to stop and hover, I would close both fists. The troops bailed out of the bird and went up the hill to where Ron and the rest of the team were. The rest of the sorties all followed in one by one and we did not lose any birds.

The NVA was now getting into the game, and the LZ started getting small arms fire and mortar rounds were impacting on the mountaintops to my left.

The 'pink teams' did their jobs and eliminated the mortar tube which was located on the mountain top directly behind me. The cobras took out the tube before they could adjust their fire. Then we started getting small arms fire from the other hill top to our north. One of the Loaches fired a marker rocket and the cobras came in with their mini guns and rockets eliminating any further attempts by the enemy to flank the LZ. During all this an RPG round impacted behind me.

As skinny, as I was I often had the local mama-san tailor my pants. Baggy pants made to much noise walking through the jungle and often got snagged on branches and thorns. As I squatted down in reaction to the explosion, I ripped the entire inseam of my leg out. Now with the prop blast from the helicopters I had my back to the valley and was flashing the enemy with my butt and leg.

The last sortie dropped his troops and the reinforcement was over. I joined the rest of the team somewhat embarrassed.

We spent the night further down the hill away from Bravo Company because we knew they would be mortared, and they were. We sat up all night basically back to back the six of us. It was a long night. Reflecting back during that night I realized this was the second time during my tour that I could have easily been killed. I did not know it then but in just another week, I would once again stare down death. The next morning, we got word we were to be taken out and Bravo would search the valley below.

We got out OK and later learned we had broken up the plans of a battalion to set up a new base camp in that valley. We had picked a fight with a battalion of troops of the 27th NVA regiment.

If not for the artillery support and the two 'hunter killer teams' out of Dong Ha the NVA would have made mincemeat out of us. Bravo made several contacts and had fire fights over the next few days as the NVA was not happy with us.

Chapter Eleven Scorpions & Lost Friends;

November started with a mission to 'Scorpion Hill'. This was an old ARVN observation post in the Thon Ai Tu area. The hill itself wasn't much just a big bump in a large open area of pines and brushwood, but it did give clear lines of site over swamp and fields of rice patties to the south and was situated just south of RD 604.

This was a walk out mission from Camp Red Devil to the hill was about three clicks. We assembled by the eastern gate after being dropped off by jeep. The team consisted of me, Ron, Doc, Byler, Medley and Al Edison.

We were all wearing cammo fatigues with no insignias and just our boonie hats. We were standing around putting paint on our faces. Don Medley was tall and had very long red hair. He always kept it tucked under a boonie hat so none of the NCO's or Officer's would see it. All of our weapons had silencers on the end of them. We did not look like a typical Army unit.

A jeep with one passenger and a driver approached the gate. The passenger was a signal corps captain. We were outside the gate and no one saluted. The jeep stopped and the captain demanded to know who we were and what outfit we were with. Before Ron could say anything Medley stepped up to the jeep and said, "Who wants to know?"

The Captain is now looking us up and down taking it all in, "No one saluted, are you all enlisted men?"

Medley now full of himself drapes his weapon across his arms takes off his boonie hat letting his long hair out and responds with, "No and we aint officers either." Ron steps up and says "Captain, if anyone asks you did not see us, is that clear?"

The captain is now thinking he has stumbled on to a MACV SOG Team, usually comprised of Special Forces and CIA types. "Yes sir I understand, move out private," the Captain said to his driver and off they went into the base where the MP's did salute him.

These guys were what the marines called 'salty'. I was thinking back to the time I dressed up as LT Kamble to get lunch. We left the gate a little quicker than usual and stared our three click walk to 'Scorpion Hill'.

The terrain was all open, small swamps and open grasslands with some scrub brush. We covered the three clicks or about three point nine miles in about three hours.

The hill itself was a short 150-meter climb and once on top we set out our claymores and got our NDP set up. The hill was infamous because of its scorpion population. The entire hill was crawling with nests.

The rainy season was starting and the temperature during the day was not bad but at night, it could get downright cold and drop to sixty degrees. This particular night was OK and it went by without any incidents.

Just before dark, Ron and I talked about a few things. In June, I was promoted to Specialist 4 and with just sixty-five days left in country, Ron suggested I should get my sergeants stripes. He indicated that when we got back to base he would put me in for the NCO promotion board.

All I would have to do was look good in a clean uniform, fresh haircut and shave and answer a few technical questions about weapons, radio procedure and map reading. I had all of these skills already so I would be a sure thing to get my stripes before I went back to the world. Coming back in January I would still have eighteen months before I would have to re-up or get discharged. It was also unit policy that anyone with fifty days or less would be pulled from the field. The thought of no more missions in the bush was good news for sure.

The next morning, we all awoke to warm weather. Ron was using his bayonet to torment a scorpion he had found. We all gathered around to watch this little thing about the size of your thumb nail repeat its attacks on Ron's bayonet. This little guy had some attitude to be sure; Medley made the comment to be careful because where there was one there was more.

I felt an itch on my left calf and reached down to scratch it. The pain I felt was like an electric shock that went up my entire leg. I grabbed my calf just below the knee with both hands and started screaming "bug juice bug juice, "while hooping on my right foot. The pain was getting worse as the scorpion that had crawled up my pant leg kept stinging me. The rest of the team watched in surprise as I continued to hop around.

Finally, I collapsed in a heap and fell unconscious. Doc Byler grabbed my pants at the belt buckle and began to pull off the pants. Once my pants were off, they found the scorpion hiding away in the crotch of my pants. If he had hit me, one more time from that position I would have flown back to the world on my own.

Laying there unconscious my leg turned an ugly shade of purple and red and swelled up like a balloon. Ron had no choice but to call for a medevac.

"Red roamer 3, this is Reaper One 6, request medivac at grid, Yankee delta 559279, negative contact, over."

"Reaper One 6, copy negative contact, sitrep, over."

"Red roamer 3 this is Reaper One 6, one man down from scorpion stings, current status ineffective over." Ron was telling battalion the team was combat in-effective because a man on the team was injured seriously enough that the team could no longer fulfill its mission.

"Copy Reaper One 6, dust off at grid Yankee delta 559279, standby."

"Reaper One 6, this is Red Roamer 3, authenticate Eagle Wing, over."

Battalion was asking us to verify who we were. Ron had anticipated this and looked up the response for today's challenge.

The NVA would if they could use captured radios to draw in medevac helicopters so they could ambush the choppers when they came in for landings. NVA troops knew how to read maps and if anyone knew English could determine from the captured code books what the call signs would be. What they did not know was the key used to break the code in the authentication codes.

"Red roamer 3, this is Reaper One 6 actual, I authenticate, Stuka Junker, over."

"Roger, Reaper One 6, your medivac inbound, ETA ten mikes, call sign is Dust-off 719er, over."

"Copy Red Roamer ETA ten mikes, Dust-off 719er, out."

The guys carried me and my gear down to the base of the hill and waited for the medevac bird to arrive. I was still out of it so I don't remember any of this. The guys told me later what happened while was out.

My leg by this time I was told was really swollen; they would not be able to put my pants back on so I was naked from the waist down.

"Reaper One 6, this is Dust-off 719er, inbound your POS in two mikes pop your smoke, over."

"Dust-off 719er, this is Reaper One 6, smoke out, over." Ron tossed the smoke grenade so the pilot would know where we were and to verify the color of the smoke.

"Roger Reaper One 6, I see snow white, over."

"Reaper One 6, roger snow white, out."

I regained consciousness as we all got on the bird to RTB. Lying half-naked on the deck of the chopper, I heard the door gunner ask "What the hell happened to him?" "Scorpion stings, "was the answer from Doc. "No shit, man that's looks like a world of hurt. "

The door gunner was right I was in a world of hurt, I passed back out on the ride back to base and I don't remember getting off the chopper or being taken to the Battalion Aid station.

The next thing I do remember was waking up in the aid station on a cot covered by a poncho liner and still not wearing any pants. I was really woozy and thirsty. I sat up on the cot and the medic came over with a canteen of water.

"How are you feeling? "He asked as I drank from the canteen My mouth felt like a cotton ball and the water tasted great. "Dizzy. "I replied.

He told me that I had been there most of the day and that the thirst I had was a result of the medication and anti-venom they gave me. He looked under the poncho liner and noted that the swelling in my leg had gone down.

He called the doctor over who checked me out and let me know that I could return to my unit when the dizziness left. I asked what happened. The doctor told me he found thirteen individual scorpion stings from my upper outside calf to my upper inner thigh. They had shot me up with anti-venom and packed my leg in ice for the swelling. The doctor also told me that there would be no permanent effects from the stings and after a few days of rest, I would be fit for duty.

I was able to put my pants back on but I could not find my boots. The medic told me that my team had taken those back to the Recon area along with my other gear. He called over to my company on the field phone and let them know I was ready to go.

The doctor gave me a two day no duty profile, so I would be sitting on my butt for a couple of days.

Doc Byler and Ron showed up about a half hour later and we drove back to Recon's area.

I had to settle for LRRP rations because I had missed the evening meal at the mess hall. The guys wanted to go to the canteen for beer but I was too tired, I hit my bunk and was out like a light. I spent the next two days taking it easy and talking with the guys who were all saying how bad my leg looked when I came in.

Johnny Rickets noted he thought the door gunner on the medevac was going to puke, when I was carried off the bird. I had made it back to the aid station about zero nine thirty so I was there all day. The medical staff of Bravo Company at 75th Support Battalion did a great job.

I learned later that the smaller the scorpion the worst the venom was. The one that got me must have been related to the one Ron was tormenting.

The mission was cut short and none of the guys were complaining. We got word a few days later that we would be going back out on Saturday the 7th.

The 7th came around to fast I along with everyone else were enjoying the days off. Team one was assigned to go out and check an area ten clicks west of Camp Red Devil along RT 604 which was heavily travelled tank and track road that ran southwest from QL 1 the main highway that ran the length of Vietnam. This mission had five men assigned to the team. Ron and I would go out with Don Medley, Alvin Edison & Doc Byler.

The choppers ran late that day we spent most of the morning at the LZ waiting for our birds. We got our slick around eleven hundred hours mounted up and left the base. It was a short fifteen-minute ride to our insert point and the slick let us off right on the RT 604 road.

This road was not heavily travelled except for tanks and tracks so there weren't any civilian vehicles to be seen. During our wait for the bird, we agreed to travel on the northern side of the road about 100 meters or so away from it.

The terrain was small rolling hills of high grass and small spots of scrub trees and bushes. We set up an NDP on top of a small hill about 25 meters' high that gave us good visibility around our area.

We were also able to set our claymores at the base of the hill giving us additional protection. Ron and I decided to do a little look around the road to our south and east. We left Medley, Edison and Doc at the NDP and headed out.

Once we got to the road we travelled southwest on it a little ways and found some fresh NVA tennis shoe tracks going back to the northeast.

We followed the tracks back up the road where they turned off to the south side of the road just beyond the point where we entered the road from the NDP. We had moved about fifty meters off the road checking some of the trails in the area. We had good line of sight all around us but there were definitely places where the enemy could hide.

I told Ron "We should head back," when we heard a single shot coming from the NDP. We both took off running through the high grass towards the road.

Once we reached the road, I was in front of Ron and when I got to the northern side of the road, I saw a small sap ling of a bush no more than a foot high in my path. For some unexplained reason I hurdled that bush like I was in the Olympics. To this day, I have no idea why I did it.

I wasn't thinking about it then the NDP was about 100 meters off the road and when Ron and I got there, we saw the guys walking around the grass at our position looking for something.

Medley told us he was setting up his sleeping position when he spooked a badger. A nasty little creature to be sure, Medley had shot it when it snapped and charged him. The badger was gone but we did find its blood trail going off into the grass headed west. Based on the amount of blood we decided to let sleeping dogs lie. The badger would most likely bleed to death and would no longer be a problem. We called into the battalion TOC marked our position with marker rounds and used those two points as pre-labeled arty support missions. We joked about the badger maybe cutting this mission short but I was not volunteering to be the one it attacked. I had enough of the local critters after my morning with a scorpion.

The night passed without any trouble either from the enemy or the badger. We were in an open area but the small hill we were on had an old bomb crater that had the grass grow back over it. We should have had a great view of the stars but it was overcast and damp. The rainy season was starting up.

We got up at dawn had some chow and coffee and planned the days' strategy. We spread out the map and showed everyone what Ron and I had found the day before. We would travel south cross the road and recon the area where we found the trails.

We pulled in the claymores called battalion TOC to let them know we were on the move, then geared up and moved out.

Ron took the point, something he did often followed by Medley, myself, Edison the RTO and Doc Byler was pulling drag. We had walked about 100 meters to the south and had just reached the road. Medley jogged up a few steps to catch up with Ron, why I don't know but as he did I noticed that the clacker for his claymores was about to fall out of one of the pockets on his rucksack. I jogged a few steps to catch up to Medley. The three of us were now bunched up together when the mine went off. Whoump!

The blast from the massive explosion killed Ron instantly Medley and I were thrown to the ground by the shock wave. He landed right on top of me. At first I thought I had been shot in the head, the pain in my left ear was piercing and my entire head hurt as if I had been hit with a heavy object. I was lying face down with what felt like an enormous weight holding me down and it was pitch black. I could not see and found it hard to breathe. Coming to my senses, I realized Medley was lying on top of me. I could hear him screaming but it sounded like he was in a tunnel far away. My first thought was ambush.

Somehow, I mustered enough strength to throw Medley off of me. I came to my feet with my weapon ready and the fire selector switch on full auto.

I saw a small clump of low trees and bushes off to my right, the perfect spot for the enemy to be. I was now expecting to see the muzzle flashes of their weapons but there was no incoming fire.

Medley was lying at my feet on his back facing me, he had both hands over his face and blood was flowing through his fingers. He was in severe pain and screaming "my eyes, my eyes."

I called out "Ronnie," and turned to look behind me. Edison and Doc Byler were standing about 15 meters away a look of shock and surprise on their faces. I called out again, "Ronnie," why wasn't he answering me I looked at Doc and said, "Doc, take care of Medley," then I told Edison "get that whip antenna up now."

Doc was at Medleys side in a flash, and Edison got his rucksack off and got the whip antenna on the radio up quickly. "Ronnie," I called again, I looked at Edison he was looking behind me to his left with sadness in his eyes.

I looked back in the direction he was staring at" Ronnie," I called again.

What was left of his body lay just about five meters away. Now I knew why he was not answering my calls. I took the radio handset from Edison and squeezed the mike.

"Red Roamer 3, Red Roamer 3 this is Reaper One 5 over."

"Reaper One 5."

"Red Roamer 3, I need emergency dust-off 100 mikes south of my NDP over."

"Reaper One 5 are you in contact?"

"Negative, no contact, no enemy activity."

"Roger Reaper One 5, be advised all flights are grounded due to weather, over."

I looked up at the sky it was about zero seven hundred but it was still somewhat dark out. The cloud ceiling was very low and thick.

This was bad, Medleys wounds were serious and if the medevac could not come, we would have to walk out. We were about nine clicks from base.

I keyed the mike, "Red Roamer 3, I really need that bird, over." I didn't realize it at the time but I was shouting into the handset. I could barely hear the responses, and I was using my right ear, I turned to Edison, "Al turn up the handset."

"Copy, Reaper One 5, standby." The radio operator at TOC was probably giving someone an update, the next voice to respond was the old man himself. "Reaper One 5, this is Red Roamer 6, what's your sitrep, over."

"Red Roamer 6, I have one KIA and one serious WIA, over."

"Roger Reaper One 5 How much money do you have over?" This was standard for us to use dollar and coin denominations to count personnel.

"Reaper One 5, we are a buffalo nickel, over."

"Copy, standby Reaper One 5, I'll get your bird, over".

Doc had finished treating Medley his entire face was covered with a bandage and he was quiet. I leaned down put my hand on his shoulder and told him, "We going to get you out Don you'll be OK." He nodded his head and asked "Where's Ron?" I told him Ron was gone.

Doc was now behind me feeling around my head. He was also looking around the rest of me and asked "Are you OK?" I told him my head hurt, I could not hear anything with my left ear and everything else sounded like it was in a tunnel and far away. My left ear hurt like hell, it felt like I had something sticking in my ear and buried inside my head. It was like I wanted to pull whatever it was out of my head and ear.

"Reaper One 5 this is Red Roamer 3 your medevac is on its way call sign is Dust-off 713, ETA your POS ten mikes over."

"Copy, Dust-off 713, ten mikes."

"Reaper One 5 this is Red Roamer 6, load your whiskey and kilo on Dust-off 713, engineers will be at your POS in thirty mikes you will RTB your team when they arrive, over."

I told doc the medivac was on its way. "You should go on the medivac with Don," he said. I replied "No way, I'm not leaving."

"Red Roamer 6, copy RTB when engineers arrive, cannot, I say again cannot load kilo, over."

The radio went blank, the info I just sent must be being discussed a few minutes later the response came back.

"Copy, Reaper One 5, engineers will evac your kilo, what happened."

"Reaper One 5, anti-tank mine, over."

I few minutes passed, I told Edison to grab a smoke grenade, then we heard the 'whoup whoup' of the chopper blades.

That sound any grunt who served in Vietnam will tell you is like hearing angels sing. It means help, supplies or the ride back to base is on its way. "Reaper One 5, this dust-off 713, we are inbound to your POS, over."

"Reaper One 5, roger," I turned to Edison and told him to be ready to pop smoke.
"Reaper One 5, this is dust-off 713, pop your smoke over."
"Roger, smoke out." I nodded to Edison, he pooped the smoke and threw it into the middle of the road.
"Roger, Reaper One 5, I have 'goofy grape', over".
"Roger, 'goofy grape', area is mined do not land, you have to hover, over."

The chopper came in from the east following the road, he was low not more than 100 feet off the ground but not too fast, he passed right over head and continued flying west for about 300 meters. Then he turned and started back to us.

For a brief minute, I thought he had missed us but then he came back on net. "Reaper One 5, this is dust-off 713 your area is clear, no enemy activity, get your wounded man ready, over." "Roger, remember do not land area may be mined, over."

The bird came in slow and low and dropped right on top of the road where the smoke grenade was thrown. "Don't land, don't land area is mined," I shouted into the handset. The bird dropped softly on its skids and the on board medic waved for us to get Medley on board.

Once Medley was on, the Co-Pilot gave me thumbs up and the chopper lifted off. "Reaper One 5, we have your man, we'll take good care of him, over." It was just the three of us now, all we had to do was wait, for the engineers.

"Dust-off 713, this is Reaper One 5, sorry I yelled, over."

"No sweat GI, Reaper One 5, good luck, dust-off 713 out."

"Reaper One 5, this is Red Roamer 6, over."

"reaper One 5."

"I have Reaper 6 with me, identify your kilo and whiskey, do not use any one's real name, do you copy, over."

I thought for a minute, Captain Glosser was with the company commander, "Roger, Red Roamer 6, kilo's last name sounds like city in Ohio, whiskey is the red haired hippy, over."

I was describing both Ron Zakrin (Akron Ohio) and Medley. My methods worked as the CO came on net.

"Roger, this is Reaper 6 copy your message, who is left on your team, over."

"Reaper 6, I have echo six Ben Casey and light bulb man, over."

"Copy that, identify yourself, over."

"Reaper 6, this is Reaper One 5 actual, alphabetski up country from one niner, niner, over". My last name was a long polish name with the usual 'ski' at the end.

I was also indicating I came from down south from the 199th Infantry Brigade.

"Copy, Reaper One 5, engineers are inbound your POS, ETA five mikes, RTB the rest of your team, call sign Sapper One 6, how copy over."

"reaper One 5, copy ETA, 5 mikes, Sapper One 6, over."

I looked over at Ron's remains and the experience I had nine months ago at FSB Nancy, came back to me. A few minutes later, we heard the choppers coming in from the east. "Reaper One 5, this is Sapper One 6, over."

"Reaper One 5."

"Reaper One 5 pop your smoke we are inbound your POS, over".

I took a smoke grenade off my pack, pulled the pin and tossed it on the road where Al had tossed the last one. "Reaper One 5, smoke out."

"Roger Reaper One 5, mellow yellow smoke."

"Roger, Sapper One 6, mellow yellow". The two birds came in from the east and set down facing west on the road right on top of the smoke. The engineers jumped off with their equipment and the NCO in charge came up to us.

We showed him where the mine had exploded, where Ron's remains where, he told us they would take care of everything and that we should get on the chopper. I called the TOC to update our status, "Red Roamer 3, this is Reaper One 5, we are RTB, over."

"Copy, Reaper One 5, Red Roamer 3 out."

The first chopper took off, and the second hovered a bit and turned around to face east. We loaded our gear on the bird and lifted off. I stared at the spot where Ron remains lay and watched as we lifted off and then he was gone.

The ride back to Camp Red Devil was about 10 minutes. When we landed, everyone from Echo Company was there to meet us.

They took all of our gear off the chopper and loaded it all on to the jeeps they brought.

Captain Glosser met us and said, "You need to de-brief the CO, OK." "Yes sir," I said, we walked into the TOC & Lieutenant Colonel Davis was waiting for us.

There was a large map on the wall of the battalions AO. I showed the Colonel where we had set up our NDP and what Ron and I had found yesterday. I let him know we were on our way this morning to check out the area to the south of the road.

"OK, Ski we'll look into this, are you OK?" I told the Colonel my head and left ear hurt and that my hearing was bad in my right ear. He turned to Captain Glosser and said, "Get him to the aid station right away." I left the TOC, and Captain Glosser drove me to the aid station.

I was treated by the doctor who put drops in my ears, and was given some meds for the head ache and told to get some rest.

I went back to the E Company area and went to my bunk. Once there I played Henry Mancini's, 'A Warm Shade of Ivory'.

I listened to this often to mellow out, wrote a letter home to my Mother and just lay on my bunk. Doc Byler came by he had to fill out some type of form for me because I was treated in the field. He didn't stay long I guess he figured I was not in the mood for company. I missed lunch and dinner chow, I found I just wasn't hungry.

Sgt. Bill Senford came by, he was Ron's best friend, and they had arrived from NCO school together. Bill said, "Let's go to the canteen Ski a couple of beers will do you good."

"I really don't feel like drinking, but thanks anyway." Bill sat there a second or two and said, "It's not a request, you can walk or be carried, the rest of the guy's need to see you."

Reluctantly I went with Bill to the canteen; most of Recon was there, including some new guys that just transferred in from the world. Imagine their prospective just arriving to their unit and sitting in on an impromptu memorial service. I sat at the table and someone gave me a beer.

Bill raised his beer can and gave a toast to Ron. We all touched cans and drank. All of the guys were supportive. They asked about the details, and I answered all of their questions. Before long, we were all telling stories about Ron. Al Edison sat quietly and finally said, "Thanks for getting us out Ski." Everyone drank up and we had to be tossed out after the canteen closed. If not for the medication and the beer, I don't think I would have slept much. The next day was spent cleaning my weapon, and just taking it easy. Later in the morning, I got word the LT wanted to see me at the CP. I walked the short distance from my hooch and met him in the front room.

He told me I was short enough that the Captain wanted me out of the field and that I was going to be pulling CQ duty from seventeen hundred to midnight. I had fifty-six days left in country. There would be no more humping the boonies for me.

I was getting concerned that maybe I had done something wrong, call it survivors guilt. The LT assured me that my conduct that day was everything they would have expected. No one was blaming me for Ron's death, if anything my actions that day saved Medleys eyesight. He told me they got word that Medley was doing fine and would be going home, the doctors were able to treat his wounds and the fact that he got treatment so quickly made the difference. It was good news, but I still had this nagging feeling I did something wrong. That afternoon we had a formal memorial service in the base chapel.

Sgt. Ronald Zakrin was going home; his body was recovered by members of A Company, 7th Engineer Battalion who relieved us that day.

Ron had been married on November 11, 1969 before he was assigned to NCO school at Ft. Benning. Bill Senford told me he had sent flowers to his wife Tina just before we went out on his last mission. I was still feeling guilty and it was haunting me.

CQ duty was easy enough, just sit at the desk, answer the phone, and log the sitreps from battalion TOC.

There was no change in the way the rest of the guy's treated me. I was still a member of the platoon. Barnie Jackson even asked me my opinion on the design of the 'Grim Reapers Recon' patch the guys were talking about.

We got more replacements so there were a bunch of new guys in the platoon. They had a lot of questions. New guy's always do.

'RJ' the company clerk informed me there was an R&R slot for Sydney, Australia open and if I wanted it, I could go. Australia was a prime R&R location, round eyed women and real booze. It would be just like going home except everyone talked funny. I was signed up and ready to go on the 30th. Then the Army pulled a fast one. On Monday the 23rd of November, I got word the Army was tired of me and would send me back home on the 28th of November.

I was going home thirty-eight days early. Needless to say, I was thrilled. The only problem was if I took my R&R to Australia, I had to return to Vietnam and would stay until my original DEROS date of January 5th, 1971. The other option was leave Vietnam for good on the 28th of November. Most guys will tell you when you leave the Nam do not test fate and return thinking you can leave again. I cancelled my R&R. I was going home, never to return to the big green hurt.

I wrote a letter to 'Mom Peg' to let her know I would be arriving on the 29th from Seattle. I asked her in the letter not to let anyone know so it would be a surprise. So much for those plans, she let everyone know I was coming home.

Alex Worley was also from Philly and he was going home early on the 30th. I was sitting in the mess hall after getting the news having evening chow when Worley was walking just outside yelled out, "Shoorrtt", I responded with "Shorter." "Screw you Ski," he replied. Everyone laughed, except the new guys; they had a long hard year in front of them.

The last few days passed slowly, I could not get out of the Nam fast enough. When the time came for me to go everyone was happy for me. We all shook hands, promised to write, and I wanted Barnie to be sure to send the new patch to me. Doc Byler told me the orders for my Purple Heart Medal would catch up to me.

I still had this nagging feeling that I had done something wrong, and I felt guilty about the medal. I took a bus to Quang Tri Combat Base and processed out. We turned in all our gear and were told we could not take any undocumented weapons, ammo or other contraband home with us. My SKS that I had brought up from the 199th was cleared first through Army Customs and then Vietnamese Customs. I then took a C130 flight from Quang Tri to Tan Son Nhut Airbase.

We were given clean khaki uniforms with our rank, brass and ribbons. The busses took us to the terminal and we were moved to a secure area in the terminal to await boarding. Officers first, followed by NCO's and then the grunts. Everyone on the plane was in a festive and anticipatory mood and when that freedom bird went wheels up everyone was cheering, goodbye Vietnam. Little did we know, although we were no longer there we would never actually leave. The Nam followed us home.

Chapter Twelve Back in the World;

Leaving Tan Son Nhut airbase was the first leg of a long trip home. Arriving at McCord AFB, we were put on buses to take us to Ft. Lewis Washington we had to process back into the world. It was late November and no one was going home in Khaki's. After changing into new dress green uniforms, we had our leave and next assignment orders cut. Some guys were getting out of the Army others like me had some time left in their enlistments. I had another eighteen months to go. The clerk let me know that I did not have orders for some of the ribbons I was wearing, but after I explained the circumstances, he thought that the orders had just not caught up yet.

The Air Medal I was told was for the hot LZ mission when we were reinforced. The Purple Heart orders were only twenty days old. The clerk told me, "Check with personnel at your next duty station, you have thirty days leave so they should catch up by then." He let me know that I would also receive detailed orders of my next posting by mail at my home address. I was put on another bus that took us from Ft. Lewis to Seattle Airport and booked a flight to Philadelphia.

Walking through the terminal in my new uniform and carrying a Chinese SKS on my shoulder the local protest group against the war was eager to let me know that they did not approve of me.

I passed two Seattle Policemen and gave them a questioning look. The protestors called out, "Go home you fascist pig. You are not welcome here, baby killer."

They had an area roped off for the protestors and I was far enough away from them that they could not spit on me as some veterans will tell you. The cops gave me their best advice, they had seen it all before, "Go home, get out of that uniform and put it all behind you." Getting out of the uniform would be easy enough, putting it all behind me was something else.

I was forced to check the SKS into luggage after multiple assurances it would be there for me in Philadelphia. I settled into a window seat by myself and waited for the flight to take off.

The flight from Seattle would take about six hours. I was due to arrive in Philly around 8 PM. Between the flight times from Tan Son Nhut to McCord AFB, crossing the International Date Line, and now the three hour difference from Seattle to Philly my internal clock was in a tail spin.

I was looking forward to landing in Philly and being able to see the city from the air as we landed. One of the stewardesses on the flight took a shine to me and provided me with anything I needed. I sat on the port side of the aircraft in the first aisle behind first class. She brought me a sandwich and bags of peanuts, and although I had just turned nineteen, twelve days ago, she also treated me to all the cold beer I wanted.

Between the beer and my jet lag, I was not aware that her intentions were not just for beer and peanuts. I was going home so getting lucky with a 'Stew' as they were called was not on my radar. With just about two hours before landing, I was out like a light. We landed on time and my 'Stew' friend had to wake me to let me know we had arrived.

I got up fixed my tie, buttoned my blouse, grabbed my cap and the only carryon luggage I had, which was no more than a large manila envelope containing my orders and quickly headed to the door. My 'Stew' friend asked, "Is this your final stop soldier, I have an overnight lay over?"

I turned at the door and said, "Hey thanks for everything, and I'm home, no more travelling for me." Then I turned and headed into the terminal. I went to the baggage claim area that in those days was right where you got off the aircraft.

I was looking for my SKS, and it was nowhere to be found. I checked with the airline lost and found and was told they would research this and get back to me. They took my contact info and gave me a receipt. I wasn't happy but what else could I do. The airline made good however and the SKS showed up three days later and was hand delivered to me at my house.

After dealing with lost and found, I went back to the terminal area and started looking for directions to get a cab. That's when I saw my mother. There were only two flights from Seattle to Philly that day and she waited for each one. She didn't see me her back was turned so I went up and tapped her on the shoulder. She turned and threw herself into my arms.

She was crying and holding my face with both hands and kissing me over and over. "Hi, Mom how the fuck are you?" I asked. She never noticed what I said, but I realized I would have to be aware of who I was with when I spoke. She finally composed herself and still holding my face stared at me.

She was very happy to see me but I also noticed she was looking at me in strange way, as if she wasn't sure about something. My Dad and Brother showed up next and we were all hugging and backslapping, happy to be back together.

We left the terminal and my Brother drove back to my house on Ogden St. He took the Schuylkill Expressway back and seeing the city skyline was a welcome sight. After exiting at Girard Ave, we turned off Poplar St. made a right on 30th St. and then left onto Ogden. The entire street was covered with flags and welcome home signs. This was completely different from my experience in Seattle.

My Aunt Betty that lived next door was out of the house to greet me as I got out of the car. Uncle Bill was filming my arrival with an 8mm movie camera. After hugs and kisses we went inside, there was only one more home coming greeting to make.

Caesar was my dog a shepherd, collie, and mutt mix. He was in the kitchen, his tail was down, ears back and a low long growl was coming from him. "Caesar, hey buddy, come here," I said. His nose was up sniffing the air, he never moved, I stooped down and called him again but still no response. I stood up and stepped towards the kitchen. The low growl was loud now and there was a flash of teeth. I couldn't understand it we were buddies, why was he acting this way?

He started poking at the door to the basement with his nose and paws and eventually got the door open and made it down the stairs. What I didn't know then was the smell of Vietnam was still on me.

That same smell we all experienced the first time we got off the plane the one we said we would never forget. I could no longer smell it. My senses had adjusted to it. He could smell it though and he knew it was death, destruction and misery.

Eventually a few days later, he was happy to see me but that initial encounter troubled me. Animals have a sense that we humans do not. Caesar knew who I was but he also knew there was something different.

I Came Home, But It Wasn't Me.

EPILOGUE

During the production of this work, memories that I have carried for forty-five years in some cases became clearer and in others reemerged from those places where I buried them. The deepest wound to be opened was when I wrote about the closeness and brotherhood I felt of assisting to get home two of the men killed at FSB Nancy just two weeks into my tour. I had done my duty for them and although we had never met, the horrible task of placing their damaged bodies into body bags so that every part of them would be returned to their families is something I feel emotionally attached too. Then the realization that this same task was something I failed to do for my friend and team leader on my last day in the field hit me hard. The burden of guilt that I carried for all these years was suddenly revealed to me as the words I wrote jumped off the page. The question that nagged me from that day Ron was killed was finally answered. I had left him there in the place where he died and did not perform my duty for him as I had done for others I never knew. I was home alone and wept over the shame of my sin. I still do. His body was recovered by strangers who performed their morbid duty because of my failure and then carried that same memory all their lives as I did.

On that day in January 1970, my memory all these years was of three men killed. Two that I placed in the body bags and the first man I saw who was so critically wounded. I often thought about them and wondered who they were. Now I know from my research that it was actually 13 men killed that day, and with the wonders of the internet their names and in some cases, their faces are now known to me. Like my team leader Ron, "They Came Home, But It Was Them". The men that were sent to Vietnam and died there were returned to their families as they were on the day they arrived. Their souls and who they were live on in the memories and hearts of their loved ones. Those memories are cherished by those who knew them. For those of us who returned we carry forever the burdens of the duty we were asked to do. So too do our families and friends. This one year of our lives haunts us and remains to this day the one thing in our lives that has influenced our remaining days in this world. Our children and grandchildren hear from our families who we were before we left for Vietnam and wonder how did the man they knew become so different. They need to know. If we all bury the pain, then it will all die with us. That cannot be allowed to happen. In order for our love ones to know us and remember our sacrifice and service, then our future generations must hear the story that needs to be told. We owe it to ourselves and to them.

The sacrifice of our brothers must never be forgotten. They cannot tell their story. We must speak for them. As we remember all of them their individual lights like the stars of a clear night sky shine brightly in a vast sea of darkness, their sacrifice will be forever lit even to those who never met them. The Wall in Washington DC will always reflect back to the visitor their names and their sacrifice but they will never know how or why unless we speak for them.

My family now knows why I am the man I am today. I wonder if I earned the right to come home and tell my story even if it is forty-five years later. You may wonder the same but that is a question to be answered by future generations. That question can only be answered if we all tell our story.

We used to say to each other "Don't mean nothing;" well it does so listen up. If you are a veteran of Vietnam, please seek help. Do not carry your burden alone, your brothers will welcome you and help you. I know I see them often and they are helping get me through my days. If you are a family member or friend of a veteran of Vietnam, educate yourself about the Nam and PTSD. This will help you to understand the person you loved and how they changed. The why they changed may be harder to find out but you will learn to cope with them as they struggle to be the person you once knew.

Like all of my brothers, I came home, and I want to be me. They too came home and they want to be themselves.

Reference Information Book One

Echo Recon 4th Battalion 12th Infantry Regiment

199th Light Infantry Brigade

"Vietnam Order of Battle" by Shelby R. Stanton

"They Fought Together" by Robert J. Gouge

"These Are My Credentials" by Robert J. Gouge

"Hearts" The Story of a Reconnaissance Squad Leader by H. E. Shockley

After Action Reports of the 199th Light Infantry Brigade;

AD507858 Lessons Learned Period Ending 31 Oct 1969

AD511159 Lessons Learned Period Ending 30 April 1970

AD513911 Lessons Learned Period Ending 31 July 1970

AD878026 Operation Keystone Robin Period Ending 12 October 1970

"Redcatcher" Brigade Newsletters from 1 January 1970 to 26 August 1970

US Army Topographical Map Series L7014 developed by National Imagery and Mapping Agency and US Army Corps of Engineers 29th Engineer Battalion with the following adjoining map sheets;

6431-4 6431-1 6531-4

6431-3 6431-2 6531-3

6430-4 6430-1 6530-4

Personal correspondence from letters written home by the author and post war correspondence with Hank Shockley, Mike O'Malley, Tom Ward, Ed Davis and Dave Kiefer.

Reference Information Book Two

"Grim Reapers Recon"

Echo Co. 1st Battalion 11th Infantry Regiment

5th Infantry Division (Mech Vietnam)

"Vietnam Order of Battle" by Shelby R. Stanton

DOA Form DD1300 dated 18 November 1970

WANX-AA Task Force 1-11 Combat Action Report Operation Wolfe Mountain Period Ending 26 February 1971

US Army Topographical Map Series L7014 developed by US Army Corps of Engineers Topographical Command and the National Geographic Directorate, Vietnam with the following adjoining map sheets;

6342-1 6442-4

6342-2 6442-3

Personal correspondence from letters written home by the author and post war correspondence with Tina Cleland Petro, Dennis Headley, Tom Combs, and Bernie Mack.

Glossary

A

Agent Orange - Defoliant/herbicide containing 2,4,T Dioxin
AK47 - Soviet/Chicom 7.62mm assault rifle
AN/PVS-2 - Smaller Starlight Scope for use on individual weapons
AO - Area of Operations, your "neighborhood". Ours were Cochise-Green & Walker
APC - Armored Personnel Carrier, usually an M-113
ARVN - South Vietnamese Army Soldiers
AW - Automatic Weapons

B

Baseball Grenade - Defensive Fragmentation hand grenade: explodes on impact
Base Camp Commando - See REMF
BDA – Bomb Damage Assessment
Beaucoup – Many or very much
Bic - Vietnamese for "understand" "No bic" means "I don't understand"
Blue Legs – Infantrymen

BOQ- bachelor quarters for travelling personnel.
Break Brush - To travel off a trail to avoid mines and booby-traps
Break Squelch - To press the transmit button on the radio handset
without speaking: Twice for all-clear, once for enemy near.
Bug Juice - Insect Repellent

C

C4 - Plastic Explosive in Claymores we used for heating coffee
C and C - Command and Control Ship, usually a Huey, sometimes a Loach
CAP – Combat Air patrol
CAR-15 - Carbine version of M-16 with collapsible stock - Officers only
C Rations - Dog food left over from WWII and canned for GIs in Nam
CHAM – Montagnard tribe in coastal areas
Charlie - Viet Cong, from phonetic alphabet for VC, Victor Charlie
Charles - Formal reference to Charlie
Chieu Hoi - Literally "Open Arms" - RVN Amnesty program for NVA/VC
Chinook - a CH-47 cargo helicopter nicknamed shithook
CIB - Combat Infantryman Badge (a mark of honor among grunts, justifiably so)

CIDG - Civilian Irregular Defense Group - Usually Montagnard tribesmen led by U.S. advisers, usually Green Berets
Claymore - antipersonnel mine (from Gaelic "claidheamh mor" pronounced like "Claymore" meaning Broad Sword)
Click – 1 kilometer or 1000 meters.
Cockadau - derivative of Vietnamese slang, meaning, "To kill"
CONUS – Continental United States
CP – Command Post
C-Rats – C Rations, canned meat and other meals
CQ – Charge of Quarters, night time desk clerk & watchman

D

Danger Close - an air strike or artillery mission within 100 meters of your location
Dee-Dee - To leave
Delta Tango - Designated Targets - Preselected artillery targets located in daylight for use at night
DEROS – Date of Return from Overseas
Detcord - Explosive that looks like rope- used to daisy-chain claymores
Dinky-dao - (pronounced "dinky dow") Crazy, Americanized Vietnamese
Donut Dolly - Women from the American Red Cross

Dumbo - A C-123 Provider of the USAF
DMZ – Demilitarized Zone, border between North & South Vietnam
Duster - an M42, an old M24 tank chassis with two 40mm AA guns in an open turret
Dustoff - Medical evacuation helicopter, usually a Huey

E

Elephant - Radio code for an M48-A3. Also the real thing: 'Nam was crawling with them
Elephant Grass - tall, sharp-edged grass found in the highlands of Vietnam
EOD - Explosive Ordnance Disposal
ETS - Estimated Termination of Service - the day you got out of the Army

F

FAC - Forward Air Controller, usually flying around in an O-1 Birddog
Fast Mover - FAC radio code for an F100, F105, or F4C aircraft
Fifty - the .50 caliber M2HB machine gun
FDC – Fire Direction Center
FNG - F______ New Guy, the term applied to everyone whose name you couldn't remember
FO - Forward Observer, an artilleryman, usually an officer

Frag - Offensive Fragmentation hand grenade: five second fuse
Friendlies - Other US or allied troops on the battlefield
Friendly Fire - Officially called "Misadventure" by the DOD.
Fire Mission - radio request to the artillery to drop some HE on the bad guys
Fox Four - FAC terminology for an F-4 Phantom in the ground support role.
FSB - Fire Support Base: usually a battery (3 105mm howitzers) of guns with a perimeter
FTA - F___ The Army
FUBAR - F_____ Up Beyond All Recognition
Funny Money - Military Payment Certificates, scrip issued in lieu of dollars

G

Goofy Grape - Radio code for purple smoke
Grunts - Infantrymen
Guns - short for gunships
Gunship - Usually a UH1B Huey, later a UH1G Huey Cobra
Gun Target Line - You don't want to be on it.
Gun Truck - Cargo truck with added armor and machineguns for convoy escort

H

HE - High Explosive
Hershey Bar – 2nd Lieutenant
HHC - Headquarters and Headquarters Company
H & I - Harassing and interdicting artillery fire
Hoi Chanh - an enemy soldier who took advantage of the Chieu Hoi program
Hook - short for a CH-47 Chinook
Horn - the radio
Hre - Tribe of Montagnard, 110,000 strong.
Huey - sometimes UH-1A appeared as HU-1A that led to name "Huey", ***the*** image of Vietnam

I

IFFV - 1st Field Force Vietnam
II Corp - The AO for the 1/69 Armor, included Binh Dinh, Kontum, Pleiku provinces
Illum - Illumination rounds fired by artillery, mortar, M79, or dropped by aircraft
In-Country - on the ground in South Vietnam
Indian Country - Area controlled by Charles
IP - Initial Point - A reference point in the attack

J

Jarai Tribe of Montagnard, living in the Pleiku area
JCO- Jungle Combat Orientation training
Jungle Boot - Special boots with stainless steel shank and holes to drain water out
Jungle Fatigues - tropical weight jacket and pants
Jungle Penetrator - bullet shaped device for extracting wounded in triple-canopy rain-forest
Jungle Rot - Any of a number of fungal infections caused by moisture in Vietnam

K

KHA - Killed Hostile Action
KIA - Killed In Action
Kit Carson Scout - North Vietnamese Regulars who defected and acted as scouts for US troops
Klick - a kilometer, 1,000 meters

L

La Dai - Come here!
LAW - Light Antitank Weapon - M-72 - Fired 66mm round from disposable launcher
LBE - Load Bearing Equipment, web gear, system for carrying canteen, ammo, pack, battle dressing
LBJ - Long Binh Jail, the Army Stockade in Long Binh
Lima Delta - Line of Departure: point of no return in an attack
Lima Papa - LP - Listening Post
Little People - radio code for ARVNs
LLDB - Vietnamese abbreviation for Luc Luong Dac Biet, Airborne Special Forces
Loach - Light Observation Helicopter, usually an OH-6 (Hughes 500C) but also OH-58 (Bell Jet ranger)
LOH - Light Observation Helicopter (Loach), usually a Hughes 500C but also Bell Jet ranger
Louie Lime - Radio Code for Green Smoke
LP- Listening Post
LRRP - Long Range Reconnaissance Patrol - 5 or 6 man team dropped into Indian country
LRRP Rations - freeze dried food developed for LRRPs tasted better than "C" Rations
LT- short for lieutenant pronounced as "el tee"

LZ - Landing Zone (note that some were Fire Support Bases and had names)

M

M-2HB - Caliber 50 machine gun (HB = Heavy Barrel)
M-3A1 - Caliber 45 submachine gun (M-3 was older variant)
M12 – Winchester Model 1912 .12 gauge pump action
M14 – Standard Infantry Rifle replaced by M16
M16 – standard Infantry rifle
M-18A1 - Claymore antipersonnel weapon, threw out 700 steel balls, lethal to 50 meters.
M-26A1 - Fragmentation hand grenade (offensive)
M-33 - Fragmentation hand grenade (defensive) aka "baseball grenade"
M-34 – White Phosphorus Grenade
M-42 - Duster (twin 40mm Bofors antiaircraft cannon on M-41 chassis)
M-48A3 - Main Battle Tank used in Vietnam because of its thick hull
M-55 - Quad .50 caliber machine-gun mount.. Range 7,275 meters
M-60 - in Vietnam, the 7.62mm squad machine gun of the infantry; belt fed, air-cooled; 600 rounds per minute

M-67 - 90mm recoilless rifle; range 450-800 meters; an Anti0Tank weapon, it was used to bust bunkers in Vietnam
M-72 - LAW (Light Antitank Weapon) 66mm rocket in disposable launcher
M-79 - 40mm grenade launcher, aka "Thumper"; range (HE) 400 meters
M-113 - Armored Personnel Carrier fitted with Chrysler 209HP gasoline engine
MACV - Military Assistance Command Vietnam
Mad Minute - Random firing of all perimeter defensive weapons to discourage infiltration
Meo - Laotian term for Hmong tribesmen, meaning "savages".
Mike Mike - Millimeter
Moi - Literally, "savages". Vietnamese term for Montagnard tribesmen
Montagnard - French Lit. "Mountaineer" Originally from Polynesia, they were the original inhabitants of the coastal region of Vietnam
MPC - Military Payment Certificates, scrip issued in lieu of dollars

N

Napalm - Thickened gasoline. Resembles Jell-O in bombs, maple syrup in a Zippo-track
NCO – Non-Commissioned Officer, Sergeants

NCOIC - Non-Commissioned Officer In Charge
NDP - Night Defensive Position
Nickel - radio code for a junior NCO or a 5 man recon team
No Bic - I don't understand
Number One - The Best
Number 10 - The worst
Nung - Tribe of Montagnard, 15,000 strong; the fiercest of the Montagnard CIDG troops.
NVA - North Vietnamese Army

O

OIC - Officer In Charge
One Three - RTO
One Four - The platoon Sergeant
One Five – Asst team or platoon leader or squad leader
One Six - The platoon leader or Team Leader
One Six Actual - The platoon leader or Team Leader Identifying himself
OP or Oscar Papa - Observation Post
OPCON- Operational Control

P

P-38 - Can opener that came with C-Rations
PFC – Private First Class
Piaster- Vietnamese Currency
Poncho Liner - lightweight, camouflage blanket for use at night in Central Highlands. Very useful
Pop Smoke - to ignite a smoke grenade for identification and wind direction for Hueys
POS - Position
PRC-25 - AN/PRC-25 man portable FM radio set
PRC-77 - AN/PRC-77 man portable secure FM radio set
Punji Stake - sharpened bamboo stick booby trap smeared with excrement to cause infection

Q

Quad-50 - Four Caliber 50 machine guns (M2HB) mounted on a gun truck for convoy defense
Quick Reaction Force - Helicopter-borne infantry with gunships able to react to enemy attacks

R

Red Ball - Radio code for a hard surface road
Red Legs - Artillerymen, aka Cannon-Cockers
Renago - Tribe of Montagnard, 10,000 strong.
Rootin Tootin Raspberry - Radio Code for Red Smoke
REMF - Rear Echelon Mother F_____
Remington Raider - "Stretch" Grohman term for REMF (above); anyone typewriter-armed; see also "Smith-Corona Commando"
Rhade - Tribe of Montagnard, 120,000 strong; of Maylay-Polynesian descent, continued to build houses on stilts.
RF/PF - Ruff Puffs Regional Forces/Popular Forces, usually without weapons (see ARVN)
Rock N' Roll - an M-16 on automatic
Round Eye - Caucasian, usually a female
RPD - (Ruchnoi Pulyemet Degtyarova) Soviet made squad machinegun, 7.62mm
RPG2 - Rocket Propelled Grenade Launcher, Soviet made
RPG7 - Later model Rocket Propelled Grenade Launcher, Soviet made
RRF - Rapid Reaction Force
RTB – Return to Base
RTO - Radio Telephone Operator
Rucksack - Also, ruck: packs carried by grunts

Ruff Puffs - Regional Forces/Popular Forces, usually without weapons (see ARVN)

S

SA - Small Arms
Sappers - NVA/VC whose job it was to blow things up; also an engineer
Search and Avoid - Typical ARVN mission
Shithook- A CH-47 2 rotor helicopter
Short - Very little time left in-country
Sinh Loi - Sorry about that!
Sitrep - Situation Report, made hourly to next higher headquarters
SFC – Sergeant First Class / Platoon Sergeant
SKS - Soviet/Chicom 7.62mm carbine
Slick - a UH1D with no seats (slick floor) used for carrying troops
Snake - slang for AH-1 Hueycobra attack helicopter
SOG – Special Operations Group
Spectre - Radio code for the AC-130 Gunship, which we called Spooky
Spooky - Radio code for the AC-47 Gunship the REMFs and Saigon reporters called "Puff"
Starlight Scope - AN/PVS-2 Image Intensification Device, turned night into day

T

TAOR - Tactical Area Of Responsibility
Tango Charlie - Radio code for Tank Commander (also Track Commander)
Tee Tee - very little
Thumper - an M-79 grenade launcher, so called because it made a hollow "thump" when fired
Tien Lien - Vietnamese phrase for "forward" or "charge"
TOC - Tactical Operations Center: a huge bunker where the old man lives with his staff
TOE - (also TO&E) Table of Organization and Equipment; Army rules for personnel & equipment
TOT - Time On Target - Artillery fire from different batteries timed to explode at the same time.
Tracks - the collection of track blocks on a tracked vehicle (REMFs say treads) also an M113 APC

U

UCMJ - Uniform Code of Military Justice
UH-1A - sometimes appeared as HU-1A that led to name "Huey", the symbol of the Vietnam War.
Uncle Ho - Ho Chi Minh

USARPAC - United States Army Pacific
USARV - United States Army Vietnam
URC-10 - AN/URC-10 Survival Radio used by LRRPs
UTM - Universal Transverse Mercator - grid system on topo maps

V

Viet Cong - Literally, Vietnamese Communist. The Former Viet Minh were co-opted by communist sympathizers
Viet Minh - Literally, Vietnamese Nationalist: movement started by Ho Chi Minh to get French out of Indochina
Voting Machine - Nickname for ARVN tanks because they only came out during a coup d'état

W

Web Gear - canvas belt and shoulder straps used for packing equipment and ammunition on infantry operations
Whispering Death - Charles' name for a B-52 strike. He couldn't hear or see them
WHA - Wounded Hostile Action
WIA - Wounded In Action
Willie Pete - White Phosphorous round or grenade (evil stuff)
White Mice- South Vietnamese Policemen

X

XM-177E2 - CAR-15, short-barrel, collapsible-stock version of M-16 rifle
XM-203 - 40mm grenade launcher attachment for M-16 rifle
XO - executive Officer, the second in command of a unit.

Y

Yankee Station - Tonkin Gulf Area of South China Sea patrolled by US Navy
Yards - Affectionate GI term for Montagnard

Z

Zippo Track - An M-113 APC converted to a mechanized flame-thrower M132A2
Zulu Time - Greenwich Mean Time (now UTC) about twelve hours later than our time zone in 'Nam

Printed in Great Britain
by Amazon

47420174R00200